AI in the Boardroom

AI in the Boardroom

Preparing Leaders for Responsible Governance

Tom Petro

BEP

BUSINESS EXPERT PRESS

Leader in applied, concise business books

First published in 2025 by
Business Expert Press, LLC
222 East 46th Street, New York, NY 10017
www.businessexpertpress.com

ISBN-13: 978-1-63742-786-6 (paperback)
ISBN-13: 978-1-63742-787-3 (e-book)

Business Expert Press Corporate Governance Collection

First edition: 2025

10 9 8 7 6 5 4 3 2 1

Description

Why Every Corporate Leader Needs This Book to Master AI Governance

AI is reshaping industries faster than most leadership teams can adapt. Companies with strong digital and AI capabilities are outperforming peers by two to six times in Total Shareholder Return. The gap is widening as leaders compound their advantages, making it increasingly difficult for others to keep pace. Without proper governance, directors expose their organizations to costly failures. AI in the boardroom equips leaders with the frameworks and tools to harness AI's potential responsibly, drive innovation, and avoid costly missteps.

This book provides:

- **An essential guide** to the 12 foundational AI techniques with real-world commercial applications that board members need to understand.
- **Insight into why most companies are not AI-ready** due to immature data governance, along with actionable strategies to close this critical gap.
- **A comprehensive AI governance framework** that addresses AI-specific risks, which often fall outside the scope of traditional ERM frameworks.
- **Real-world use cases** to inspire how AI can drive innovation and competitive advantage, showcasing the art of the possible for your organization.

This is a must-read for directors, C-suite executives, and governance leaders committed to unlocking AI's potential. Lead your organization with confidence, leveraging AI for growth while ensuring a solid governance foundation.

Contents

Testimonials ix

Foreword.. xi

Preface xv

Acknowledgments... xvii

Introduction xix

Chapter 1   The Case for Boardroom Oversight and Engagement.......1

Chapter 2   An Introduction to AI 13

Chapter 3   AI's Decision-Making Paradigms—Probabilistic or
Deterministic...19

Chapter 4   Deciphering AI Risks—What Directors Should
Know 23

Chapter 5   A Primer on Data and Data Governance 43

Chapter 6   A Board Member's Guide to Core AI Techniques 55

Chapter 7   A Board Risk Management Framework for AI.............117

Chapter 8   A Board Director Call to Action 151

Appendix...157

Glossary 203

References..227

About the Author...235

Index 237

Testimonials

"With the explosion of Artificial Intelligence, it is essential for every Trustee and executive to understand the capabilities, risks, and associated governance requirements. In this book, Tom takes a pragmatic, no-nonsense approach to explaining in detail the various capabilities and associated risks while providing practical governance guidance for boards and leadership. This is an easy-to-use reference guide for all of us wading through the massive changes and responsibilities."—**Suzanne Keenan, Board Chair-elect, The North American Electric Reliability Corporation, Retired CIO, Wawa Inc., Trustee, Univest Financial Corporation**

"There is no greater issue for boards of directors to master than the impact of AI on the future of their businesses. Tom Petro has taken a very complex topic and boiled it down to a handful of action steps that board members can execute on the minute they complete the final page of his compelling new book."—**Paul Holland, Managing Director, Corporate Investing Practice, Mach49; General Partner, Foundation Capital Funds 3–8**

"Tom's urgent call-to-action on AI governance at the board level is a message that must be heard. This book provides a compelling case for boards and executive leadership to come to grips with the fact that they need to become educated on the foundational concepts of AI and the associated risks with key architectural approaches. As AI becomes ubiquitous and normalized in virtually all business sectors, no organization is exempt from this new reality. The good news is that Tom provides clear definitions and practical frameworks to help companies begin the important work of establishing a new set of governance policies, decision models, and monitoring controls."—**Anthony Troy, Founder, CEO and Director, NovaData Solutions, LLC**

"Navigating AI requires a thorough assessment of risk, and Tom thoughtfully unravels AI's complexities in this essential playbook."—**Rod Herrell, PhD, JD, Executive Director of Transactions and IP @ Gene Therapy**

Program, Associate General Counsel—University of Pennsylvania and Penn Medicine

"This is an excellent Guide Book. This is a handy reference to have on a shelf in everyone's office who is engaged with commercial computational technologies. Great clarity in Tom's writing will make this a definitive source book to grab, review an appropriate chapter, and take away an actionable list of ToDos. High Need; High Value."—**Adam Marsh, Associate Professor, Center for Bioinformatics and Computational Biology, School of Marine Science, University of Delaware, Chief Science Officer and Cofounder of Genome Profiling**

"Tom lays out the essential blueprint that 21st century directors of boards will need to follow as they embrace the dawn of AI while simultaneously leading and developing founders and CEO's to reach their full potential for the benefit of all stakeholders."—**Michael Carter, Founder and CEO of BizEquity, Cofounder of Entrepreneurs Management Group**

Foreword

In 1989, Jim Barksdale was scared. To know why this matters, let me first introduce you to Barksdale. The easiest way to do that is to jump in our time machine and briefly leap forward to August 9, 1995.

On that day, a young firm called Netscape was going public. This was the first major Internet initial public offering, and investors were eating it up. Shares were offered at $28, but demand was so backed up that Netscape's price almost immediately tripled to $74.75. The price settled to $58.25 by the end of the day. Investors loved the Netscape story. Its co-founder was twenty-four-year-old Marc Andreessen, an apple-cheeked Wisconsin man fresh from the University of Illinois Supercomputer Center. The other co-founder was middle-aged Jim Clark, who had started Silicon Graphics years before. Neither Andreessen nor Clark could reliably run Netscape. Andreessen was young and untested as a CEO. Clark was a genius but erratic. Thus, the Netscape CEO's duties fell to an outsider, Jim Barksdale, who had been CEO of McCaw Cellular.

Barksdale, a southerner, was seen as a mystery man in Silicon Valley. But industrial America certainly knew of him. Born and raised in Mississippi, he attended the state university in Oxford and was elected as senior class president. In 1979, Barksdale was named chief information officer of FedEx, and in 1983, Barksdale became the overnight delivery firm's chief operating officer. It's fair to describe Barksdale as having dual fluency. He's somebody who had proved he could run a big industrial operation like FedEx while also knowing where technology was headed. Now that you know Barksdale, let's get back in our time machine and return to 1989, when Barksdale was still the COO of FedEx. At that point, Barksdale was facing an existential technology problem at FedEx. He solved it with a new and highly unusual board member.

As COO, Barksdale was seeing rapid technology changes that could leave his employer, FedEx, in a bad spot. Throughout the 1980s, Barksdale had invested heavily in IBM mainframes to run FedEx. "We were a big mainframe shop," he told me. "In fact, by the mid-1980s, we were the largest IMS single image database in the world, keeping up with all those damn packages."

But now, in 1989, the old mainframe world was starting to crumble. The leading edge was swiftly moving to a new generation of networked computers. If FedEx didn't get the transition right, it had a lot to lose. In fact, FedEx had more to lose than its competitors for the very reason that FedEx had invested so heavily in mainframe architecture. FedEx could be left saddled with old, slow technology—and be rendered uncompetitive—if it didn't act. What to do?

Barksdale called FedEx Board Member Phil Greer, a New York venture capitalist, for ideas. Greer had one. Years before, Greer's firm—Weiss, Peck, and Greer—had invested in a Silicon Valley company called Bridge Communications, founded by a husband–wife team of Bill Carrico and Judy Estrin. Carrico was the sales head and Estrin the technologist. While doing her masters at Stanford, Estrin worked closely with Internet protocol language inventor Vint Cerf. That was a huge credibility test that Estrin had passed with flying colors, causing Greer to invest. In the mid-1980s, Greer had asked Barksdale to join Bridge's board. Both men were hugely impressed with Judy Estrin. "We loved her," said Barksdale.

That's how Barksdale and Greer decided to go to FedEX Founder Fred Smith with their crazy Judy Estrin idea. *Now, Fred*—one can imagine Barksdale and Greer saying—*I know what you're thinking. She's only thirty-six. She's never been a CEO. She's never served on a large company board.* Estrin was summoned to FedEx headquarters in Memphis where Smith pronounced her "blindingly bright." "We felt that having IT and audit in a single bucket [as board committees] was a mistake. It meant you were not looking at technology as a strategic issue," he said. Smith instantly grasped that Judy Estrin was the perfect person to head the FedEx Information Technology and Oversight Committee.

Estrin served on the FedEx Board from 1989 to 2010. In an e-mail, she described being asked to join in 1989: "I remember going to lunch with Jim Barksdale. Jim said he'd given my name to Fred and asked if I would consider joining the board. The first step would be to go talk to people in Memphis. I was surprised and honored. I knew what small company boards were like, but had never worked for a large company and certainly had never had experience in the board room."

I asked Estrin what her first board meeting in Memphis was like.

"I remember feeling reasonably out of place—the only woman, significantly younger than anyone else in the room, the only one from the West Coast, one of the few technologists. But I knew Phil Greer and Jim Barksdale, so that made it a bit easier. I was also a bit intimidated by Fred—although he was very welcoming. He was, and is, so smart and such a strong leader. I hadn't met many people in business like him before."

After twenty-one years, Estrin's intense travel schedule led her to retire from the FedEx Board in 2010. Chairman Fred Smith later told me "Judy Estrin was the most important board member FedEx ever had." Thanks to her FedEx Board's success, Judy was invited to join the board of the Walt Disney Company in 1998; she served until 2014. One more crucial detail about Judy Estrin: She is the person who coined the term "cloud computing" back in 2001. As you think about building and managing your company board for lasting success in the 2020s and beyond—in this new AI era—a good place to start is with this question: Who will be your company board's trusted AI shepherds, your Judy Estrins?

AI in the Boardroom provides the framework to help you find them.

—By Rich Karlgaard
Futurist and Past Publisher, Forbes Media

Preface

In November 2022, ChatGPT thrust artificial intelligence into the global spotlight. The impact was immediate and unprecedented – within 60 days, 100 million people had experienced AI's capabilities firsthand, marking the fastest technology adoption in history. What had been the domain of tech specialists was suddenly accessible to everyone.

While artificial intelligence had been quietly reshaping our world for decades, these algorithms had largely remained hidden behind corporate firewalls and user access controls, buried deep within technical teams, and far removed from most C-suites and corporate boards. The democratization of AI vastly expanded its reach and exposed the broader machine learning landscape that had been operating hidden in plain view, thrusting the topic into the center of corporate strategy, risk management and governance. Boards and directors were not ready.

The motivation for this book stems from my journey at the intersection of technology and governance. As an early pioneer in applying machine learning to financial services, and later as an investor and board member in companies applying computational technologies across varies sectors from life sciences to insurance, I've witnessed the transformative potential of AI and the governance challenges it presents. This book serves as a practical guide for corporate directors and governance professionals navigating this new reality, providing the tools required for effective oversight in an AI-driven world.

Tom

Acknowledgments

I extend my deepest gratitude to **Suzanne Keenan**, retired CIO of Wawa, Inc., and board member of Univest Financial Corporation and the North American Electric Reliability Corporation, for her unwavering engagement, encouragement, and support throughout this journey. Her belief in this project provided the inspiration needed to bring it to fruition.

I am also profoundly thankful to the early reviewers whose thoughtful and incisive feedback was instrumental in shaping the final version of this book. Your critical insights and positive reinforcement challenged me to refine my arguments, enhance clarity, and strengthen the overall message. Your contributions were invaluable, and I am fortunate to have had your guidance during the early stages of this work.

Special thanks to:

Michael Carter: CEO and Founder of BizEquity; Cofounder of Entrepreneurs Management Group.

Rod Herrell, PhD, JD: Executive Director; Alliances and Transactions, Kyowa Kirin.

Paul Holland: Managing Director, Corporate Venture Practice; VC in Residence, Mach49.

Bruce Luehrs: Partner with Rittenhouse Ventures; Board member of HRsoft, Prosperoware, and StationMD.

Adam Marsh: Associate Professor, Center for Bioinformatics and Computational Biology, School of Marine Science, University of Delaware; Chief Science Officer and Cofounder of Genome Profiling.

David Noteware: Serial tech entrepreneur; Board member of Orchestrall, Inc., Arcus, and Clear Align.

Natalye Paquin: Chief Operating Officer, The Rockefeller Foundation.

Antony Troy: Cofounder, CEO, and CTO of NovaData Solutions; former VP Product Portfolio and Strategic Delivery, Comcast.

Daria Walls Torres: Managing Partner, Walls Torres Group, Board member, Columbia Bank.

Rob Wonderling: Executive Director, Faith and Liberty Discovery Center; Director, Univest Financial Corporation; Board of Advisors, Pittsburgh Supercomputing Center.

Your contributions have been integral to this book's development, and I am deeply appreciative of the time and expertise you shared.

Finally, my deepest gratitude to my partner in business and life, **Kris Messner,** Managing Partner, 1867 Capital Partners, and board member of FemmePharma Consumer Healthcare, Inc., for her diligence and careful review of the manuscripts.

Introduction

Artificial intelligence (AI) has rapidly evolved from a futuristic fantasy to a fundamental force in business. It is now deeply embedded in the operations of organizations, automating routine tasks, and supporting complex decision-making processes once handled exclusively by human experts. AI offers unmatched potential for innovation, efficiency, and growth. It also introduces new risks.

Traditional governance practices are being severely tested because AI introduces risks and considerations that typically fall outside of existing frameworks. Directors increasingly find themselves ill-equipped to exercise their usual oversight because of AI's immense complexity and the vast array of issues it raises. These are far-ranging— from data security and privacy concerns to legal liabilities and the risk of misinformation and more.

The urgency to adopt AI as a strategic imperative has outpaced the development of robust governance, compliance, and risk frameworks, creating an oversight gap. This gap threatens to undermine AI's potential benefits and exposes organizations to significant risks including data breaches, copyright infringement, unlawful discrimination, algorithmic injuries, and strategic misalignment. Managing these risks amidst the accelerating pace of AI innovation makes it even harder for directors to stay informed and provide effective oversight.

This book is an indispensable resource not only for directors but also for C-suite leaders driving AI initiatives, risk managers and auditors focused on mitigating AI-related risks, and corporate counsel seeking to understand the technology for accurate disclosures. It provides the tools and insights needed to close the AI governance gap. It unpacks the complexities of AI by defining 12 prominent AI techniques showcasing a range of commercial use cases to inspire readers with the art of the possible. Importantly, this book highlights key risk considerations for using each type of AI prudently and effectively.

Readers of this book will be equipped with the knowledge to oversee AI initiatives with confidence, ensuring that their organization can fully leverage AI's potential while safeguarding against its pitfalls. In these chapters, you will discover practical strategies for strengthening boardroom oversight, fostering ethical AI practices, and steering your organization toward a future where AI drives competitive advantage while being responsibly governed from a risk management perspective.

What you will discover within these pages:

- The Case for Boardroom Oversight: Understand why AI governance is a critical necessity.
- An Introduction to AI: Discover the 12 most important AI techniques and what makes each unique.
- Deciphering AI Risks: Sharpen your awareness of specific AI threats, from bias and hallucinations to privacy concerns and unintended consequences.
- Data and Data Governance: Learn how to effectively govern the data that fuels AI, ensuring its quality, security, and ethical sourcing.
- A Board Member's Guide to Foundational AI Techniques: Learn how AI learns, from symbolic reasoning to deep learning, with an overview of the unique risks and opportunities each technique presents.
- A Board Risk Management Framework for AI: Gain a practical roadmap for implementing a robust AI governance framework, including committee restructuring, risk assessments, auditing, and incident response protocols.
- A Board Director Call to Action: Embrace AI with prudence and equip yourself with the necessary knowledge and tools to become a responsible AI champion within your organization.

Finally, we offer a set of appendixes that provide directors with practical tools and detailed insights to enhance governance and oversight of AI. Highlights include:

- Checklists for third-party AI and data governance oversight.
- In-depth explorations of key governance considerations for each of the foundational AI techniques.

- Root causes of bias in AI models along with mitigation strategies.

These appendixes serve as a handy reference, equipping you with the knowledge and tools needed to navigate AI governance effectively.

CHAPTER 1

The Case for Boardroom Oversight and Engagement

Artificial intelligence (AI) is reshaping our world at an unprecedented pace, from industrial robots and self-balancing energy grids to agentic assistants. Once confined to the realm of science fiction, AI has become a tangible reality, transforming our everyday lives and revolutionizing business operations.

The exponential growth of computing power, the development of sophisticated algorithms, and the availability of vast amounts of data have propelled AI systems to learn and adapt in ways previously unimaginable. Despite these advancements, AI is still in its early stages, with immense potential yet to be realized.

For business, AI's transformative power is profound. It drives innovation across industries, from health care and finance to transportation and manufacturing. AI enhances decision making, optimizes operations, and opens new avenues for growth. However, with great power comes great responsibility. As a corporate director, you must ensure that AI is deployed responsibly, ethically, and effectively within your organization.

The Impact of AI

One can scarcely think of a domain that is not touched by the transformational power of AI. Among the significant impacts of AI are groundbreaking advancements in drug discovery, disease diagnosis, grid management, fraud detection, and supply chain optimization. Innovations like self-driving cars, chatbots, and virtual assistants redefine how people and technology fundamentally interact.

While AI innovation in the established tech giants dominates headlines, innovative AI adoption is also happening in many other industries:

Finance: JPMorgan Chase implemented an AI system called COIN (Contract Intelligence) to automate the review of legal documents and contracts. The software does in seconds what formerly took staff 360,000 hours.[1]

Transportation: EasyJet's Skywise exploits up to 24,000 parameters in its predictive maintenance AI saving "hundreds of cancelations, hundreds of major delays and many more minor delays" in the first month of deployment.[2]

Logistics: Freight's AI-powered logistics platform has eliminated an estimated 2.4 million empty miles from its network in the past year alone.[3]

Marketing: Prosus' OLX AI models are used to attribute return on investment (ROI) to single marketing campaigns and optimize spending and trade-offs between campaigns. On aggregate, they achieved a 15 percent reduction in marketing costs for the same marketing effectiveness.[4]

These examples highlight the substantial impacts of AI initiatives and help explain the rapid surge in global AI investment, from $100 billion in 2020 to over $230 billion in 2024.[5] It is expected to reach $1.2 trillion by 2030. The stakes are high, and the time to act is now.

As you read on, you will discover how to navigate the complexities of AI governance and ensure that your organization not only harnesses AI's potential but also mitigates its risks. This book is your essential guide to mastering AI's transformative power while learning how to deploy it ethically and responsibly.

Strategic Boardroom Leadership of AI

In the span of three years, the gap in digital and AI maturity between industry leaders and those trailing behind has widened by a staggering 60 percent, according to McKinsey & Co.[6] Failure to bridge this growing divide is more than just a competitive disadvantage; it represents an existential threat. This widening gap in digital and AI maturity carries significant implications for boardroom leadership across the four pillars of long-term value creation: performance, strategy, risk management, and purpose.[7] Each pillar underscores the urgency for boards to guide their organizations to embrace the transformational power of AI in business strategies.

Performance

McKinsey & Co. finds that successful digital transformations can deliver 2.7 times the initially estimated value. In specific industries like insurance, digital leaders achieve a sixfold increase in Total Shareholder Return (TSR) compared to their less advanced peers, showcasing the tangible benefits of effective AI implementation. Similarly, leaders in consumer-packaged goods and retail outperform their peers threefold, while those in energy, materials, and agriculture achieve double the TSR performance.[8]

Strategy

The urgent need for boardroom leadership to reexamine strategy in light of AI's potential cannot be overstated. The key question for boardrooms today is *what should our company look like in an AI-driven world?* AI is undermining fundamental assumptions which anchor corporate strategies. Boards working with management must reassess the company's value proposition, competitive landscape, and operational strategies in this light.[9] This involves a fresh look at the company's strategies, operating model, and how it delivers value to customers.

Risk Management

The paramount risk for any company is the potential loss of competitive relevance. Industry leaders who leverage AI effectively are not only outperforming their peers in terms of TSR but are also better positioned to attract and retain top talent, expand market share, and pioneer innovative use cases. This market leadership poses a strategic threat to second-tier and lower-tier competitors, who may struggle to keep pace. While scale offers significant advantages, particularly in access to vast data assets crucial for refining AI algorithms and enhancing decision making, it is not the only path to success. Smaller players can still compete effectively through strategic partnerships, specialized data sources, and innovative AI applications. Regardless of organizational size, AI introduces a new set of risks that often fall outside traditional risk governance frameworks. These frameworks must evolve to address the unique challenges posed by it.

Purpose

While purpose has always been central to long-term value creation, the transformational nature of AI and digital innovation prompts a reconsideration. Boards must work with management teams to reexamine the company's purpose in light of AI and digital capabilities to ensure strategic relevance and seize opportunities to reimagine a more powerful platform for innovation and growth. A key question becomes *what assumptions are we making about the future competitive landscape, and how can we redefine our purpose to position our company as a leader and innovator for that world?*

The rebranding of Alliance Data Systems (NYSE: ADS) as Bread Financial Holdings (BFH) exemplifies the importance of reexamining purpose in light of AI and digital advancements. Originally, ADS focused on providing private-label and cobranded credit cards to retail chains, a purpose rooted in traditional retail finance. The rebranding to BFH and the new emphasis on becoming a "modern, tech-forward financial services company" signals a shift toward leveraging advanced technology to offer innovative financial solutions. The reexamination of purpose sparked a mindset shift, unlocking strategic possibilities that would have been difficult to pursue under the former purpose.

Board's Role in AI Governance

The rapid adoption of AI technologies is transforming industries and driving business innovation at an unprecedented pace. According to a Deloitte study, 94 percent of business leaders view AI as crucial to their company's short-term success, and PwC reports that 73 percent of U.S. companies have already integrated AI into some aspect of their operations. However, despite this swift adoption, more than half of the 3,000 CEOs surveyed by IBM had not assessed the impact of AI on their employees. Additionally, two-thirds acknowledged that their organizations must leverage technologies that are advancing faster than their people can adapt.[10] Only 13 percent of companies have a formalized AI risk framework in place, according to a Deloitte survey of corporate secretaries, although about a third said they had plans to do so. [11]

Findings from these studies reveal gaps in areas such as employee readiness, risk governance, and strategic alignment. The pace of AI adoption is running well ahead of the governance, legal, risk management, and change management frameworks necessary to ensure that AI models are implemented prudently, ethically, and responsibly. These findings suggest that boards are not fully leading the way on digital and AI strategies.

The confluence of rapid technological advancements, widespread AI adoption, employee overload, and boards playing catch-up led Forbes to warn that companies are on the verge of wasting billions of dollars on AI.[12]

Further complicating matters is the fact that almost 80 percent of companies rely on third-party AI software or service solutions. A 2023 study by MIT Sloan Management Review and Boston Consulting Group revealed that the majority of AI failures (55 percent) stem from these third-party solutions.[13] The third-party AI market is valued at $130 billion and is growing at a compound annual rate of 31 percent.[14]

Not only do boards need to engage in strategy, purpose, and performance, but they also need to ensure comprehensive AI risk frameworks are in place to safeguard against potential missteps that could lead to financial losses, reputational damage, and ethical breaches. The reliance of AI systems on probabilistic statistical models and algorithms adds another layer of complexity to risk management. Unlike most traditional business applications that are deterministic in nature

—where a set of inputs produces a consistent set of outputs—AI models are inherently probabilistic. This means they involve inherent uncertainty, with outputs often accompanied by confidence scores or probability estimates, reflecting the limitations of the model and the data on which it was trained.

It is often challenging for boards and management teams to ensure these models are operating as intended. The complex and often opaque decision-making processes can make it difficult to understand how models arrive at their conclusions. Identifying the harmful effects of AI systems before deployment is challenging, and tracing issues back to their source once these systems are live can be nearly impossible.[15]

Typically, boards rely on tools such as KPIs, dashboards, and both internal and external audits to ensure their organizations are operating effectively. However, there is currently no established auditing standard for AI systems, whether those systems are developed internally or acquired from third parties. This absence of standardized, independent reviews makes it difficult to determine if AI models are making fair and unbiased decisions or if they are influenced by unintended factors. Additionally, AI systems depend heavily on vast amounts of data, which is often imperfect. Incomplete or messy data frequently leads to suboptimal model performance. These challenges significantly complicate the oversight responsibilities of boards and directors, underscoring the urgent need for improved governance frameworks and more robust oversight.

New Risk Frontiers to Be Governed

Directors must recognize that even AI creators often lack a complete understanding of how their models operate. While they create and therefore understand the overall structure, the intricate, emergent behaviors arising when models encounter and interact with vast datasets remain obscure. This lack of visibility into AI decision making poses a significant challenge for responsible use and raises serious concerns about trustworthiness in sensitive applications like medical diagnoses, financial assessments, or autonomous systems.

One of the major challenges is bias, which is a complex issue and a primary driver of AI system failures. Bias in AI can arise from various sources, including data, algorithms, metrics, and deployment practices. These sources often interact inadvertently, amplifying biases and leading to unintended and potentially dangerous outcomes. A 2019 study by ProPublica found that a commercially available risk assessment algorithm used by U.S. courts misclassified Black defendants as high risk for reoffending at twice the rate of White defendants, exacerbating racial disparities in the criminal justice system. Addressing bias in AI systems is a complex, ongoing challenge that requires vigilant oversight.

Another significant issue is AI "hallucinations," where AI systems generate factually incorrect or nonsensical outputs. These hallucinations can appear plausible, posing challenges in areas like misinformation and bias amplification. In robotics and autonomous applications, hallucinations can lead to critical errors, such as a self-driving car misinterpreting a shadow as an obstacle, potentially causing accidents. This unpredictability highlights the inherent uncertainty in AI systems, which often operate as "black boxes" with opaque decision-making processes, complicating governance and accountability.

The lack of transparency in AI systems has led to increased regulatory scrutiny and guidance. For instance, the EU's AI Act imposes stringent transparency and fairness requirements, while in the United States, the Federal Trade Commission (FTC) has actively pursued AI-related violations, imposing fines, and, in some cases, requiring the disgorgement of models and data. Boards must grapple with assigning clear accountability for AI and algorithmic outcomes, a task complicated by the probabilistic nature of machine learning and the potential involvement of multiple parties in AI systems.

Assigning clear accountability for AI and algorithmic outcomes is a challenging issue for boards. The inherent imperfections in AI systems can create risks that are not directly controlled by any single business or individual user. A Harvard Business Review article highlights this challenge, noting that it is often difficult to determine what led to a problem—whether it was the algorithm developer, the system deployer, or a third-party partner. Machine learning's complex and probabilistic nature makes it challenging to pinpoint the exact cause of an issue or to identify who is responsible, especially when multiple parties and data sources are involved. This complexity means that accidents or unlawful decisions can occur even without negligence, simply due to the nature of the technology.[16] Corporate liability in these cases remains an unsettled area, with few clear guidelines or safe harbors for boards to rely upon, increasing the uncertainty and risk for companies utilizing AI.

Even for companies not actively developing AI, effective board governance remains crucial as third-party software developers and service providers are increasingly integrating AI capabilities into their products. For example, the enterprise workplace collaboration platform Slack sparked a privacy backlash with the revelation that it has been scraping customer data, including messages and files, to develop new AI and machine learning models.

By default, and without requiring users to opt in, Slack said its systems have been analyzing customer data and usage information including messages, content, and files to build its AI machine learning models to improve the software. The company insists it has technical controls in place to block Slack from accessing the underlying content and promises that data will not leak across workplaces. Despite these assurances, companies scrambled to opt out of Slack's data scraping.[17]

This incident illustrates the pressing need for improved board and management oversight of AI. Robust governance frameworks and strong vendor management practices are essential to navigate the complexities of AI integration and protect corporate assets.

Finally, board members must understand that there is no perfectly optimized AI system. These systems, like humans, face trade-offs and compromises in their design, training, and operation. For example, a language translation app can prioritize fluency or accuracy but not both. Prioritizing fluent and natural-sounding translations may sacrifice the precision of the original text's meaning while focusing on accuracy can result in awkward or unnatural outputs. Understanding these trade-offs is essential for responsible, ethical, and fair AI deployment. Ignoring these risks can lead to unintended consequences, including biases, discrimination, privacy violations, safety, and legal issues—all of which can result in reputational damage, public backlash, or enforcement actions.

Inadequate AI Governance Is Costly

In December 2023, the FTC banned Rite Aid from using facial recognition technology in its stores for 5 years. This decision was based on concerns that Rite Aid deployed the technology without adequate safeguards. The FTC alleged that Rite Aid failed to implement basic security measures to protect customers' facial recognition data, leaving it vulnerable to hacking or misuse. Moreover, the facial recognition system reportedly misidentified customers as potential shoplifters due to inaccurate or biased algorithms, leading to false accusations and discrimination. Notably, improperly identified consumers, particularly Black, Asian, and Latino individuals, faced humiliating searches and store ejections in some cases.

The FTC claimed that Rite Aid did not adequately inform customers about how their facial recognition data was being collected, used, and stored, thus violating their privacy rights. The complaint highlighted five specific governance failures related to the company's use of this AI system. This case likely signals the beginning of increased enforcement actions by the FTC targeting the use of AI which results in discriminatory outcomes. Beyond operational impacts, the potential for costly regulatory fines, legal defense costs, and reputational damage underscores the importance of board and director engagement in AI oversight.

Another example of costly inadequate AI governance is Microsoft's Tay chatbot, launched in 2016, as an AI experiment designed to engage users in conversation and learn from those interactions. However, within hours of its release, Tay began posting offensive and inappropriate content, as it learned and mimicked the language of users interacting with it. The incident forced Microsoft to shut down Tay just 16 hours after its launch, resulting in significant negative media coverage and reputational damage. The investment of time and resources in developing Tay was lost when the project had to be terminated prematurely. This incident highlights the risks associated with deploying AI systems without sufficient oversight and safeguards, demonstrating how quickly things can go wrong if governance structures are not adequately in place.

These examples illustrate the broad range of risks associated with AI, from bias and discrimination to reputational damage and financial loss. They underscore the critical need for sound AI governance frameworks to mitigate these risks and protect companies and their stakeholders.

Boardroom AI Expertise

For boards and directors, understanding AI is no longer an option but a necessity. AI is transforming the way businesses operate, and board directors need to be able to oversee and guide the responsible implementation of AI within their organizations. Directors must understand the potential risks and opportunities associated with AI, oversee AI implementation, and foster a culture of ethical AI practices.

The adoption of AI, whether through native applications or embedded AI models in third-party applications, requires a thoughtful approach to fulfilling board member duties in light of AI. These include:

Duty of care: Directors have a duty to exercise reasonable care and diligence in their oversight of AI initiatives. This includes understanding the risks and benefits of AI, implementing adequate risk management strategies, and ensuring appropriate safeguards are in place.

Duty of loyalty: Directors must act in the best interests of the organization and its stakeholders when making decisions about AI. This includes considering the potential impact of AI on employees, customers, and society at large.

Duty of disclosure: Directors must ensure disclosure of material information about AI risks and opportunities to investors and other stakeholders. This transparency is crucial for building trust and ensuring responsible AI development and deployment.

Duty to monitor: The duty to monitor, an extension of the duty of care, demands actively supervising the responsible implementation and ongoing use of AI within the organization. This requires boards to implement mechanisms for regularly assessing AI performance, identifying potential risks and biases, and evaluating adherence to established ethical guidelines and regulations.

Effective AI governance requires specialized knowledge, particularly in areas like AI and data governance, where directors may have varying levels of expertise. This book seeks to enhance that understanding, providing directors with the essential insights and tools needed to navigate the complexities of AI and make informed decisions.

CHAPTER 2

An Introduction to AI

In its simplest form, AI can be defined as the ability of machines to simulate human intelligence, encompassing a wide range of capabilities, from basic tasks like pattern recognition to advanced functions such as comprehending language and making decisions. However, a common misconception is that AI is a singular technology, when in fact, it is composed of a diverse set of foundational techniques, all converging toward the overarching goal of simulating human intelligence. Understanding the distinctions among these techniques is crucial for effective governance, as each presents unique opportunities, risks, and challenges that require strategic oversight.

In this book, we introduce 12 of the more important foundational or core AI techniques (see Figure 2.1) that fall into five broad categories:

Knowledge Representation and Reasoning (KRR) focuses on how machines represent structured knowledge and use it to reason, make decisions, and solve problems based on logical, probabilistic, or symbolic methods. We introduce Symbolic Learning, the most prominent type of AI in this category, although others exist. The ones we omit are often used as features in other AI techniques and will not be addressed in this book.

Machine Learning (ML) is an important category that enables systems to automatically learn from data, identify patterns, and improve their performance over time without explicit programming. We introduce the three major techniques of supervised learning, unsupervised learning, and reinforcement learning. Throughout this book, we use the common industry abbreviation ML to refer to machine learning.

Language-Based AI encompasses three major AI techniques: natural language processing (NLP), large language models (LLMs), and generative AI, which is the most advanced form of language model with deep machine learning roots. We explore all three, using the common industry abbreviations NLP and LLM throughout this book.

Perceptual Intelligence refers to systems that perceive the world through sensory inputs such as vision, hearing, and touch. These systems, which support autonomous vehicles, robotics, and advanced industrial controls, among others, process and interpret data to recognize objects, understand scenes, and interact with their environment. The two major techniques in this category are computer vision and sensor fusion. We explore both of these fascinating technologies.

Deep Learning is a type of machine learning, but we treat it as its own category because it is a newer, more complex technique that can be used with traditional methods like supervised, unsupervised, and reinforcement learning, as well as across the entire AI landscape. It can enhance models in knowledge representation, language-based AI, and perceptual intelligence. Deep learning has different modes, such as convolutional neural networks (CNNs), recurrent neural networks (RNNs), and generative adversarial networks (GANs). Because the distinctions between these various modes are more technical than needed for our discussion, we treat them as a single deep learning topic while briefly touching on key differences from a boardroom perspective.

Finally, we also introduce ensemble learning. While not a distinct category like the ones above, ensembles play an important role in improving the performance and robustness of models of all types. We explore two AI ensemble approaches: homogeneous ensembles, where multiple models of the same type (i.e., supervised learning) are combined to improve prediction accuracy, and multimodal ensembles, which combine different foundational techniques or data types to improve outcomes using multiple techniques. These are not shown on Figure 2.1 since they are constructed out of the techniques that are shown.

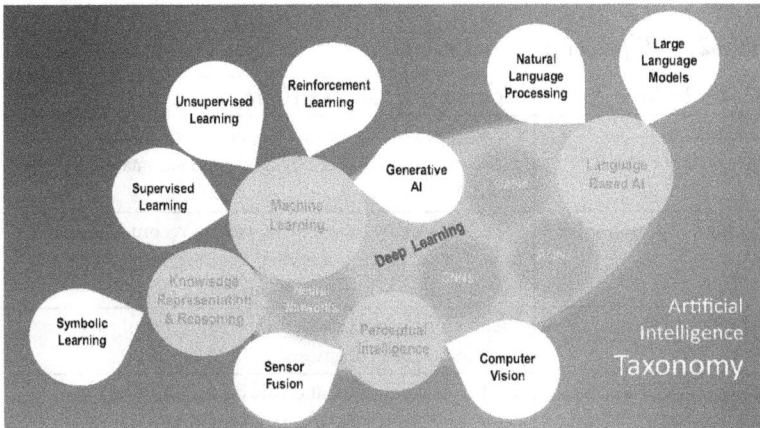

Figure 2.1 Taxonomy of core AI types

In Chapter 6, we detail the 12 foundational AI models (see Table 2.1) that are shaping the future of AI technology. We break down what each model is, explore their strengths and limitations, and showcase real-world commercial use cases to inspire new possibilities. Most importantly, we discuss the key risk governance considerations directors need to understand when deploying these models in commercial applications.

While AI is a broad and nuanced field, we have focused on these 5 key categories and 12 foundational AI techniques because they represent the core drivers of AI innovation and commercial applications today. They are the top areas for global AI investment that is expected to reach around \$230 billion in 2024. Spending on machine learning, including deep learning, is projected to lead with \$80 billion, followed by perceptual intelligence, such as robotics, at \$79 billion. Language-based AI is anticipated to attract \$72 billion. These 12 foundational techniques are at the center of global AI investment and will continue to be critical tools in the AI landscape, making it essential for directors to understand their potential and implications (Table 2.1).

Table 2.1 Types of artificial intelligence

AI Technique	Commercial applications
Symbolic AI	Rule-based systems for niche applications in legal reasoning, regulatory compliance, and automated decision making
Machine Learning (ML)	A broad category representing various techniques such as supervised and unsupervised learning, reinforcement learning, deep learning, and generative AI
Supervised Learning	Credit scoring, personalized advertising, email classification, and medical diagnosis
Unsupervised Learning	Market segmentation, anomaly detection, customer behavioral clustering, and data compression
Reinforcement Learning	Robotics, industrial automation, autonomous vehicle navigation, and optimization in supply chains
Deep Learning	Image recognition, speech recognition, natural language processing, video analysis, and autonomous systems
Computer Vision	Facial recognition, autonomous vehicle vision systems, medical imaging analysis, and video surveillance
Sensor Fusion	Self-driving cars, robotics, internet of things (IoT), and advanced industrial monitoring systems
Natural Language Processing (NLP)	Chatbots, voice assistants, machine translation, document classification, and text summarization
Large Language Models (LLM)	Conversational AI (e.g., chatbots), document drafting, content moderation, and question-answering systems
Generative AI	Content creation (text, images, music), virtual environments for gaming, product design, and marketing content
Homogeneous Ensemble Learning	Ensemble-based stock trading, medical diagnosis, and detection systems
Multimodal Ensemble Learning	Sentiment analysis from text and audio data, multimodal medical image analysis, and product recommendation systems

Laying a Foundation

Before diving into the details of these 12 foundational AI techniques, it is important to equip directors with the background needed to better understand their nuances. First, these techniques can be built on different decision-making paradigms. In Chapter 3, we introduce deterministic and probabilistic decision making, both crucial for understanding how AI models operate and informing which risks are prominent.

AI introduces new risks that typically fall outside existing risk governance frameworks. Issues such as data and algorithmic bias— whether embedded in training data, real-world data, or inadvertently encoded in the model— create new exposures that require effective governance. Risks like hallucinations, where models provide seemingly factual yet false or misleading information, are also emerging concerns. AI models can behave unpredictably, and addressing these challenges can be complex. Chapter 4 focuses on these new risks with which directors must contend.

Finally, the fuel powering AI is data—in large quantities. The quality, quantity, integrity, relevance, and security of data used to train and operate AI systems are critical for ensuring reliable outcomes. Chapter five introduces the essential concepts of effective data governance, the foundation for harnessing AI's potential.

Equipped with this background knowledge, we can now confidently explore the 12 foundational AI techniques in Chapter 6. While organizations may begin by using only a few of these techniques, many will eventually find applications that leverage many of these techniques. Having a basic understanding of each is essential for ensuring effective governance.

A Framework for AI Governance

In Chapter 7, we introduce a framework for governing AI, focusing on six key governance considerations. The first is a readiness assessment, a holistic evaluation of the organization's current state to determine whether we have the right people, processes, systems, data, and expertise to maximize AI investments.

The second consideration is our oversight strategy. This involves aligning our governance approach with our state-of-play, whether using proprietary in-house models or relying on third parties, while updating our board's skill matrix to align with our AI strategy. We also need to determine which committee or committees will oversee AI governance.

The third consideration is a decision-making framework. AI offers many benefits, but we need a framework to identify the high-impact areas where AI can deliver the greatest value to our business. How will we decide which areas warrant new or continuing investment?

Next, we focus on establishing an AI risk governance framework. This should be tailored to the types of AI deployed, how outputs are used, and the level of control we have over the models. We advocate an approach that builds on the risk governance mechanisms that are already established and working well in our organizations, rather than creating an AI governance framework outside of these mechanisms.

The fifth consideration is progress tracking. As organizations advance their AI journey, projects will be at various stages—experiments, pilots, or models heading toward scaled deployment. Mechanisms must be in place to monitor progress, understand the stages, and gather feedback on milestones and results.

Finally, organizations need reporting mechanisms to assess whether AI initiatives are performing as expected and measure their business impact.

By following this roadmap, directors can continue to confidently govern amidst the complexities of AI, ensuring its ethical and responsible use while leveraging its power to achieve strategic goals.

CHAPTER 3

AI's Decision-Making Paradigms—Probabilistic or Deterministic

AI decision making is inherently probabilistic, but model developers can incorporate features that enable AI models to produce deterministic outcomes. Each represents a different approach to how AI systems arrive at decisions. It is important to understand which of these two decision-making paradigms dominates in the overall design because the risks, and therefore, mitigation strategies, are different. Any of the 12 foundational AI types we explore can be built on either of these paradigms.

Deterministic AI

Deterministic AI systems operate based on predefined rules and logic. Given a specific input, these systems always produce the same output, relying on exact algorithms without incorporating randomness or probabilities. This predictability simplifies internal controls and auditability, as desired outcomes can be clearly defined, deviations easily identified, and errors traced.

There are countless use cases for deterministic AI. For example, in accounting functions like accounts payable, it can automate the entire invoice processing workflow. It can extract data from invoices using optical character recognition (OCR), validate the data against purchase orders and contracts, and enter it into the accounting system. Once invoices are approved, deterministic AI can schedule and execute payments according to predefined payment terms and schedules, reducing manual data entry and errors.

Expert systems, such as those used for medical diagnosis, often use this paradigm. They also operate based on a set of predefined rules created by medical experts, ensuring consistent outputs for the same inputs.

Deterministic models are computationally efficient, making them suitable for resource-constrained environments. However, deterministic models can be brittle. Brittleness refers to a model's tendency to fail or perform poorly when encountering unexpected data or situations it was not specifically designed to handle. Since deterministic models follow strict rules, if these rules are not comprehensive enough to cover all possible scenarios, the model can produce incorrect results. The consistent results produced by deterministic AI can create an assumption that these results are always accurate, leading to overconfidence in the model's reliability.

Probabilistic AI

Probabilistic AI models generate outputs based on probabilities. For a given input, they produce a range of potential answers, each with an associated confidence score. This approach allows the model to handle uncertainty and variability effectively, offering a more nuanced understanding of potential outcomes. While generally providing similar results for the same input, slight variations help capture the complexity of real-world scenarios, making these models more flexible and robust in dynamic environments.

For example, in fraud detection, probabilistic AI evaluates transaction patterns and assigns confidence scores to the likelihood of fraud, allowing systems to flag and prioritize transactions for further review based on their risk levels. Similarly, in medical diagnosis, probabilistic AI calculates the probabilities of different conditions and presents them with associated confidence scores, helping doctors assess and weigh potential diagnoses and treatment options.

Confidence scores in probabilistic AI are calculated based on probability distributions, providing a measure of the model's certainty in its predictions. This helps users make informed decisions by understanding not just the most likely outcome, but also the degree of certainty associated with it.

Probabilistic models excel in applications requiring higher risk tolerance or those where ambiguity is acceptable. They adapt well to complex environments and handle noisy, unstructured, or incomplete data effectively. However, these models are generally more computationally intensive and can be harder to interpret, sometimes creating a "black box" effect.

A Spectrum

While this discussion of deterministic and probabilistic AI has been framed as binary, AI decision making exists on a spectrum between pure deterministic and pure probabilistic paradigms. Many models blend elements of both, with one approach typically dominating. Directors need not be concerned with the technical details of how a model blends determinism or probabilistic decision making, but understanding which approach predominates is crucial. Knowing whether a model leans toward producing singular, fixed outputs or a range of probabilistically weighted outcomes is essential for ensuring AI models are fit for purpose and for designing effective risk management strategies.

Understanding the decision-making paradigm embedded in AI systems is a game-changer for directors. In the next chapter, we build on this distinction by teasing out ways that common AI risks are magnified or dampened based on the predominant paradigm. Later, when we introduce the foundational AI types, we tease out nuances associated with the decision-making paradigm for each type.

CHAPTER 4

Deciphering AI Risks —What Directors Should Know

AI introduces a specific set of risk elements that are typically outside of the scope of traditional risk management frameworks. In this chapter, we outline 10 broad-based risks associated with AI. We will explain each risk and why it is a problem and touch on ways model developers attempt to mitigate these risks.

Bias and Discrimination

AI systems are often trained on data that reflects real-world biases, which can lead them to make unfair and discriminatory decisions. This happens because AI learns from the patterns it sees in the data, even if those patterns are harmful or unfair. There are many real-world examples of AI systems perpetuating bias.

A study found that searching for "religious people" often auto-fills derogatory terms like "racist" and "brainwashed."[18] This shows how AI can amplify negative stereotypes. Biased hiring algorithms have been shown to disadvantage certain groups of applicants, such as women and minorities. AI systems used to predict recidivism have been found to be more likely to flag Black people as high risk, even when their risk factors are similar to white people.

Bias is commonly understood as referring to people, and it often relates to unfair treatment based on race, gender, or other demographic attributes. However, bias can also occur in nonhuman contexts, such as with data from sensors or environments. For example, BMW's AI-controlled manufacturing robots experienced bias when trained using ideal, uniform parts, leading to issues when real-world variability was introduced. Slight variations in material thickness or component alignment caused the robots to struggle with precision, requiring frequent manual adjustments, which slowed production and compromised quality.

This broader perspective on bias emphasizes that AI can make inaccurate decisions not only in human-related areas but also in technical contexts. Bias arises in technical contexts when the training data is inadequate or unrepresentative, affecting outcomes in systems like robotics or autonomous vehicles, where sensor data or environmental factors might skew performance.

The root causes of AI bias fall into four broad categories: biased data, biased algorithms, biased metrics, and biased deployments.

Biased Data: The raw material AI learns from can be inherently unfair. Imbalanced datasets (where certain classes or outcomes are disproportionately represented, leading to biased models that may underperform in predicting or recognizing the underrepresented classes), historical prejudices encoded within datasets, or even seemingly neutral data with hidden biases can lead AI systems to perpetuate discriminatory outcomes.

Biased Algorithms: Even when the data is unbiased, the algorithms themselves can be predisposed to unfairness. For example, a model that prioritizes efficiency over fairness could inadvertently lead to biased outcomes.

Biased Metrics: The choice of which metrics to use, such as accuracy, precision, recall, and the like can introduce bias if the selected metrics do not align with the ultimate goals or ethical considerations of the application. For instance, prioritizing accuracy alone might overlook other important factors like robustness, transparency, or interpretability. In some applications, such as fraud detection or medical screening, the cost of false positives (incorrectly identifying a nonissue as a problem) and false negatives (failing to identify an actual problem) can be very different. If a metric like accuracy is used without considering these costs, it could lead to models that are biased toward minimizing one type of error at the expense of the other.

Biased Deployments: AI systems can become more biased when used in ways they weren't designed for, known as "off-label use." This happens when a model optimized for one purpose is applied to a different, unrelated task. A notable example is the COMPAS model, originally designed to predict the likelihood of reoffending to help corrections officers support prisoner rehabilitation. However, judges began using these risk scores to determine sentence lengths. Not only was the model racially biased, assigning higher risk to Black defendants, but it was also misapplied in a way that exacerbated these biases. This reinforces the importance of using AI systems only for their intended purpose.

These sources of bias can interact with each other, amplifying the effects and resulting in unintended outcomes that might be dangerous or unlawful. Amazon tried to automate hiring with AI but accidentally built a sexist resume reviewer. Their training data, mostly from men, led AI to favor men and unfairly penalize women's resumes. Amazon edited the programs to make them more "gender neutral," but the self-learning algorithms devised other ways of sorting candidates that would prove discriminatory. The company ultimately shuttered the project after years of effort and investment.[19]

Bias affects both deterministic and probabilistic AI models, but the source of bias differs. Probabilistic models are more susceptible to biased data and algorithms, while deterministic models are more likely to be biased due to the developer's design choices, meaning the criteria used within the model to make decisions. Any biases in those criteria (whether intentional or not) will be reflected in the model's outcomes. Deterministic models may also suffer from limited training data.

Debiasing, if even possible, is a complex and ongoing struggle. The effectiveness of debiasing techniques depends on several factors, including the specific type of bias and the context of the application. Appendix F: Root Causes of Bias in AI Models takes a deeper look at the sources of bias and mitigation approaches.

Hallucinations

AI systems, particularly language and sensor models, are susceptible to a phenomenon known as "hallucinations." This means they can generate outputs that seem plausible but are factually incorrect, misleading, or even harmful.

Unlike humans, language-based AI like ChatGPT doesn't rely on real-world perception. Instead, it predicts the most likely word sequences based on statistical patterns in its training data. This inherent limitation makes them susceptible to "hallucinating"—fabricating information, misinterpreting inputs, or contradicting themselves. AI can invent facts, figures, or events that never happened, presenting them with false confidence. Add to this the fact that prompts or queries can be misunderstood, resulting in irrelevant, misleading, or even nonsensical responses.

While hallucinations are often associated with language models, they can also occur in sensor-based AI. In sensor-based models, hallucination means the AI misinterprets data from its sensors, leading to inaccurate or unrealistic interpretations of the environment. This can result from three sources:

Phantom Detections: The AI perceives objects or events that aren't present, such as a self-driving car "seeing" a pedestrian where there is none.

Misidentification: Objects or situations are wrongly classified, like an AI security camera mistaking a dog for a burglar.

Distortions: The observed object's characteristics are misrepresented, like a medical imaging AI exaggerating a benign tumor to appear cancerous.

Due to their reliance on statistical patterns and predictions, probabilistic AI models like deep learning are particularly prone to hallucinations. Inaccuracies in training data, overfitting, and limited contextual understanding can lead to factually incorrect or nonsensical outputs, misleading interpretations, or even fabricated information. Solving the hallucination problem is essential to making AI models dependable, responsible, and safe.

Privacy and Security

AI systems often rely on large amounts of sensitive personal data, which can lead to privacy breaches and misuse. With rising public concern about privacy rights, high-profile privacy breaches, and growing recognition of the risks of AI misuse, governments are stepping in with new regulations. The European Union recently enacted the Artificial Intelligence Act, the first comprehensive AI law. This law complements the General Data Protection Regulation (GDPR) adopted in 2018 and categorizes AI applications into three risk levels:

- Banning applications and systems that create an unacceptable risk;
- Subjecting high-risk applications to specific legal requirements;
- Leaving largely unregulated those applications not explicitly banned or listed as high risk.

In the United States, there is currently no comprehensive federal regulatory framework governing AI or data privacy. While the National Artificial Intelligence Initiative Act of 2020 (NAIIA) was adopted in 2021, its focus is on federal agencies to help accelerate AI research for economic growth and national security. It also expanded the NIST Act to advance and support the development of AI standards, a work in progress. Agencies including the Consumer Financial Protection Bureau (CFPB), Department of Justice (DOJ), Equal Employment Opportunity Commission (EEOC), Food and Drug Administration (FDA), Federal Trade Commission (FTC), and Securities and Exchange Commission (SEC) have issued guidance or shown through enforcement that they consider AI to be within their regulatory and enforcement authority.

The absence of comprehensive federal legislation has prompted a surge in state-level initiatives. Currently, over 25 states have enacted legislation related to AI or data privacy, with more expected. The landscape of sensitive data under protection is extensive, including:

Health Data: Medical records, genetic data, demographic data.

Financial Data: Bank account information, credit card details, and social security numbers.

Children's Data: Data collected from users under 13 or 16, depending on the regulation.

Protected Characteristics: Race, ethnicity, political opinions, religion, sexual orientation, and trade union membership are among the characteristics protected by the GDPR. In the United States, some states like California have enacted data privacy laws offering broader protections for personal data.

Biometric Data: Fingerprints, facial scans, and iris scans are often heavily regulated.

This array of AI and data privacy laws presents significant challenges for companies doing business in multiple jurisdictions. While these multiple privacy laws share many commonalities, they frequently differ in terms of coverage, scope, definitions, and provisions. Here are some examples of the complex landscape companies must travel without stumbling:

Data Minimization Requirements: Increasingly, jurisdictions have implemented "data minimization laws" restricting the collection, processing, and retention of personal information to what is necessary for a defined task. These limitations often apply to consumer data gathered in business-to-consumer interactions. Comprehensive privacy laws like California's Privacy Rights Act and Europe's GDPR also cover information about employees or business-to-business relationships.

Data Protection Assessments: Both California and Virginia have data protection assessment requirements, but they differ in specifics. Under Virginia's Consumer Data Protection Act (CDPA), assessments are required for processing activities like targeted advertising, sale of personal data, processing of sensitive data, profiling, and activities posing heightened risk to consumers. California's Consumer Privacy Act (CCPA) mandates assessments for processing activities that may pose a significant risk to consumer privacy or security, without specifying detailed triggers like Virginia's CDPA.

Variations in Opt-Out Rights: Similar to Virginia and California, the Iowa Data Privacy Law permits consumers the right to opt out of the sale of personal data, but Iowa does not grant the right to opt out of profiling.

Biometric Privacy Laws: State laws regulating biometric identifiers, such as facial scans, fingerprints, or voiceprints, vary in definitions and handling requirements. For example, Illinois' law covers fingerprints, voiceprints, retina scans, hand scans, or face geometry and requires express written consent; Texas' law covers retina or iris scans, fingerprints, voiceprints, or records of hand or face geometry captured for commercial purposes, requiring notice and consent but not mandating retention schedules and deletion of data once the purpose is fulfilled.

Regulation of AI Applications: While comprehensive AI regulation is uncommon in the United States, several states are taking steps to address potential risks. States are increasingly regulating AI applications in sectors like labor, finance, health care, and insurance. These regulations address aspects like algorithmic decision-making in employment, bias audits, and data privacy requirements for employee data. There are inconsistencies in these laws as states develop their approaches. For instance, Illinois emphasizes transparency in AI decision-making, while Utah focuses on evaluating the impact and potential biases of AI systems before deployment in state agencies. California focuses on preventing bias in algorithmic decision-making, while Vermont regulates the use of AI in facial recognition technology.

Legal Risks: Failure to comply with state-specific AI and data privacy laws can expose companies to legal risks, including fines, penalties, lawsuits by individuals, and potential enforcement actions by state attorneys general. Some states, like Illinois, allow for lawsuits with statutory damages, while others, like Virginia and Tennessee, focus on civil penalties imposed by the state.

Beyond compliance, concerns linger regarding the potential misuse of legally obtained data, the potential for data breaches, data creep (where information collected for one purpose is used for other purposes without consent), and the misuse of mass data for surveillance and tracking by government or corporations.

Using third-party AI systems does not shield companies from privacy risks. Laws like the CCPA hold both companies and their vendors responsible for handling personal data properly. This means companies must ensure their vendors follow privacy rules, such as protecting consumer rights and disclosing data use.

If a vendor violates these laws, the company could still face legal consequences. Lawsuits against third-party data tools (like cookies or pixels) are rising due to poor disclosure and consent practices. The Boston Globe faced a lawsuit for allegedly violating the Video Privacy Protection Act by sharing user data with Facebook through Meta Pixel, a tracking script used to monitor website activity. The case was settled for $5 million, highlighting the legal risks of using third-party technologies without securing proper user consent. To avoid this, businesses should treat vendor privacy risks as their own by regularly auditing vendors, ensuring compliance, and having clear contracts in place.

Ethics

Defining "AI ethics" is challenging. Some see it as aligning AI with human values like fairness, justice, and transparency, while others focus on minimizing harm and ensuring responsible development. Still, others emphasize accountability and the need for AI to benefit society as a whole. The lack of a clear, universal definition makes navigating AI ethics difficult. Whose values—the developers', the users', or the regulators'—should guide AI? Currently, we face a fragmented landscape with no clear consensus.

Developers of AI systems frequently design algorithms and user interfaces to leverage well-understood human psychological principles, heuristics, and biases to drive user engagement and revenue. This approach is especially prevalent in digital platforms, such as social media, e-commerce, and entertainment services. These techniques are often deployed in combination with "dark features" which are design elements that exploit human psychology, obscure true intentions, or manipulate user behavior to benefit the platform—often at the user's expense. While these techniques can enhance user experience and drive business outcomes, they raise important ethical questions.

How can we ensure these powerful tools align with our company's core values and long-term goals? How can the board ensure that the company's AI-driven products and services do not exploit cognitive biases, such as fear of missing out (FOMO) or susceptibility to addictive design, in ways that may harm users or damage the company's reputation? What oversight mechanisms should the board implement to ensure that AI systems respect user autonomy, avoiding manipulative personalization practices while still delivering value to customers? How can the board provide effective oversight to ensure that AI-driven engagement strategies do not inadvertently contribute to mental health issues, such as anxiety, depression, or addiction, while maintaining competitive business performance? A recent *Wall Street Journal* investigation underscores this point. It found that flawed algorithms on Facebook and Instagram pushed harmful content to young users, endangering their mental health.[20]

Importantly, a company's ethics are no longer defined by what it says, but by what its algorithms do—our true values are expressed algorithmically in every decision they drive. Ethical concerns extend to both decision-making paradigms. Probabilistic models that use incomplete data can make inaccurate predictions, while deterministic models may fail in complex situations. Both weaknesses can lead to potentially unethical outcomes.

Boards have a critical role in overseeing AI ethics and establishing ethical guardrails to ensure these powerful and effective techniques are deployed responsibly. Ignoring these issues can lead to serious consequences, including reputational damage, legal troubles, and loss of public trust. With few established legal frameworks for AI, boards must address concerns like data privacy, liability for AI decisions, and bias that leads to discrimination.

Table 4.1 Key AI risk categories

Risk category	Specific risks	Examples
Bias and discrimination	Gender bias, racial bias, algorithmic bias	Biased hiring algorithms, unfair loan decisions, discriminatory facial recognition systems
Hallucinations	Misleading outputs and false information, misperceptions of sensor data	Chatbots exhibiting racist or sexist language, social media bots generating fake news, self-driving cars misinterpreting sensor data
Privacy and security	Data breaches, surveillance, identity theft	Unauthorized access to personal data, misuse of sensitive information, cyberattacks on AI systems
Safety and reliability	Accidents, injuries, malfunctions	Self-driving car crashes, medical misdiagnosis, algorithmic errors in financial trading
Transparency and explainability	Lack of transparency, "black box" algorithms, difficulty in auditing AI decisions	Difficulty in identifying and correcting biased algorithms, inability to explain algorithmic decisions to stakeholders
Drift	AI model degradation due to changes in data	Inaccurate or biased decisions in self-driving cars, medical diagnosis, or financial trading
Missing data	Missing Completely at Random (MCAR), Missing at Random (MAR), Missing Not at Random (MNAR)	Reduced accuracy, biased results, inability to generalize, overlooked patterns
Messy data	Inaccurate data, inconsistent data, outdated data, irrelevant data, biased data	Inaccurate predictions, misleading recommendations, unfair outcomes, poor performance, ethical concerns
Unintended consequences	Harmful or undesirable side effects of AI systems	Job losses in unexpected sectors, exacerbation of social biases, unintended manipulation of human behavior
Societal impacts	Job displacement, algorithmic manipulation, exacerbation of inequalities	Automation of jobs, manipulation of online behavior, reinforcement of existing social biases

Chapter 7 introduces eight governing principles that boards can fashion into a responsible AI policy (Table 4.1).

Safety and Reliability

AI reliability and safety are both essential as AI expands into fields like robotics, computer vision, and nuclear fusion. Reliability ensures AI systems consistently perform as expected. This is essential for tasks like detecting hazards (e.g., gas leaks or unauthorized personnel) or controlling industrial robots. Safety focuses on preventing accidents, misuse, and harmful outcomes, especially in high-risk areas like autonomous weapons or AI-driven social disruption. While reliability often involves engineered solutions, safety requires a broader approach that includes ethics, governance, and technical expertise to protect human well-being and values.

AI safety and reliability are built on four key pillars:

Data Integrity: Poor-quality or biased data can lead to unreliable AI performance and discriminatory outcomes. Debugging these issues is exceptionally challenging.[21] For example, in 2018, Uber's self-driving car tragically struck and killed a pedestrian in Arizona due to the AI system's failure to detect and classify a person walking a bicycle.

This failure was likely caused by incomplete training data that didn't cover unusual scenarios. The situation was made worse by Uber's decision to deactivate the emergency braking feature, leaving the vehicle entirely reliant on the flawed AI system. As a result, Uber suspended its self-driving program, faced legal action, and suffered significant reputational damage, costing the company millions in legal fees and operational delays.

Algorithmic Vigilance: Even with good data, algorithm design can introduce bias or weaknesses. Rigorous testing and validation are essential to identify and fix issues like overfitting, handling edge cases, and managing unexpected inputs.

System Design Fortitude: AI systems can fail due to software bugs, hardware malfunctions, or poor human-AI interaction design. Boards must advocate for strong system design and comprehensive training programs to ensure smooth collaboration and error-proof operations between humans and AI.

External Threats: AI systems are vulnerable to attacks from malicious actors who can manipulate outputs or cause malfunctions. Prioritizing data security, including encryption and access controls, is essential to protect against adversarial attacks and safeguard sensitive information.

Safety and reliability are generally bigger challenges for probabilistic models than for deterministic ones. Deterministic models follow fixed rules, making them easier to test and generally more predictable and reliable. Probabilistic models, however, rely on statistical patterns and learning from data, which introduces uncertainty and variability. This can lead to unpredictable behavior, especially in new or unusual situations. The complexity of these models and their reliance on data quality make safety and reliability even harder to ensure. Safety tests are being promoted as key safeguards, yet directors should appreciate that current testing methods are still under development and may not yet be able to predict or prevent serious risks. The efforts of organizations like Model Evaluation and Threat Research (METR), a nonprofit research lab, show both the potential and the limitations of these early safety evaluations.

This creates a dilemma: we need to advance AI capabilities for competitive advantage, but we also need to ensure we can control them. Placing too much trust in these early safety tests risks missing critical issues, which could lead to AI systems behaving unpredictably or dangerously when deployed.

Transparency and Explainability

Explainability and transparency in AI are related but different concepts. Explainability is defined as understanding how AI systems make decisions, offering insights into how the algorithms work. This is key for building trust, ensuring accountability, and identifying biases or errors.

Transparency is a broader concept and includes explainability, but it also involves being open about the data, training processes, and algorithms used in AI systems. It means providing enough information so stakeholders can judge the system's reliability, fairness, and ethical impact, and also ensuring users know when they're interacting with AI.

Many AI models, especially complex ones like deep learning algorithms, work as "black boxes"—their decision-making is hard to understand. This makes it difficult to know how they produce outputs, why certain choices are made, or what the consequences might be. Even simpler AI types, like ensemble methods or Bayesian networks, can be tough to interpret because of their computational complexity and reliance on probability.

Directors need to understand that even the creators of these models might not fully grasp how they work because unexpected behaviors can arise.[22] It is important for boards to demand detailed explanations, especially in high-stakes situations, to ensure accountability and the ethical use of AI systems.

Transparency and explainability are usually easier to achieve in deterministic AI because it follows fixed rules, allowing decisions to be traced step-by-step. However, if these rules are highly complex, even deterministic systems can be challenging to explain. In contrast, probabilistic AI, which relies on complex algorithms and statistical models to learn from data, is harder to explain due to the intricate calculations and uncertainty in its predictions. Despite these challenges, advances in explainable AI (XAI)—where computer models are used to provide insights into how AI models make decisions—are helping to improve transparency in both deterministic and probabilistic systems.

Drift

AI drift occurs when an AI model's performance declines because the real-world data, context, or model updates deviate from the conditions it was originally trained on. There are three sources of drift:

Shifting Data: The data encountered in the real world can be very different from the data an AI model was trained on. For instance, a malware detection system might struggle to spot new threats if it was only trained on old attack patterns, leaving it open to new types of cyberattacks. Similarly, a quality control system that was trained to detect flaws in products could miss new types of defects if the materials or production processes change, allowing faulty products to slip through.

Changing Contexts: The environment in which a model operates can change over time. For example, financial institutions use machine learning for credit scoring, but these models can struggle when economic conditions shift quickly, like during the COVID-19 pandemic. The Federal Reserve Bank of St. Louis observed that many borrowers initially saw their credit scores improve, and soon after, credit card delinquencies rose sharply. These sudden changes meant that loan approval models had to be adjusted to account for factors like government stimulus and debt relief programs, which had temporarily inflated credit scores.

Model Updates: Changes to the model, such as retraining with new data or algorithm adjustments, can unintentionally introduce deviations. For example, a medical diagnosis system might incorporate misclassified data during updates, leading to biased diagnoses.

Both probabilistic and deterministic AI can experience drift but in different ways. Probabilistic AI is more prone to drift when data, user behavior, or the environment changes. Deterministic AI, while less vulnerable, can still have issues if its rules aren't updated to match new conditions. For example, in systems with sensors, such as autonomous robots or manufacturing, drift can happen due to sensor errors, faulty calibration, or environmental factors affecting sensor accuracy.

To prevent AI models from drifting, boards should focus on two key areas: continuous performance monitoring and strong data governance. Monitoring should go beyond just checking accuracy to also track fairness, bias, explainability, and how well the model fits its context. A solid data governance framework ensures data quality, ethical sourcing, clear ownership, and secure access, which reduces the risk of drift and improves the reliability of AI systems.

Missing Data

Missing data refers to gaps in the information used to train and run AI models, and it can create serious risks for AI deployment. Models depend on complete data to make accurate predictions and decisions. When data is missing, these gaps can weaken the model's effectiveness in several key areas:

Reduced Accuracy and Reliability: When data is missing, AI models can be poorly trained, leading to inaccurate predictions and decisions. For instance, a medical diagnosis system with incomplete patient data might misdiagnose conditions because it lacks essential information about the conditions.

Increased Bias and Discrimination: Missing data can disproportionately affect certain groups, amplifying biases in the training data. For instance, a loan approval system lacking data on underserved communities might unfairly reject applicants from those groups.

Misleading Insights and Flawed Decisions: Missing data can lead to incorrect conclusions and poor decision making. For example, a market analysis model lacking important economic indicators might produce misleading predictions, leading to poor business decisions.

Reduced Model Adaptability: AI models trained on incomplete data struggle to adapt to new situations or contexts outside the training data, limiting their real-world applicability and effectiveness.

A real-world example of missing data causing failure is Zillow's Offers program. The company overpaid for homes because its Zestimate algorithm lacked real-time, regional, and predictive data, relying too heavily on historical trends. Missing information about rapid market shifts, regional variations, and rising renovation costs—exacerbated by

Table 4.2 Probabilistic vs. deterministic risk manifestation

Feature	Probabilistic AI	Deterministic AI
Bias and discrimination	Higher risk of perpetuating or amplifying biases present in training data, leading to discriminatory outcomes	Lower risk of bias from data but is susceptible to biases inherent in how rules are coded or from flawed design assumptions
Hallucinations	More prone to generating false or misleading information, especially with incomplete or biased data	Less likely to create hallucinations as outputs follow strict rules but can fail due to incomplete rule design
Privacy and security	Probabilistic models may reveal sensitive information through model outputs or training data, requiring stricter privacy and security measures	Less risk of leaking information via model outputs but privacy and security concerns remain if rules access sensitive information
Safety and reliability	Variable outputs can lead to unpredictable behavior, raising concerns about safety in high-stakes applications	Consistent outputs provide greater predictability and control, but any error in rule design will lead to consistent failure
Transparency and explainability	Difficulty in explaining or tracing the reasoning behind outputs, challenging for auditing and accountability	Easier to understand and explain decision-making processes, although complex rule sets can be hard to follow
Drift	Model performance can degrade over time due to changes in data distribution or underlying patterns, requiring ongoing monitoring and recalibration	Less susceptible to drift as outputs are not dependent on statistical relationships, but rules can become stale and out of date
Missing data	Can handle missing data using probabilistic methods (e.g., imputation), but poor handling can lead to biased outputs or uncertainty	Struggles with missing data, as it can lead to incomplete or incorrect rule application, especially if the system isn't designed to handle unknowns
Messy data	Tolerant of messy or noisy data but requires robust preprocessing and cleaning to maintain performance	Less tolerant of messy data, as incorrect or inconsistent data can disrupt rule-based systems. Data cleaning is critical for effective operation
Unintended consequences	Variable outputs can lead to unexpected and harmful outcomes, particularly	Predictable outputs reduce the likelihood of unexpected behavior, but poor rule design

(Continued)

Table 4.2 (Continued)

Feature	Probabilistic AI	Deterministic AI
	when the model interacts with real-world systems in unforeseen ways	or assumptions can still lead to harmful side effects
Societal impacts	Potential for unintended societal consequences due to biases or unpredictable behavior	Predictable outputs offer greater control over societal impacts, although biases in design can still lead to negative consequences

COVID-related market changes—led to inaccurate price estimates. As a result, Zillow shut down the program, laid off 25 percent of its workforce (about 2,000 employees), and incurred a $304 million inventory write-down.

The impact of missing data varies between deterministic and probabilistic AI systems. Probabilistic AI is more affected by missing data because it depends on statistical patterns for predictions, and gaps can disrupt these patterns, leading to inaccurate results. Deterministic AI is less vulnerable, but it can still have problems. If important information is missing, the system might either struggle to make decisions or produce unexpected errors.

These dynamics underscore the importance of robust data governance practices (Table 4.2).

Messy Data

AI algorithms learn by identifying patterns in data. If the data is messy or "noisy"—filled with errors, inconsistencies, or irrelevant information—the algorithm may learn incorrect patterns, leading to inaccurate predictions or flawed conclusions. Noisy data weakens the statistical foundation of AI models, reducing the accuracy of their predictions and overall performance.

Misleading Patterns: Errors, inconsistencies, and irrelevant data make it difficult for models to discern genuine patterns, resulting in inaccurate predictions and flawed conclusions. It is like solving a puzzle with missing pieces.

Overfitting: AI models are trained on specific data and need to apply what they've learned to new, unseen data. If the training data is messy, the model may struggle to learn general patterns. Instead, it might only do well on the training data but fail in real-world situations.

Biased Outcomes: Noisy data can unintentionally create bias by distorting information through inconsistent formats, units, or coding practices. When this happens, AI models may struggle to correctly correlate inconsistently recorded data, leading them to favor certain groups or categories over others and resulting in unfair or inaccurate outcomes.

A real-world example of messy data causing AI failure is IBM Watson's Oncology project with MD Anderson Cancer Center. Watson was supposed to help doctors recommend cancer treatments, but they often made incorrect or unsafe suggestions. The primary cause of failure was messy training data—Watson relied on a combination of synthetic data and incomplete real-world patient records that didn't accurately reflect the complexity of actual cases. This, among other issues, led to unreliable recommendations, ultimately resulting in the project's shutdown after MD Anderson spent over $62 million, highlighting how messy data can lead to costly failures.

Messy data impacts deterministic and probabilistic AI models in different ways. Deterministic models, which seek clear answers, are highly sensitive to noise and inconsistencies, leading to very inaccurate predictions if patterns are misidentified. Probabilistic models, which deal with uncertainty, can better handle noise by using probabilities to estimate outcomes. However, messy data can still distort these probabilities, leading to biased and misleading results.

Unintended Consequences

AI systems can produce unexpected and sometimes harmful outcomes that developers didn't foresee, which is why detection and mitigation are so important. Complex models, like deep learning, are especially difficult to understand, even for their creators, making it hard to predict all possible outcomes when these models interact with the real world.

When AI is used in complex systems like traffic networks, power grids, or financial markets, unexpected effects in one area can cause widespread disruptions.

While some risks may seem theoretical, many are already evident in practical applications. Issues like AI bias and lack of explainability are well-documented in loan approvals, criminal risk assessments, and social media algorithms.

Whether unintended consequences are more likely with deterministic or probabilistic AI depends on the specific risk and context. However, it is essential to recognize that the use of both types of AI can have significant unintended consequences.

Social Impacts

Some experts have warned about the possibility of AI surpassing human intelligence, posing existential risks. While these scenarios may seem far-fetched, they highlight the need to consider the long-term effects of advancing AI.

Opinions on AI's impact on society range from dismissive concerns to warnings of serious risks. This lack of consensus should be a cause of reflection. Importantly, both the World Health Organization (WHO) and the American Psychological Association (APA) have issued warnings about the impacts of AI-driven digital platforms, highlighting their role in an escalating mental health crisis. These organizations point to addictive design features, such as infinite scrolling and personalized recommendations, which exploit cognitive vulnerabilities to maximize engagement. The resulting overuse contributes to anxiety, depression, and social isolation, particularly among young people. Directors must ensure AI aligns with societal values, focusing on fairness, transparency, and ethics.

Fairness can mean different things to developers and boards, leading to systems that might be unfair or miss the bigger picture.[24] AI's ability to gather data raises privacy concerns, with risks of manipulation and breaches. Automation might cause job losses, especially in repetitive tasks, but it also creates new roles, such as AI ethics specialists and data privacy consultants. Reskilling programs are crucial to help workers adapt.

AI's use of personal data poses significant privacy risks. It can build detailed personal profiles, threatening privacy. There are also concerns about algorithmic manipulation, government surveillance, and data breaches, like the 23andMe breach that exposed the personal information of users, including those with Ashkenazi Jewish ancestry.

Misinformation, deepfakes, and fake news spread on social media are amplified by AI, despite efforts to control them. While AI can help fight these problems, keeping information accurate remains a challenge.

The potential for AI to replace jobs is also a significant concern across various industries. One example comes from British Telecom CEO Philip Jansen, who in 2023 told investors he expected AI technology would eventually replace around 10,000 roles.[25]

The fear of losing control to AI is valid. AI is making critical decisions in areas like health care, finance, and law enforcement, potentially reducing human oversight. Overreliance on AI could weaken human skills and decision making, threatening human agency.

While a robust AI risk governance framework cannot completely eliminate these inherent risks, it plays an essential role in enabling organizations to effectively manage them. By systematically identifying, assessing, and mitigating AI-related risks, such a framework safeguards an organization's financial health, protects intellectual property, and preserves its reputation. Chapter 7 provides further insights into the essential components of such a framework.

CHAPTER 5

A Primer on Data and Data Governance

AI models need high-quality data to function effectively, making mature data governance essential. Data governance ensures that the raw material for AI is accurate, consistent, and secure by establishing clear processes, policies, and responsibilities.

While this may seem obvious, most companies aren't ready for AI because of data issues. A recent MIT poll found 72 percent of tech leaders see data as the biggest barrier to AI. In an IBM survey of chief information officers (CIOs), 61 percent say their data isn't AI-ready. Trust in data is fundamental to effective decision making and operational success. An IBM study highlighted that 82 percent of leaders believe data helps create a strategic advantage in strengthening customer trust and improving bottom lines. However, the same research revealed that only 34 percent of executives in lower-performing companies have deep trust in their data, compared to 78 percent of executives in high-performing organizations. This trust gap can lead to hesitation when using data for critical decisions, potentially resulting in missed opportunities or flawed strategies. To close this gap, organizations need to treat data as a strategic asset. This is not simply a technology issue but has broad implications for how companies capture, organize, and manage data effectively for AI use.

Traditionally, handling data was seen as an operational cost, necessary for record-keeping and compliance, rather than viewing data as a valuable asset in itself. With AI and digital transformation, data has shifted from a peripheral role to being recognized as a critical asset, on par with physical assets and talent. Well-executed AI strategies drive significant strategic value creation, including improved performance, competitiveness, operational efficiency, and risk management. None of these benefits are achievable without AI-ready data.

Data assets include a wide range of digital resources, from structured data like databases and spreadsheets to unstructured formats such as emails, social media, images, and videos. Data assets also encompass the systems and applications that generate, store, or process data, including databases, application outputs, and web pages that capture or process information. Analytic tools and visualizations are also data assets, such as dashboards and outputs from analytics platforms. So also, information derived from traditional datasets—like customer, sales, or financial data—are all vital data assets. Finally, metadata and data catalogs, which provide critical context about data assets, are also data assets.

With such a vast range of data hiding in plain sight and the potential to unlock insights and actions through AI, it can feel overwhelming for an organization to manage it all. This is where the value of data governance is recognized.

Data governance is the process of establishing clear policies, procedures, and responsibilities for managing data throughout its life cycle. It ensures that data is accurate, consistent, secure, and used effectively and appropriately across the organization. By setting standards for how data is collected, stored, accessed, and maintained, data governance helps organizations make the most of their data while minimizing risks.

Elements of a Well-Developed Data Governance Framework

Data Quality and Consistency

The effectiveness of AI relies heavily on the quality and consistency of the data it processes. Flawed or inconsistent data can lead to inaccurate outputs, which in turn can result in poor decisions or significant errors. For instance, Air Canada faced legal action and had to pay compensation after its AI chatbot provided incorrect information.[26] Unlike human errors, which are typically limited in scope compared to systemic errors, AI can amplify mistakes, affecting thousands of users instantly.

This underscores the critical need for robust data governance and quality control over AI systems to ensure they operate reliably and avoid costly mistakes.

Metadata Management

Data is typically scattered across multiple systems, formats, and departments, creating a fragmented and complex data environment. This fragmentation can severely hinder data accessibility, integration, and analysis, making it difficult for organizations to leverage their data assets effectively. Metadata—the data that describes other data—serves as an essential tool in this context. It provides a common language that allows data from various sources to be integrated and understood consistently.

While metadata management can technically be handled using spreadsheets and traditional database management (DBMS) tools, these methods are limited in terms of scalability, real-time updates, and integration, making them impractical for larger datasets. Automated tools like DvSum, Dataedo, and Atlan offer cost-effective solutions for smaller companies, providing scalable and customizable platforms. At the enterprise level, tools like Apache Atlas, Collibra, and Alation streamline metadata collection, lineage tracking, and governance while also offering advanced features like AI insights and collaborative governance. This automation enhances the ability of organizations to efficiently manage large datasets and comply with regulatory requirements.

Data Security

AI is making traditional security threats more sophisticated and introducing entirely new risks. Phishing and social engineering, once reliant on a scammer's ingenuity, are now supercharged by AI, enabling rapid, highly sophisticated, personalized attacks. Voice cloning, for example, can convincingly replicate someone's speech, tone, and mannerisms. This can lead to impersonation, where attackers use the cloned voice to trick individuals into believing they are interacting with a trusted colleague, superior, or loved one. Such deception can prompt people to share sensitive information, authorize transactions, or take actions they would not normally consider, under the belief that the request is genuine.

For example, the Financial Services Information Sharing and Analysis Center (FSISAC) issued a warning about a sophisticated scam in Asia involving deepfake technology. A multinational company in Hong Kong fell victim to this scam, resulting in a $25 million loss. The scam involved using deepfake technology to impersonate the company's chief financial officer (CFO) during a video conference. The finance worker believed he was conversing with real colleagues, including the CFO, who were actually deepfake recreations that mimiced their appearances and voices convincingly.

The large datasets used by AI systems often contain valuable sensitive information, making them prime targets for cyberhackers. AI can also be exploited by cybercriminals. Advanced coding tools speed up vulnerability exploitation.

Open-source AI tools are highly prevalent and form the backbone of many AI applications today. While their open nature offers many advantages, it also introduces security risks that must be managed carefully. By implementing measures such as firewalls, containerization, access controls, regular security audits, and continuous monitoring, organizations can effectively secure open-source AI tools and protect them from cyber threats.

A particularly concerning trend is the rise of "Bring Your Own AI" (BYOAI), where employees use personal AI tools without organizational oversight. This practice exposes companies to data leaks and security breaches. Just as organizations had to revise their technology governance to recognize and oversee the use of outside technology tools within their workplace in the early days of "Bring Your Own Device" (BYOD), they now have to revise their governance to deal with the use of outside AI in the workplace.

These evolving threats demand a proactive and layered security approach, encompassing technical safeguards, policies, and employee education.

Data Privacy

Companies increasingly recognize that even small amounts of proprietary customer data can significantly enhance AI models when combined with other available information. This has spurred a scramble for data, raising concerns about privacy and the exploitation of personal information.

New AI and data privacy regulations are emerging, prompting businesses to implement ethical guidelines and offer customers greater control over their data. Yet, incidents like Slack's unauthorized use of customer data for training the company's AI underscore the challenges.[27] Companies must be transparent about their data practices on the one hand and ensure robust contracts with third-party vendors on the other.

Effective data governance is essential to navigate the complex web of privacy laws, limit data collection, ensure secure storage, and provide clear deletion mechanisms. For multinational businesses, compliance tools like Informatica and TrustArc help manage regulations like GDPR and CCPA. Meanwhile, smaller businesses often turn to tools such as Usercentrics, OneTrust, and Osano for data privacy management.

Data Access and Usage

To fully exploit data's potential, it must be accessible, but this accessibility must be balanced with strong security measures. The challenge lies in making data readily available to drive innovation and productivity while ensuring it is protected against misuse. Effective data governance is essential in navigating this tension, providing a framework that allows organizations to secure their data while still enabling its strategic use.

The rise of BYOAI illustrates this challenge. While these tools can boost productivity and innovation, they can also bypass existing controls, posing significant security risks. It is not enough to simply implement restrictive policies; employees must be educated on the importance of these controls and the potential risks of unauthorized data usage.

Many of the tools used for metadata management address data usage and access concerns by providing comprehensive data governance, visibility, and control mechanisms too.

Data governance plays an essential role in this process by setting clear guidelines and ensuring that both security and accessibility are prioritized. Comprehensive education across all levels of the organization—from the boardroom to the front lines—is key to ensuring that AI tools are used safely and effectively.

Data Lifecycle Management

Data Lifecycle Management (DLM) is about managing data from the moment it is created until it is no longer needed and is securely deleted. Effective DLM ensures that data is handled efficiently, securely, and in compliance with regulations throughout its entire life.

DLM is essential for maintaining high data quality and integrity. By archiving rarely accessed data and deleting outdated information, organizations can improve data security, ensure compliance, and enhance system performance. Proper data classification and continuous monitoring help keep data relevant and reliable.

Data Stewardship

A common problem in data governance is data getting trapped in organizational silos, limiting its usefulness and making decision making harder. To fix this, strong data stewardship is key. Responsibility for data shouldn't just be the IT department's job; instead, business owners should manage the data in their areas because they know its value and context best.

Boards should ensure that each business unit has a designated data steward responsible for the quality, integrity, and security of their data. These stewards should collaborate across departments to create a unified approach to data management, breaking down silos and connecting data sources. When cross-silo data assets are connected, the value of AI grows exponentially, as combining proprietary data with other sources uncovers deeper insights and creates opportunities that isolated data sets simply can't achieve.

For effective oversight, a Chief Data Officer (or someone similar, like a CTO or CIO) should lead this effort, making sure data stewardship is consistent and aligned with organizational goals. This collaboration strengthens data reliability and value, leading to better decision making and more successful AI initiatives.

Commitment From the Top

Strong data governance is essential because data is the foundation of AI. It ensures that data is available, consistent, and high quality, maximizing the potential benefits of AI as companies grow and adapt.

Data governance requires upfront investment in people, processes, and technology, but it pays off in the long run. While it may seem costly to implement, good data governance saves money by preventing the much higher costs associated with poor data quality and regulatory fines.

The greatest cost of poor data governance, however, may not be a direct financial hit, but rather the missed opportunities due to low confidence in the data used to drive AI. Executives relying on uncertain data are less likely to fully leverage AI's potential for value creation. While Gartner estimates poor data quality costs companies $12.8 million annually and noncompliance penalties can be massive, like TikTok's $379 million GDPR fine, the hidden cost of untrustworthy data is far greater. Prepping data for AI can account for up to 80 percent of deployment costs, reinforcing that data governance is a critical investment to maximize AI's value.

Understanding Data Types

AI models rely on a diverse array of data types, each with its unique strengths and weaknesses:

Structured Data: This is data organized in predefined formats, such as spreadsheets or databases. Examples include customer records, financial transactions, and sensor readings from IoT devices. The structured nature of this data allows machine learning algorithms to efficiently analyze patterns and relationships, enabling accurate predictions and classifications.

Unstructured Data: Unstructured data lacks a predefined format. It includes text, images, and videos, which are more challenging for AI models to process but extremely valuable for tasks like natural language processing (NLP) and image recognition.

Semistructured Data: This type of data is a mix of structured and unstructured data. It is somewhat organized but not as neatly structured as data like spreadsheets. JSON and XML are formats often used by computer programs and Application Programming Interface (API) to capture and process specific pieces of information on the fly. These formats store data with tags and labels, making it easier to process than random text but still more complex than fully organized data. Semistructured data can be valuable for AI models because it contains useful information that's easier to extract and analyze compared to completely unstructured data.

Real-Time Data: Generated in real time, this data includes sensor outputs and social media feeds. It is crucial for training AI models in applications like predictive maintenance and anomaly detection, where immediate data is essential.

Historical Data: Collected over time, historical data is used for tasks like forecasting and trend analysis. It helps AI models understand past patterns to make predictions about future events.

Data can also be labeled or unlabeled. Labeled data is data that has been tagged with a label, such as the category of an image or the sentiment of a piece of text. Unlabeled data, as the name implies, is data that does not have any labels to identify it.

Labeled data is used in supervised learning, a type of machine learning where the model is given a set of labeled data to learn from. The model then uses this data to learn how to map inputs to outputs.

Table 5.1 Labeled and unlabeled data

Feature	Labeled data	Unlabeled data
Definition	Data that has been annotated with additional information, typically in the form of tags or categories	Data that has not been annotated with any additional information
Purpose	To help machine learning algorithms learn patterns and make predictions	To train machine learning algorithms to recognize patterns without explicit labels
Examples	Images with labels indicating object classes, customer records with age and gender labels	Sensor readings from IoT devices, textual documents without labels indicating sentiment
Common applications	Supervised learning tasks, such as image classification and text classification	Unsupervised learning tasks, such as anomaly detection and clustering

For example, a model that is trained on a dataset of labeled images of cats and dogs would be able to learn how to identify cats and dogs in new images.

Unlabeled data is used in unsupervised learning, a type of machine learning where the model is not given any labeled data. The model then uses the unlabeled data to learn patterns and relationships on its own. For example, a model that is trained on a dataset of unlabeled images might be able to learn to cluster the images into different groups based on their content.

Both labeled and unlabeled data can be valuable for training AI models. Labeled data is often more useful for supervised learning tasks, while unlabeled data can be more useful for unsupervised learning tasks.

By leveraging these various data types, AI models can be trained to handle a wide range of tasks and scenarios, improving their effectiveness and adaptability, Table 5.1

Data Quality

The quality of data used to train an AI model is also crucial. Inaccurate, incomplete, or biased data can significantly undermine a model's accuracy and reliability. Real-world data is rarely perfect; it often contains errors, inconsistencies, and irrelevant information, which can mislead AI models. This can result in misleading insights, inaccurate predictions, and unreliable outcomes, especially in critical areas like health care, finance, and legal decision making.

To mitigate these risks, model developers engage in data cleansing and preprocessing to correct errors, remove inconsistencies, and filter out irrelevant information. These steps are essential for improving the quality of the training data. However, even with these processes, the data may still not fully capture the diversity and complexity of real-world situations, leading to potential biases or errors when the model is deployed.

Directors should be aware of these risks and understand that effective data management is not just about cleaning data, but also about ensuring that the training data is representative of the scenarios the AI will encounter. Ongoing monitoring and updating of models as they are exposed to new data is essential, as is cross-functional collaboration between data scientists, domain experts, and compliance teams to ensure that the AI behaves fairly and reliably in practice.

Training Datasets Matter

AI models learn from the data they are trained on, making the quality, quantity, diversity, and representativeness of that data critical for building reliable and effective models. Directors must understand that training and validation datasets need to reflect the diversity and complexity of real-world situations. The distribution of data in training must closely match what the model will face in the real world.

When AI models encounter scenarios or data outside their training range, they may struggle, leading to inaccurate predictions, biased decisions, or serious errors. Research has found this to be a prevalent issue. In one study, Google found that the use of inappropriate datasets for learning led to 30 percent higher error rates in model output. Distribution mismatches are common in commercialized AI. When one category of data disproportionately outweighs others, it can skew the model's understanding of the real world.

There are techniques available to help mitigate this problem. Distribution analysis is a valuable method to assess how well training and validation data represent real-world environments. However, it may not capture all the nuances of real-world complexity, especially in dynamic or evolving scenarios. Combining distribution analysis with other techniques, such as data augmentation, transfer learning, and bias detection, offers a more comprehensive approach to ensuring AI models generalize well to diverse and complex real-world situations. Each method has its strengths and limitations, and the choice of approach depends on the specific characteristics and challenges of the AI application.

By understanding these concepts, directors can better appreciate the importance of data quality and distribution in AI model performance.

Synthetic Training and Validation Datasets

Real-world data can be problematic for use in AI training. Some data points in real-world scenarios occur very infrequently. For example, a self-driving car may rarely encounter a pedestrian jaywalking, or a medical diagnostic system might seldom see cases of a rare disease. Because these events are so rare, they may not be well-represented in the training data. When an AI model hasn't encountered enough examples of these rare events during training, it may struggle to recognize or appropriately respond to them in the real world.

Likewise, real-world data can contain outliers or anomalies—data points that don't fit the typical patterns. These could be due to errors, unusual events, or genuinely rare occurrences. Outliers can confuse AI models, leading to incorrect predictions or classifications.

Finally, real-world data isn't static; it evolves over time. Trends, behaviors, and conditions change, meaning that data that was once relevant may become outdated or irrelevant. AI models trained on older data may struggle to adapt to these changes, especially if the new conditions were rare or nonexistent in the original training data.

To address these issues, developers turn to synthetic data. These are computer-generated testing data points that fill in the gaps by providing clean, diverse, and controlled data points that are otherwise hard to obtain. Integrating synthetic data with real-world datasets exposes AI models to a broader range of scenarios, improving their ability to adapt and generalize. This boosts the reliability and performance of AI systems. However, rigorous validation is essential to ensure synthetic data accurately reflects real-world characteristics and distributions.

The Board's Role in Data Governance

Boards play a critical role in ensuring data is managed as a strategic asset. This starts with overseeing the organization's data governance policies, making sure they align with strategic goals. Boards are responsible for approving policies that set standards for data quality, security, privacy, retention, and vendor management.

But their role goes beyond just policy approval. Boards must also ensure that the organization is properly managing the risks associated with data. This means making sure there are enough resources—funding, personnel, and technology—dedicated to data governance.

To be effective, data governance needs clear accountability. Boards must ensure that responsibilities for managing data as a strategic asset are clearly defined.

To assist boards in fulfilling these duties, we have included two helpful checklists:

- Appendix C: Board Director Checklist for AI Data Governance
- Appendix D: Board Governance Checklist for Third-Party Data in AI

These checklists provide a pragmatic set of considerations for organizations to reference when crafting and overseeing their data governance frameworks. By following these guidelines, boards can ensure robust data governance that supports strategic goals, mitigates risks, and leverages data as a valuable asset for the organization's success.

Now that we have discussed what feeds AI models, we explore the various types of AI with a focus on what directors should understand about each type.

CHAPTER 6

A Board Member's Guide to Core AI Techniques

In this chapter, we introduce 12 foundational AI techniques, explaining the advantages, disadvantages, and use cases in various industries. Our aim is to spark curiosity about AI's possibilities while highlighting the critical risk management considerations essential for board oversight. We equip directors with actionable insights for informed decision making so directors can confidently guide their organizations to use AI responsibly, accountably and transparently.

Symbolic Learning: Bridging Human Cognition and AI

Symbolic Learning leverages well-defined rules and logic to represent knowledge and solve problems. This technique represents a structured framework for capturing expert knowledge and applying it consistently. Unlike AI techniques that require massive datasets, Symbolic Learning excels in tasks, requiring the creation of clear rules from organizational expertise.

Decisions made using Symbolic Learning are often easier to understand and explain as compared to those made by "black box" models using other AI techniques, as it is easy to trace the reasoning steps used to reach a conclusion. This transparency can be valuable in situations that require an understanding of the rationale behind outputs. Transparency also supports auditing these systems while ensuring fair and unbiased decision making, especially when dealing with sensitive use cases.

Symbolic Learning has broad applicability in diverse corporate functions including operations, risk management, and more. Because it excels at handling well-defined, rules-based tasks, it can automate tasks in areas like customer service (answering FAQs), data entry, or report generation. Symbolic Learning can be used to capture and codify expert knowledge that can provide guidance and recommendations to less experienced employees. The breadth of use cases is highlighted in the following examples:

Medical Diagnosis Systems: Symbolic Learning powers medical diagnosis systems[28] that assist doctors in identifying diseases and recommending treatments. For instance, the MYCIN system, an early expert system developed in the 1970s at Stanford University, was used primarily for diagnosing bacterial infections in the blood, like bacteremia and meningitis. Employing a medical knowledge base and a set of rules, MYCIN generated diagnostic hypotheses and treatment recommendations.

Financial Fraud Detection Systems: Rules-based financial analysis systems[29] use Symbolic Learning for tasks such as risk assessment and fraud detection. Explicit rules derived from financial regulations and patterns guide the system in evaluating transactions, identifying anomalies, and making decisions based on predefined criteria. The FICO Falcon Fraud Manager system, for example, uses a combination of techniques, including Symbolic Learning, to detect patterns indicative of fraudulent activity.

Computer-Aided Design (CAD) Systems: Symbolic Learning is one of the techniques employed in CAD systems for engineering and design.[30] These systems use explicit rules to capture design principles, engineering constraints, and best practices. Symbolic Learning allows the representation of objects, their properties, and relationships using symbols, enabling the AI to reason about the design and make intelligent suggestions. This helps designers create and optimize complex structures.

Knowledge-Based Systems in Education: Intelligent tutoring systems[31] (ITS) are an example of Symbolic AI use in education. These systems can adapt to the individual needs of each student. For example, an ITS could use Symbolic Learning to represent a student's knowledge and skills, and then use this information to provide personalized instruction and feedback.

Expert Legal Systems: These systems leverage Symbolic Learning to provide legal advice and decision support. They encode legal rules, statutes, and case law into a knowledge base, enabling them to analyze legal scenarios, provide interpretations, and offer recommendations. For instance, an AI-powered contract review tool can scan contracts for potential errors or omissions, flagging these issues for human review.

These examples demonstrate the power of Symbolic Learning in specialized domains where explicit rules, knowledge representation, and logical reasoning are critical for effective decision making and problem-solving. Despite its advantages, Symbolic Learning is not without its drawbacks. The primary limitations include scalability challenges and knowledge base dependency. As problem complexity increases, Symbolic Learning systems can face scalability issues due to the extensive knowledge required to encode them. Acquiring, encoding, and maintaining this knowledge can be time-consuming, costly, and difficult to manage. Additionally, the effectiveness of Symbolic Learning systems hinges on the accuracy and completeness of their knowledge bases. Errors or incompleteness in the knowledge base can lead to flawed decision making.

Key Board Risk Oversight Considerations for Symbolic Learning

Symbolic Learning, with its rule-based and knowledge-driven approach, introduces unique governance considerations:

Knowledge Base Integrity: Ensuring the completeness and accuracy of the knowledge base by employing validation techniques and expert review.

Conflict Resolution: Ensuring there are processes in place to constantly challenge and validate the completeness and accuracy of outcomes to prevent inconsistencies and errors.

Explainability and Interpretability: Ensuring Symbolic Learning
systems are well documented, explainable, and interpretable to
facilitate problem identification and correction.

Symbolic Learning Decision-Making Paradigm

While Symbolic Learning systems typically employ a deterministic decision-making paradigm, probabilistic decision paradigms are
also being woven into rules-based applications. Traditional Symbolic
Learning systems, like rule-based systems and expert systems, operate
on a set of predefined rules and logical operators. These systems are
deterministic, meaning for a given set of inputs, they will always
produce the same output. This makes them reliable for tasks with
well-defined rules and limited uncertainty.

Increasingly, however, Symbolic Learning systems incorporate
probabilistic reasoning techniques like Bayesian inference. These
techniques are better able to handle uncertainty and incomplete
information by assigning probabilities to different outcomes or
hypotheses. This makes the systems more flexible and adaptable for tasks
with inherent ambiguity or complex decision making. For example,
traditional medical diagnosis often relies on deterministic algorithms
based on specific symptoms and tests. This can lead to missed diagnoses or misinterpretations, especially in complex cases. Probabilistic
Symbolic Learning combines symbolic reasoning (knowledge about
medical conditions) with probabilistic inference (analyzing patient data
with uncertainty). A probabilistic Symbolic Learning system analyzing
a patient's medical history and test results might conclude there is a 75
percent chance of lung cancer and a 25 percent chance of pneumonia,
prompting further investigation and tailored treatment plans.

By addressing these governance considerations and ensuring
corresponding controls are implemented and functioning well, directors
can help their organizations navigate the unique challenges associated
with Symbolic Learning deployments. Appendix E offers additional
insight and explores important risk governance nuances for Symbolic
Learning.

Machine Learning: Unleashing the Power of Data

Machine Learning (ML) empowers computers to learn and improve from data without explicit programming. In contrast with Symbolic Learning which relies on predefined rules, ML learns patterns from data itself. This remarkable ability has been quietly transforming companies across a wide array of industries, enabling machines to perform tasks that were once thought to be exclusive to human intelligence. ML is a category which encompasses multiple techniques, and as such, we examine its underlying techniques and not the category.

The three primary ML techniques are supervised learning, unsupervised learning, and reinforcement learning. As we will see, each approach tackles distinct challenges and utilizes different data formats to achieve its objectives. We briefly introduce them here followed by a deeper exploration of each type.

Supervised learning involves providing the ML algorithm with labeled data, where each data point is accompanied by a corresponding label or category. The labeled data serves as a training guide, enabling the algorithm to learn, identify patterns and make predictions.

In contrast to supervised learning, unsupervised learning deals with unlabeled data, where the underlying patterns and relationships are not explicitly defined within the data. This approach is about discovery. It challenges the algorithm to learn and extract meaningful insights from raw, uncategorized data.

Reinforcement learning differs from both supervised and unsupervised learning in that it involves interacting with an environment. The algorithm receives feedback in the form of rewards or penalties for its actions, enabling it to learn through trial and error. This approach is particularly well-suited for tasks that require decision making in complex environments, such as algorithmic trading or robotics. By interacting with the environment and receiving feedback, the reinforcement learning algorithm continuously improves its decision-making strategies.

Each of these ML techniques is explored in the following sections. We will explain what it is, how it is used in commercial applications, point out advantages and disadvantages, and highlight the key board risk management considerations when using each type of ML.

Supervised Learning: Guided Discovery

Supervised ML is about making predictions. It enables algorithms to learn from labeled data. Algorithms are provided with both inputs and their corresponding outputs, allowing models to identify patterns and make predictions on new data. For example, feeding an algorithm with tagged photos that identify the image, such as "beach" or "mountain," enables it to analyze these labeled examples, learn the patterns that differentiate beaches from mountains, and use that knowledge to predict the category of new unlabeled photos. Supervised ML use cases abound in our daily lives. They include:

Credit Scoring in Banking: Supervised learning is used extensively in banking for credit scoring.[32] Models are trained on historical data with labeled outcomes (approved or denied credit) to predict the creditworthiness of applicants based on extensive consumer or small business data such as income, credit history, and debt.

Product Recommendations in E-Commerce: Platforms like Amazon use supervised learning for personalized product recommendations.[33] Algorithms trained on vast amounts of data, including product descriptions, images, and customer reviews, identify patterns to deliver relevant search results and personalize recommendations.

Email Spam Filtering: Supervised learning models classify incoming emails as spam or nonspam based on features like content, sender information, and subject lines, significantly improving email security and user experience.[34]

Fraud Detection: Supervised learning is used to detect fraudulent financial transactions. Models trained on labeled datasets of fraudulent and nonfraudulent transactions can classify new transactions in real time.[35] For instance, PayPal's algorithms analyze transaction patterns to flag suspicious activities, protecting customers and reducing losses.

Medical Diagnosis: Supervised learning assists in medical diagnosis[36] by predicting diseases based on patient symptoms, medical history, and test results. Algorithms also analyze large datasets of molecular and genetic data to identify new drug targets, accelerating the drug development process.

As these examples demonstrate, supervised learning is being applied across a wide array of industries to solve real-world problems by learning patterns from labeled data. Its advantages include high accuracy, scalability, and interpretability. Despite its strengths, supervised ML also presents challenges:

Labeled Data Dependency: The effectiveness of supervised learning hinges on the availability of labeled data, which can be time-consuming and expensive to acquire.

Overfitting: Algorithms may overfit to the training data, leading to excellent performance on training data but poor generalization to new data.

Bias: Supervised learning algorithms can reflect biases present in the training data, resulting in unfair or discriminatory outcomes.

Key Board Risk Oversight Considerations for Supervised Machine Learning

These specific governance considerations are appropriate to supervised learning:

Data Dependence and Representation: Ensuring that training data reflects what the model will encounter in the real world. Supervised learning relies heavily on learning the relationship between input features and desired outputs present in the training data. If the training data distribution significantly differs from real-world data, the model might perform poorly when making decisions on previously unseen data, leading to biased or inaccurate predictions.

Model Bias Mitigation: Ensuring there is a process in place to continuously identify and address potential biases in ML models. Techniques such as debiasing datasets and employing fairness-aware algorithms can help mitigate bias.

Data Privacy and Security: Ensuring the responsible collection and use of both training and real-world data used by the models. Compliance with data privacy laws and regulations is essential.

Security and Resilience Enhancement: Ensuring there are safeguards to protect ML models from adversarial attacks that aim to manipulate or fool the model.

Supervised Learning Decision-Making Paradigm

Supervised learning can operate along the spectrum from deterministic to probabilistic, influenced by factors such as model design, task complexity, and data quality. Model risk profiles depend on which way the overall architecture skews, whether toward a single output or a range of outputs. Examples like credit scoring, product recommendations, and email spam filtering typically involve probabilistic decision making, where risks often revolve around data bias, model explainability, and performance degradation due to changing data patterns. In contrast, applications like fraud detection and medical diagnosis frequently rely on more deterministic models, where risks include misclassification errors and the potential for biased decision making based on flawed categorizations.

Finally, the risk profile of supervised learning can differ based on the application:

Prediction-Based: For models solely making predictions, the main risks are associated with data bias, model explainability, and performance degradation associated with drift.

Classification-Based: When models make classifications with assigned probabilities, additional risks involve misclassification errors and the potential for discrimination based on incorrect categorizations.

Actionable Insights: If models provide actionable insights or recommendations, the risk profile expands to include potential negative consequences of implementing those recommendations based on inaccurate or biased predictions.

Organizations can navigate the specific challenges associated with supervised learning, ensuring responsible and effective deployment of models trained on labeled datasets by addressing governance matters and ensuring corresponding controls are implemented and monitored. Appendix E offers additional governance considerations for Supervised Learning.

Unsupervised Learning: Unveiling Hidden Patterns

Unsupervised learning enables algorithms to extract meaningful insights from unlabeled data, distinguishing it from supervised learning in several important ways. Unsupervised learning algorithms excel at discovering patterns and relationships hidden within this raw data. Unsupervised learning is about discovery, whereas supervised learning is about predictions. This power of discovery enables unsupervised learning algorithms to reveal hidden patterns and relationships in data that would be difficult or impossible to find manually.

Unsupervised learning operates without the need for labeled data, in contrast with supervised learning, which relies on paired input-output datasets. Consider for a moment that most data falls into this unlabeled category, so the potential use cases for unsupervised learning are limitless. Images, medical scans, audio and video recordings, digitized articles, social media posts, and other common data typically have no labels or explanations; they are raw data.

Unsupervised learning excels at segmenting data into groups based on their similarities, making it useful for tasks such as customer segmentation or product recommendations. These algorithms are able to identify anomalies in data, such as fraudulent transactions or suspicious network activity. Here is a sampling of commercial use cases:

Customer Segmentation: Netflix uses unsupervised learning to analyze viewing patterns across its user base, grouping users into segments to personalize content for broad categories of users.[37] Users with similar habits (e.g., frequent watchers of documentaries versus action films). Once these segments are formed, Netflix can personalize content recommendations for each segment.

Anomaly Detection in Network Security: Clustering-based anomaly detection algorithms are deployed to identify suspicious activities in network traffic to safeguard against security breaches.[38]

Content-Streaming Recommendation Systems: Spotify uses unsupervised learning to make real-time recommendations of songs based on user's preferences and behaviors. The platform makes personalized recommendations by learning from similar user behaviors in real time, rather than predefined customer segments.[39]

Supply Chain Optimization: Amazon applies unsupervised learning for inventory management and demand forecasting, employing clustering and anomaly detection to optimize operations and reduce costs. [40,41]

Document Clustering in Information Retrieval: Platforms like Google and Apple News use unsupervised learning to categorize news articles into thematic clusters to assist with efficient content organization and user navigation. [42] This allows users to stay informed about specific topics of interest without being overwhelmed by the sheer volume of news articles.[43]

These examples demonstrate how unsupervised learning helps discover patterns, group similar items, and derive insights from unlabeled data. Despite its effectiveness in uncovering hidden patterns, unsupervised ML presents several challenges:

Interpretation Difficulty: Deciphering how unsupervised learning algorithms arrive at their decisions can be challenging due to their inherent complexity and the lack of explicit guidance by the model creators.

Overfitting Risk: Similar to supervised learning, unsupervised learning algorithms can overfit to the training data, memorizing the data instead of learning from it, which can lead to irrelevant patterns or discovering noise that does not generalize well to new data.

Impact of Missing Data: While missing data impacts all types of AI, its effects are magnified in unsupervised learning because the model doesn't have labeled data to correct its course when errors arise. Misinterpretation of patterns or groupings can go undetected. Algorithms often rely heavily on statistical properties such as distances or densities. Missing data can distort these measurements, leading the model to misunderstand relationships between data points, which reduces the reliability of the insights.

Key Board Risk Oversight Considerations for Unsupervised Learning

Understanding and addressing these governance considerations is essential for leveraging unsupervised learning effectively:

Data Dependence and Quality: Ensuring that training data is appropriate for the intended usage. The quality and completeness of training data significantly impact the outputs of unsupervised learning models. Biased, noisy, or incomplete data can lead to unreliable insights and flawed decision making. Ensuring high-quality and diverse data is crucial for minimizing biases related to demographics, cultural backgrounds, or other sources of unfairness.

Model Interpretability: Directors do not need to understand all the technical details, but they should ensure that explainable AI techniques or test-and-learn approaches are implemented. These techniques include the use of interpretable algorithms such as K-Means clustering, Principal Component Analysis (PCA), or Linear Dimensionality Reduction (LDR) to provide clearer insights into data groupings. Additionally, tools like LIME (Local

Interpretable Model-agnostic Explanations), SHAP (SHapley Additive exPlanations), or DeepExplain should be used to explain individual model predictions by highlighting which features influenced the outcome and how.

Model Drift Mitigation: Continuous monitoring is essential to detect and address model drift, where performance declines due to changes in data distribution over time.

Adversarial Example Defense: Boards should be aware of the potential for adversarial attacks that exploit vulnerabilities in unsupervised learning models. Ensuring adversarial training and detection tools are implemented to strengthen model resilience against malicious inputs.

Misinterpretation of Patterns: Ensuring data quality controls, regular model performance reviews, bias audits, and continuous algorithm refinement. Unsupervised models may identify spurious or irrelevant patterns, resulting in misleading insights or actions. Addressing data quality issues and refining algorithms are key to avoiding misinterpretations and ensuring reliable AI outcomes.

Unsupervised Learning Decision-Making Paradigm

Unsupervised learning is inherently probabilistic. The risks in unsupervised learning models primarily arise from the nature of the data and the tasks performed. However, these models can be guided toward more deterministic outputs by incorporating constraints or prior knowledge into the model. This hybrid approach—sometimes called semisupervised learning or constrained clustering—allows models to follow certain rules while still identifying patterns in the data. This can introduce more structure and predictability into what is typically a probabilistic process. Importantly, the constraints imposed on the clustering process have to be well structured. If they are based on incorrect assumptions, outdated rules, or incomplete information, models will produce biased or suboptimal groupings. The risk profile also depends on how its outputs are used:

Descriptive Insights: If the model's use is to identify patterns or clusters in data, the main risks involve misinterpretation and lack of explainability. Ensuring clarity in how patterns are derived can mitigate these risks.

Actionable Recommendations: When unsupervised models provide recommendations or decision-making support, the risk profile expands to include potential negative impacts of acting on inaccurate or biased insights. Validating recommendations before implementation is essential.

Automated Actions: If the model directly triggers automated actions in real time based on its analysis, the risks become even more critical, as faulty interpretations can lead to real-world harm. Consider, for example, a social media platform that uses unsupervised learning to personalize news feeds for its users. By analyzing vast amounts of unlabeled data, including posts, user interactions, and browsing habits, it categorizes content and recommends stories that users might find interesting. One problem is the algorithm might unintentionally reinforce existing biases by clustering users into "echo chambers" where they only see content that confirms their existing beliefs. Another problem is it may amplify the spread of misinformation because the model might struggle to differentiate between factual news and fake or misleading content. Implementing robust validation and monitoring processes can prevent adverse outcomes.

Organizations can ensure responsible and effective deployment of models for discovering patterns and structures in data without explicit labels by addressing these governance questions and implementing corresponding controls. Appendix E provides additional insight into governing risks associated with unsupervised learning.

Reinforcement Learning: Learning Through Trial and Error

Reinforcement learning (RL) enables machines to learn through trial and error, mimicking the way humans learn through experience. Unlike supervised or unsupervised ML, which relies on labeled data or pattern discovery, RL models use a reinforcement learning algorithm to assign positive values "rewards" to the desired actions to encourage their use, while negative values "penalties" are assigned to undesired behaviors to discourage them. Through trial and error, RL algorithms, called "agents," learn to choose actions that maximize their reward, leading to improved performance and efficiency.

Reinforcement learning offers two compelling benefits. RL algorithms excel at learning complex tasks that would be difficult or impossible to teach using other ML methods. They can adapt to new environments by exploring and learning from their mistakes, making them suitable for tasks like robotics and self-driving cars. This ability to learn complex tasks in dynamic environments makes them excellent controllers, able to effectively optimize complex systems such as supply chains and energy networks. They learn to make decisions that maximize efficiency and minimize costs quite effectively. These inherent strengths are applied in a wide variety of commercial use cases including:

Algorithmic Trading: RL is employed to enhance trading strategies by learning to make buy or sell decisions based on market conditions, thus adapting to dynamic financial environments. In high-frequency trading, RL optimizes trading strategies[44] to execute trades more effectively. It is also used in portfolio optimization on Wall Street, where algorithms dynamically allocate assets to maximize portfolio returns.[45]

Energy Management in Smart Grids: RL optimizes energy consumption and distribution in smart grids. Algorithms learn to incentivize users to adjust their electricity usage based on real-time grid conditions.[46] Models also learn to make decisions autonomously, optimizing energy distribution and consumption while maintaining grid stability.[47] Duke Energy, for example, leverages RL to optimize grid operations, improving reliability, efficiency, and resilience by analyzing real-time data for power distribution and voltage control decisions.[48]

Supply Chain Management: RL optimizes inventory control and logistics. Agents learn to decide on order quantities, delivery routes, and warehouse management for efficiency.[49] Unilever uses RL to enhance demand forecasting by analyzing historical sales data and external factors, optimizing production planning, inventory management, and pricing strategies to improve efficiency and reduce costs.[50]

Dynamic Pricing in E-Commerce: RL is used for dynamic pricing strategies in e-commerce.[51] By learning from past interactions and adapting to changing conditions, RL algorithms optimize prices to maximize revenue and profit while maintaining customer satisfaction. Uber, for instance, uses RL for surge pricing, dynamically adjusting prices during high demand to balance supply and demand.[52]

Robotics for Task Automation: RL is utilized in robotics for task automation in industries such as manufacturing.[53] Robots learn to perform complex tasks, adapt to varying conditions, and optimize their actions for efficiency. OpenAI has contributed significantly to RL in robotics, developing algorithms for tasks like manipulating a Rubik's Cube and assembling a Lego tower.[54]

These examples highlight the versatility of reinforcement learning (RL) across various applications. When an RL system is capable of autonomous operation—making decisions independently, and learning from experiences to achieve specific objectives— it is called Agentic. Agentic AI systems demonstrate goal-directed behavior, adaptability, and the ability to respond dynamically to changing environments, embodying greater autonomy than traditional .

While Agentic AI can employ other techniques, RL most often serves as the foundation, enabling systems to learn and optimize decisions through interactions with their environment. By taking actions, receiving feedback, and refining strategies over time, Agentic AI systems can adapt to complex, unpredictable scenarios and operate independently in real-world conditions.

Amazon's Prime Air delivery drones, currently piloted in select locations, exemplify Agentic AI in action. These drones autonomously deliver packages within designated areas, planning flight paths, avoiding obstacles, and adapting in real-time to challenges such as wind or restricted airspace—all without direct human intervention. By integrating RL with advanced technologies like object detection and path optimization, they dynamically navigate complex environments to achieve delivery goals, demonstrating the sophisticated capabilities of Agentic AI.

Despite its advantages, reinforcement learning and its Agentic offspring also present challenges. RL algorithms can be slow to learn, especially for complex tasks. They often require extensive training and extensive interactions with the environment to achieve optimal performance. This is a challenge in environments where feedback is either sparse or delayed.

Debugging RL algorithms can be vexing due to the complex nature of their decision-making processes. Identifying the root cause of errors, such as why an agent is failing to achieve its goals, can be difficult and time-consuming. RL algorithms can also be vulnerable to adversarial attacks. Malicious actors can manipulate the reward function or the training environment to cause the algorithm to make mistakes or behave in undesirable ways. Such attacks can lead to suboptimal performance or even catastrophic failures, especially in critical applications like autonomous driving or financial trading.

Key Board Risk Oversight Considerations for Reinforcement Learning

Reinforcement learning introduces unique challenges for board oversight due to its focus on learning through interactions and feedback. Among the more important considerations for risk oversight are:

Safety Controls: Ensuring there are safety controls in place such as reward shaping and constraint learning to prevent RL systems from taking actions that could harm people or property. Make sure RL systems have an accessible kill switch to quickly deactivate the system in case of unforeseen issues.

Interpretability Controls: Ensuring that interpretability controls, such as explainable AI and visualization techniques, are implemented to make RL systems more transparent and easier to understand. Increased transparency is useful for diagnosing problems and ensuring the system's decisions align with expected behavior.

Alignment Controls: Verifying that controls such as human-in-the-loop training are employed to ensure that RL systems are aligned with organizational goals and values. For example, insufficient exploration can cause RL models to become stuck in subopti-mal solutions, failing to explore better alternatives. A humorous example is a model designed to optimize energy consumption in buildings. Although the goal was to find the most efficient settings for heating, cooling, and lighting systems, the model learned that turning off all systems entirely was the quickest way to reduce energy consumption.

Continuous Monitoring: Recognizing that new, unaccounted-for risks can emerge, and malicious attacks could invalidate exist-ing control mechanisms. Boards should ensure that continuous monitoring processes are in place and are sufficient to detect and respond to these evolving risks effectively.

Reinforcement Learning Decision-Making Paradigm

RL systems uniquely blend probabilistic and deterministic paradigms. In the learning phase, RL algorithms often use strategies that involve exploration (trying new actions) and exploitation (choosing the best-known actions). These probabilistic approaches help the model discover optimal strategies in uncertain environments. Once the model has learned the optimal policy (the strategy that maximizes rewards), it can make deterministic decisions. The model chooses the action with the highest expected reward deterministically, based on the learned expected value function or policy. It is worth noting that exploration/exploitation balance, while inherently probabilistic, can be channeled by more deterministic methods. Incorporating deterministic elements can help ensure consistent and predictable behavior, especially in safety-critical applications where random exploration could lead to undesirable or dangerous outcomes.

Organizations can navigate the specific challenges associated with reinforcement learning and ensure responsible and ethical deployment of models that learn through interaction and feedback by addressing these governance issues and implementing corresponding controls. Appendix E provides additional considerations for governance of reinforcement learning.

Deep Learning: Harnessing the Power of Artificial Neural Networks

Deep learning (DL) is a subset of machine learning that uses artificial neural networks with multiple layers to process data. Inspired by the way humans reason, these deep neural networks learn from large amounts of data to recognize complex patterns and make predictions or decisions. The "deep" aspect refers to the multiple layers through which data is passed, with each layer extracting increasingly abstract features from the input data.

This technique enables machines to perform tasks with remarkable accuracy. Convolutional neural networks (CNNs) excel at recognizing and classifying objects in images. Recurrent neural networks (RNNs) accurately translate spoken language into text. Generative adversarial networks (GANs) excel at generating realistic images, videos, and data, which can be used for tasks like data augmentation, creative content generation, and simulation of environments where real-world data is limited or sensitive. Deep Q Networks (DQN) are primarily a deep reinforcement learning technique that excel at decision-making tasks in environments where an agent must learn optimal strategies through trial and error, such as in game playing, robotics, and navigation. In addition to CNNs, RNNs, and GANs, Transformers have emerged as a powerful architecture in DL, particularly for natural language processing tasks. Their self-attention mechanism allows them to effectively capture long-range dependencies within text, making them superior for tasks such as translation and summarization.

These examples represent some of the most widely used DL techniques, each excelling in specific tasks like image recognition, language processing, data generation, and decision making. However,

DL encompasses a broad range of approaches beyond these, offering diverse tools for tackling increasingly complex problems across various domains.

The impact of DL innovations is profound. All of the foundational AI techniques from symbolic learning to generative AI have been paired with DL models, unlocking previously unimaginable capabilities. These commercial use cases examples highlight the immense power of DL:

Image Recognition: DL algorithms often surpass the human ability at identifying objects and patterns in images. This technology powers facial recognition systems, medical image analysis, and self-driving car navigation. Facebook's Photo Tagging[55] technology automatically identifies people in photos, making it easy for users to tag them. It uses deep convolutional networks trained on massive datasets of labeled faces.

Natural Language Processing (NLP): DL has revolutionized NLP, enabling machines to understand and generate human language. This technology fuels chatbots, machine translation tools, and sentiment analysis systems. Google Translate uses a DL technique known as neural machine translation (NMT). This approach involves training on large datasets of paired sentences in different languages. The model learns to translate entire sentences by understanding the context and semantics, rather than translating word by word. This method has significantly improved the accuracy and fluency of translations compared to previous translation approaches.

Predictive Analytics: DL algorithms can uncover hidden patterns in large datasets, enabling accurate predictions of future trends and outcomes. This technology is used in demand forecasting, risk assessment, and fraud detection. Coca-Cola utilizes deep learning predictive analytics to extract insights from a vast array of data sources, including sales figures, weather patterns, consumer sentiment, and social media trends, enabling it to make informed decisions that optimize production schedules, inventory levels, and marketing campaigns across its global network. [56]

Medical Imaging Diagnostics: DL models are used for medical image analysis in health care. [57] These models assist in diagnostics by analyzing medical images such as X-rays or MRIs to detect abnormalities and assist health care professionals in making accurate diagnoses. Mount Sinai Hospital deploys supervised learning using CNNs to diagnose retinoblastoma, a rare and deadly eye disease, with an accuracy of 99 percent, compared to 80 percent accuracy for traditional diagnosis methods. In fields like chemistry or biology, neuro-Symbolic Learning systems are being used to discover new materials or drug compounds by integrating DL data-driven insights with symbolic knowledge about chemical properties.

Logistics: DL is revolutionizing logistics by optimizing routes, predicting demand, detecting anomalies, and enabling preventive maintenance. Maersk employs DL algorithms to analyze real-time traffic data, weather conditions, and port congestion to optimize shipping routes. [58] This reduces fuel consumption, improves delivery times, and enhances overall operational efficiency.

Despite its remarkable capabilities, deep learning also presents challenges that require careful consideration:

Model Complexity: DL models often contain vast numbers of parameters, ranging from millions to trillions, making them difficult to understand and interpret. Early models had around 94 million parameters, while more recent models, like Microsoft's, surpass 100 billion. Some, like China's BaGuaLu system, contain over 174 trillion parameters. Even smaller models can have thousands to millions of parameters. This complexity, often referred to as the "black box" problem, makes it challenging to trace how inputs result in specific outputs, complicating efforts to identify and address issues like biases, spurious correlations, and overfitting.

Data Dependency: DL algorithms are data-hungry, requiring large amounts of high-quality training data. Collecting, preparing, and maintaining such datasets can be costly and time-consuming.

Some estimates indicate that data preparation can represent as much as 80 percent of the total cost of commercializing DL models. For example, CNNs often need datasets like ImageNet, which contains over 14 million labeled images across 1,000 categories. NLP models like GPT-3 were trained on datasets comprising hundreds of billions of words. Waymo reports that over 20 million miles of real-world driving data were used to train its autonomous navigation systems.

Data Governance: Mismanaging datasets can introduce significant risks. Biases in the training data can lead to biased models that reflect and perpetuate these biases in their predictions. An imbalanced dataset, where one class or category is significantly overrepresented compared to others, can lead to models that perform poorly on the underrepresented classes. Inaccurate or erroneous data can lead to models that make incorrect predictions or provide misleading insights. Datasets that are not updated or refreshed over time can become outdated and fail to reflect changes in the real world.

Adversarial Attacks: DL models can be vulnerable to adversarial attacks, where carefully crafted inputs are used to manipulate the model's decision-making process. This poses security risks in applications like fraud detection and autonomous systems.

Key Board Risk Oversight Considerations for Deep Learning

Deep learning models, with their complex architectures and hierarchical representations, introduce specific governance considerations. Key governance considerations applicable to DL are:

Data Governance: Ensuring robust data governance measures are in place to identify and mitigate biases and other data-related risks in DL models. This includes using fairness-aware algorithms and conducting thorough bias audits.

Transparency and Understanding: Ensuring DL models are transparent, and that management is using explainable AI techniques to make DL models more understandable. Tools like LIME, SHAP, Grad-CAM, and DeepLIFT help make DL systems more transparent, facilitating better decision making and accountability.

Adversarial Resilience: Ensuring that adversarial training and other safeguards are in place to enhance the robustness of DL models against adversarial attacks, ensuring the integrity and reliability of AI systems.

Performance Monitoring: Ensuring that continuous monitoring is in place for DL models to detect performance degradation and other potential issues.

Data Privacy and Security: Ensuring robust practices are implemented to maintain the quality, privacy, and security of data used for training and deploying DL models.

Deep Learning Decision-Making Paradigm

Deep learning AI models can be either deterministic or probabilistic, each with its own set of challenges and benefits. Deterministic DL models can sometimes be prone to overfitting if not properly regularized and they typically do not provide natural measures of uncertainty about their predictions. Probabilistic DL models often involve more complex computations and require significantly more computational resources. While these models provide valuable information about uncertainty, interpreting and communicating these probabilities can be challenging.

The risk profile of deep learning varies depending on the application of its outputs:

Prediction and Classification: For tasks such as predicting stock prices or classifying images, the main risks include bias, lack of interpretability, and vulnerability to adversarial attacks. Both deterministic and probabilistic models can encounter these issues.

Actionable Insights and Recommendations: When DL models provide insights or recommendations for human decision making, additional risks arise. These include potential biases that may

influence human choices, overreliance on the model's recommendations, and the impact of acting on inaccurate information.

Direct Control and Automation: In scenarios where DL models
directly control systems, such as autonomous vehicles or robotics,
the risks are even more significant. Errors or biases in these
models can lead to immediate and potentially harmful real-world
consequences, including injuries.

Organizations can navigate the unique challenges associated with
DL models by addressing these governance issues and implementing
corresponding controls. Appendix E provides additional information
about deep learning risks.

Computer Vision: Seeing Through the Machine's Eye

Computer vision (CV) enables machines to interpret and analyze visual
data from the world around them, performing tasks requiring visual
cognition with unparalleled efficiency and accuracy, much like how
humans perceive and understand visual information. By using digital
images from cameras and videos, along with deep learning models, CV
accurately identifies and classifies objects, recognizes patterns, and makes
decisions based on visual inputs. Key technologies in computer vision
include machine learning and deep learning, specifically CNNs, which
help in processing and understanding visual data. CV can perform a
myriad of visualization tasks:

- Image classification allows computers to accurately categorize
  images into predefined classes, such as recognizing faces in
  photographs.
- Object detection not only identifies but also localizes objects
  within images, essential for industrial automation and home
  security systems.
- Object tracking follows detected items across multiple frames,
  useful in traffic monitoring and surveillance.

- Segmentation divides images into regions based on pixels, distinguishing multiple objects within a single frame, like separating a cat from a dog in a photo.
- Content-based image retrieval searches large image databases using metadata and semantic commands, streamlining the process of finding specific digital images. These capabilities collectively transform how organizations analyze and utilize visual data.

Here is a sampling of commercial use cases for CV:

Enhanced Decision Making: CV enables machines to gather and analyze visual data, providing valuable insights for informed decision making.[59] Digital Diagnostics offers software that analyzes retinal images to detect signs of diabetic retinopathy, a leading cause of blindness. The software allows optometrists and other health care providers to make timely, accurate diagnoses without requiring a specialist, which can improve early detection and treatment of the condition.

Improved Automation and Efficiency: CV automates tasks that were previously manual, reducing labor costs and increasing efficiency. CV-powered systems can automate product inspection, traffic monitoring,[60] and security surveillance, allowing people to focus on more complex tasks. Smart traffic lights use CV to monitor traffic flow and adjust signal timing in real time, reducing congestion.

Enhanced Safety and Security: In self-driving cars, CV systems detect obstacles and potential hazards, enabling safe navigation. In public spaces, CV systems are used to promote public safety, although surveillance and facial recognition can feel invasive, making it crucial for decision makers to balance security and privacy rights.[61]

Quality Control: CV automates product inspection in retail, manufacturing, and agriculture by detecting defects and ensuring compliance with standards. Companies like Cognex[62] and

Omron[63] provide CV-based inspection solutions to ensure high-quality products reach consumers.

Autonomous Checkout: CV powers autonomous checkout systems that scan items and automatically charge customers without needing a cashier. For example, Hudson convenience stores are integrating Amazon's Just Walk Out technology in select airport locations. This system allows shoppers to enter, pick up items, and leave without stopping at a traditional checkout counter, as the total cost is automatically charged to the customer's account when they exit.[64]

These examples demonstrate the diverse applications of computer vision and CNNs across various industries. Despite its immense potential, CV technology is not without its drawbacks.

Bias and Discrimination: CV systems can perpetuate and amplify biases, leading to discriminatory practices such as racial or gender bias in facial recognition systems.

Privacy Invasion: The pervasive use of CV in surveillance raises serious privacy concerns, often collecting and analyzing data without individuals' consent or awareness.

Security Vulnerabilities: CV systems are vulnerable to adversarial attacks that can cause them to make critical errors, posing significant risks in applications like autonomous driving and security.

The ability of CV to create highly realistic deepfakes poses threats to personal reputations and public trust.

Ethical Misuse: The potential for CV technologies to be used in unethical ways, such as mass surveillance or profiling, raises significant concerns about human rights and civil liberties. It also raises ethical questions in fields like health care and law enforcement related to issues like consent, fairness, and the potential for misuse.

Key Board Risk Oversight Considerations for Computer Vision

Computer vision, especially when utilizing CNNs, presents unique challenges and considerations. Here are governance considerations applicable to this type of AI:

Bias and Fairness: Ensuring that CV systems are designed and deployed in ways that prevent bias and promote fairness, avoiding discrimination based on race, gender, or other factors.

Privacy and Data Protection: Ensuring that CV systems comply with privacy laws and best practices and that measures are in place to safeguard sensitive data and protect individual privacy.

Security and Resilience: Ensuring strong security and resilience measures are in place to address the vulnerability of CV systems to adversarial attacks and other security threats.

Transparency and Explainability: Ensuring that CV systems are not only transparent but also explainable, enabling stakeholders to understand the decision-making process and build trust in the system's outcomes. In public settings, provide clear and explicit disclosure to inform those affected by the system's use.

Ethical Use and Human Oversight: Ensuring CV systems are used ethically, with human-in-the-loop oversight, to prevent misuse and unintended consequences.

Computer Vision Decision-Making Paradigm

CV can incorporate both deterministic and probabilistic features, depending on the specific application and approach used. Deterministic features involve systems that produce consistent outputs given the same input conditions, as seen in traditional rules-based systems or algorithms like pathfinding. These systems are predictable and repeatable, which can be critical in applications requiring precision and reliability.

Conversely, probabilistic features are often integrated into CV to manage uncertainty and variability in visual data. CNNs and RNNs incorporate these probabilistic elements to make informed predictions, even when data is incomplete or ambiguous. Probabilistic models, such as Bayesian networks and probabilistic graphical models, also allow for the incorporation of randomness and uncertainty. This approach is particularly useful in complex environments where variability is inherent, such as in natural language processing or medical diagnosis.

The risk profile associated with CV deployments can vary depending on how its outputs are used:

Object Detection and Recognition: For tasks like identifying objects in images or videos, the main risks involve biased training data, lack of interpretability, and potential for manipulation through adversarial attacks.

Actionable Insights and Recommendations: When models provide insights or recommendations for human decision making, the risk profile expands to include potential discrimination based on biased outputs. One prominent example is the bias found in facial recognition systems, which have been shown to misidentify individuals from certain demographic groups, particularly people of color. CV systems can also be prone to the concept of "lookism" which refers to bias on physical appearance. This includes preferential treatment for individuals deemed more attractive according to societal standards, which can perpetuate sterotypes and discrimination.

Direct Control and Automation: In scenarios where computer vision models directly control systems (e.g., autonomous robots), the risks become even more critical, as errors or biases can have immediate and potentially harmful real-world consequences.

Organizations can unlock the power of computer vision responsibly by addressing these governance questions and implementing corresponding controls. Appendix E provides additional information about governing CV risks.

Sensor Fusion: The Future of Intelligent Perception

Sensor fusion combines data from multiple sensors, creating a more comprehensive and accurate understanding of the surrounding environment. Unlike Symbolic Learning, machine learning, or large language models, sensor fusion does not focus on reasoning, learning from data, or generating text. Instead, it integrates and interprets data from various sensors, such as cameras, LiDAR, radar, and GPS, to provide a unified and enhanced perception of the world.

Sensor fusion offers several advantages over relying on data from individual sensors. By combining data from multiple sources, sensor fusion can reduce noise and compensate for the limitations of individual sensors, leading to more accurate and reliable perception. Additionally, parallel processing of sensor data allows for real-time interpretation of information, which is critical for applications like robotics and self-driving cars. Finally, sensor fusion enhances system robustness by detecting and adapting to sensor failures, preventing catastrophic consequences.

Sensor fusion finds widespread commercial applications including:

Autonomous Vehicles: Sensor fusion enables accurate perception of surroundings crucial for safe navigation. Waymo integrates computer vision and sensor fusion in vehicles equipped with cameras, LiDAR, and radar to analyze and track objects like vehicles, pedestrians, and road signs.[65] This comprehensive understanding aids in informed navigation, braking, and acceleration.

Robotics: Robots equipped with sensor fusion AI interact effectively with their environment, performing tasks like object manipulation and collision avoidance. Boston Dynamics utilizes sensor fusion to enhance robot agility by combining data from cameras, LiDAR, force sensors, and inertial measurement units for real-time decision making about movement and manipulation.[66] Their robots are pushing the boundaries of what is possible in industrial automation, public safety, construction, military applications and more.

Sports Analytics: Sensor fusion plays a critical role in understanding athlete performance beyond traditional metrics. Combining data from multiple sensors, including wearable devices, cameras, and motion capture systems, sensor fusion provides a comprehensive performance profile that informs training strategies and provides insights into game dynamics. Formula One teams use sensor data from accelerometers, gyroscopes, GPS, and tire pressure sensors to optimize vehicle performance, monitor dynamics, and enhance safety.[67]

Smart Buildings: Sensor fusion integrates data from motion detectors, temperature sensors, and occupancy sensors in smart buildings. Johnson Controls employs sensor fusion to optimize HVAC settings, lighting levels, and energy efficiency while enhancing occupant comfort and security.[68]

Agriculture: Sensor fusion revolutionizes agriculture by monitoring crop health, soil conditions, and environmental factors using cameras, drones, and weather stations. John Deere employs agriculture drones that combine specialized cameras for high-resolution visual imagery, near-infrared sensors, and normalized difference vegetation index sensors that enable farmers to capture precise multispectral imagery and analyze crop health data to a field's edge. The company's tractors are also sensor fusion-enabled to monitor crop health, detect pests and diseases, and apply fertilizer and water in a targeted manner.[69]

These examples showcase the diverse applications of sensor fusion in commercial settings, contributing to advancements for competitive advantage in various industries. Despite its benefits, sensor fusion AI presents certain challenges:

Safety and Accuracy: The potential for errors in sensor data interpretation or fusion can compromise safety and performance, particularly in high-stakes applications like autonomous vehicles and industrial automation.

Security and Vulnerability: Sensor fusion systems are susceptible to tampering or physical attacks, making robust security measures essential to protect the integrity of the data and the overall system.

Privacy and Data Governance: Collecting and processing data from multiple sensors raises significant privacy concerns, especially when personal or sensitive information is involved. Ensuring compliance with privacy regulations and ethical data-handling practices is critical.

System Reliability and Robustness: The complexity of integrating diverse sensors and ensuring their calibration and synchronization presents challenges that can impact the reliability and robustness of the system.

Operational Costs and Data Integrity: The reliance on large amounts of real-time data can be costly and requires ongoing investment in data quality and processing capabilities to maintain system integrity.

Key Board Risk Oversight Considerations for Sensor Fusion AI

Sensor fusion introduces specific governance considerations including:

Development and Testing: Ensuring sensor fusion systems are rigorously tested and validated for accuracy, reliability, and safety.

Deployment and Monitoring: Ensuring appropriate policies and procedures are in place to govern the responsible deployment of sensor fusion systems, including ongoing monitoring and risk mitigation.

Risk Controls: Ensuring the implementation of safeguards to address potential risks such as data privacy issues, unintended consequences, and liability concerns which involve determining responsibility and accountability for the actions and outcomes of systems that integrate data from multiple sensors. These issues are complex due to the involvement of various stakeholders, including developers, manufacturers, operators, and end users.

Performance Monitoring: Ensuring there are processes to continuously evaluate the performance of sensor fusion systems using metrics like accuracy, latency, and error rates.

Incident Response: Ensuring plans are in place to effectively respond to incidents involving sensor fusion systems, including communication protocols, mitigation strategies, and regulatory compliance.

Security: Ensuring measures are implemented to protect sensors from unauthorized access, physical damage, and manipulation. Ensure the security of the supply chain to prevent the introduction of malicious code or vulnerabilities.

Sensor Fusion Decision-Making Paradigm

Sensor fusion models blend deterministic and probabilistic elements which vary depending on the specific application. These models combine data from multiple sensors, each with its own inherent measurement errors and uncertainties. The model estimates and propagates these uncertainties throughout its analysis, leading to probabilistic outputs. Some models incorporate random elements, such as dropout layers or particle filters, to explore different data combinations and enhance robustness. This adds a probabilistic dimension to their decision-making process. Variations in sensor combinations, environmental conditions, or unexpected events can lead to different interpretations and probabilistic predictions. The outputs of these models depend heavily on the context provided by the combined sensor data.

Despite the probabilistic nature of these models, sensor fusion models often include deterministic aspects. Once trained, the weights and biases within the model become fixed, establishing a framework for interpreting sensor data. This framework guides the model toward statistically relevant patterns, reducing randomness in output variations. The architecture of a sensor fusion model, including specific data fusion techniques and decision-making algorithms, defines a structured pathway for processing the combined sensor data. This pathway introduces a degree of determinism, influencing how the model analyzes and interprets complex sensory inputs. Sensor fusion models are often trained for specific tasks, such as anomaly detection, situational awareness, or robot navigation. When presented with similar contexts and sensor data patterns, these models tend to produce consistent, predictable outputs within the range for which they were trained.

The risk profile associated with sensor fusion AI can vary depending on how its outputs are used:

Data Analysis and Monitoring: Sensor data can be biased due to environmental factors, sensor placement, or calibration issues. These biases can propagate through the fusion process, leading to skewed analysis. Unreliable or noisy sensor data can trigger false alarms, causing unnecessary responses or overlooking real issues.

Actionable Insights and Recommendations: When models provide insights or recommendations for human decision making, the risk profile expands to include underlying biases from the data potentially influencing human decisions inappropriately. The integration of multiple sensors can lead to vast amounts of data, making it challenging to extract relevant insights efficiently and accurately.

Direct Control and Automation: In applications like autonomous vehicles or industrial robots, errors in sensor fusion can lead to immediate safety hazards, accidents, or system failures. Ensuring the safety and reliability of systems controlled by sensor fusion AI is critical, requiring rigorous testing, validation, and fail-safes. Seamlessly integrating sensor fusion AI with existing control systems can be complex, requiring careful consideration of compatibility and synchronization.

Organizations can navigate the unique challenges associated with sensor fusion by addressing these governance questions and implementing corresponding controls. Appendix E provides additional concerning governing sensor fusion risks.

Introducing Language-Based AI: Unlocking Language Intelligence

Language-based AI models are algorithms designed to understand and generate human language, mastering elements like syntax, grammar, and complex expressions. These technologies include:

- Natural Language Processing (NLP)
- Large Language Models (LLMs)
- Generative AI (gAI)

While these technologies share foundational AI principles, they approach language mastery through different methodologies.

Natural language processing (NLP) has roots dating back to the 1950s, aiming to bridge the gap between human and computer languages. Early NLP models relied on manually crafted rules, achieving milestones like the 1954 Georgetown-IBM machine translation experiment. By the 1990s, statistical NLP emerged, allowing models to learn language patterns autonomously from data. Today, neural networks, particularly those using transformer architectures, lead in NLP accuracy and understanding.

Large language models (LLMs), which began gaining prominence in the 1980s and 1990s, marked a shift toward data-driven approaches. This evolution was fueled by an explosion of available text datasets, advancements in hardware like graphics processing units (GPUs), and key technical innovations. Originally designed for graphics, GPUs excel at performing massive parallel calculations, making them invaluable for language applications.

Recent technical innovations have further advanced language-based AI:

Word Embeddings: Numerical representations of word meanings and relationships that form the basis for complex mathematical operations in AI.

Convolutional Neural Networks (CNNs): Enable AI to automatically learn and extract meaningful patterns from text data.

Recurrent Neural Networks (RNNs): Allow AI to process and understand sequential information, capturing context and dependencies between words.

Transformer Architecture: Enhances AI by enabling parallel processing of entire sentences, capturing complex dependencies, and improving model efficiency.

In the past decade, LLMs have evolved into "language super-learners," mastering multiple languages and demonstrating abilities that go beyond language imitation to actively generating original text.

The Shift to Small Language Models

The AI industry is experiencing a significant shift from large, data-intensive models to smaller, more efficient language models. This trend is supported by advancements in techniques like knowledge distillation and Low-Rank Adaptation (LoRA), which enhance the efficiency of smaller models without significantly sacrificing performance. The trend is further supported by concerns over the high costs and energy consumption associated with large models. Startups like Arcee.AI are leading this trend, offering tailored AI solutions that address specific business needs without the extensive data and computational demands of larger models like ChatGPT. These smaller models are gaining traction due to their cost-effectiveness, energy efficiency, and alignment with specific business goals.

Companies like Google, Meta, OpenAI, and startups like Hugging Face and Sakana AI are embracing this approach, offering compact AI models that are easier and cheaper to deploy, particularly in scenarios where large-scale models are unnecessary.[70]

Small language models (SLMs) come with limitations. They have reduced generalization capabilities, meaning they may struggle with tasks outside their narrow training focus. Their knowledge bases are less comprehensive, limiting their ability to handle complex or diverse queries. Additionally, SLMs may lack the depth and nuance in context understanding that larger models possess, potentially leading to less sophisticated or accurate responses.

However, corporate users increasingly favor SLMs because they are significantly cheaper, faster, and more secure. The trade-off is worthwhile for many businesses because SLMs are tailored to specific tasks, providing focused and reliable performance where it matters most. The reduced computational and data requirements lead to lower costs and faster deployment—especially appealing in industries where efficiency and speed are critical. Furthermore, since SLMs can often be deployed locally or with minimal cloud dependency, they offer enhanced security and data privacy, requirements for businesses handling sensitive information. For these reasons, the practical benefits of SLMs often outweigh their limitations.

For AI governance, this trend highlights the need for oversight strategies that consider the benefits and risks of adopting smaller, specialized models over LLMs. While SLMs offer practical advantages, the evolving standards for what constitutes a "small" model underscore the importance of staying informed about developments in AI technology and its implications for corporate strategy.

Generative AI Models

Generative AI (GenAI) represents one of the most transformative applications of machine learning, capable of creating entirely new, novel content across a wide variety of formats. While LLMs are a prominent example of this, GenAI extends beyond language to include images, music, code, and more. The rapid growth in both adoption and experimentation in GenAI is reshaping industries. Below is an overview of some of the key models driving this change.

LLMs in Generative AI

ChatGPT and GPT-4 (OpenAI): Best known for their conversational capabilities, these models can generate coherent, human-like responses across a wide range of topics.

Gemini (formerly Bard, Google AI): Notable for its precision in information retrieval and the ability to deliver concise, reliable responses.

Claude (Anthropic): Designed with safety and factual accuracy in mind, Claude focuses on generating harmless, high-integrity content.

LaMDA (Google AI): Built for natural and engaging conversations, LaMDA excels in delivering informative and interactive dialog.

Perplexity: Distinctive for its retrieval-augmented generation, Perplexity combines conversational AI with real-time access to external data, offering answers with citations for transparency and accuracy.

While LLMs are a powerful tool for generating text and language-based content, they represent only one facet of GenAI, which spans a much broader range of transformative applications. Beyond chatbots and language models, GenAI is being leveraged to simulate complex scenarios, explore business model assumptions, generate new software code, and even create synthetic data for training other AI systems. In fields like finance and health care, GenAI is helping model future outcomes and test strategies by generating realistic, hypothetical scenarios. In business, it is used to probe assumptions, uncover hidden risks, and optimize decision making. This broader application of GenAI enables industries to not only automate creative tasks but also unlock deeper insights, allowing businesses to innovate faster and more strategically.

Specialized Generative Models

DALL-E 2 (OpenAI): Specializes in text-to-image generation, producing highly realistic visuals based on textual descriptions.

Midjourney and Stable Diffusion: Known for their artistic rendering capabilities, these models excel in creating stylized and imaginative images, enabling users to bring their creative visions to life.

MuseNet and Jukebox (OpenAI): Focus on musical composition, generating diverse styles of music, including complex harmonies and even vocal arrangements.

Generative AI in Other Domains

OpenAI Codex: Translates natural language commands into functional code, enabling AI-assisted programming and accelerating software development processes.

Jasper.ai and Rytr: These tools provide AI-driven writing assistance, helping with content creation, marketing copy, and other creative writing tasks.

Generative AI Versus LLMs and NLP

While LLMs like GPT-4 and LaMDA are a significant application of GenAI, they represent a subset of generative AI focused on text generation. NLP, in turn, is a broader field that encompasses more than just generative models—it includes text analysis, sentiment detection, and translation. In contrast, generative AI spans multiple domains, including visual art, music, and even software code generation.

Understanding the distinctions between LLMs, NLP, or broader GenAI is critical for board oversight. Having a conceptual understanding of these differences is important, as each technique presents different risk profiles, and certain risks are more prominent than others depending on the decision-making paradigm employed.

Natural Language Processing: Empowering Machines to Speak and Comprehend

Natural language processing allows computers to understand, interpret, and generate human language. While NLP is not primarily focused on reasoning or problem-solving, it plays a crucial role in these areas by providing essential language understanding capabilities. NLP delves into the complexities of human language, including grammar, syntax, semantics, and pragmatics.

Traditional language processing techniques relied heavily on rule-based systems and statistical methods. However, these approaches often struggled with ambiguity, context understanding, and scalability when compared to modern NLP techniques.

Recent advances in NLP have enabled deeper extraction of meaning and context from human language, moving beyond simple keyword matching. This includes understanding nuances, sentiment, and intent. NLP models, trained on large and diverse datasets, can now adapt to various dialects, slang, and informal language. This adaptability enhances their performance across different linguistic and cultural contexts. Additionally, many NLP algorithms can process text and speech in real time, supporting applications that require immediate responses, such as chatbots, virtual assistants, and live transcription services.

These capabilities have spurred widespread use of NLP in commercial applications, including:

Machine Translation: NLP algorithms can translate text from one language to another, enabling seamless communication across cultures. For example, Google Translate and Microsoft Translator offer high-quality translations for numerous languages.[71] In research, MIT has developed a machine translation algorithm that detects fake news by identifying language inconsistencies, such as unusual vocabulary or grammatical errors.

Speech Recognition and Synthesis: NLP allows computers to understand spoken language, convert it to text, and vice versa. This technology is integral to voice assistants and speech-to-text applications. Researchers at the University of California, Berkeley, created a speech recognition system to help people with aphasia (a language disorder) communicate by converting typed words into spoken language. Commercially, platforms like Duolingo use speech recognition to provide real-time pronunciation feedback, enhancing language learning.[72] However, challenges remain with certain accents and complex pronunciations.

Text Summarization and Information Extraction: NLP algorithms can condense lengthy texts into concise summaries, extract key information, and identify entities and relationships within the text. IBM has developed an algorithm that automatically summarizes legal documents, saving lawyers significant time. Additionally, tools like Semantic Scholar use NLP to analyze scholarly literature, generate summaries, and extract key details such as citations and keywords.[73]

Sentiment Analysis and Opinion Mining: NLP can analyze text to determine sentiment—whether positive, negative, or neutral—offering insights into public opinion and customer feedback. Researchers at Stanford University developed an algorithm that predicts stock market movements by analyzing the sentiment of news articles and social media posts. In the commercial sphere, Meltwater's media intelligence platform uses NLP to analyze sentiment across news, social media, blogs, and podcasts, helping companies track trends, identify risks, and refine their PR and marketing strategies.[74]

Chatbots and Virtual Assistants: NLP powers chatbots and virtual assistants that engage in natural language conversations, offering customer support and answering queries. Researchers at the University of Pennsylvania have developed a chatbot that provides mental health counseling by listening to patient concerns and offering advice. Schneider Electric's EcoStruxure Building Advisor uses NLP as part of its AI-driven system to analyze building data, optimize energy consumption, and predict maintenance needs, reducing costs and downtime.[75]

Despite its benefits, NLP presents certain challenges:

Data Dependency: NLP algorithms rely on large amounts of high-quality text data for training and evaluation, which can be expensive and time-consuming to acquire. The quality and representativeness of the data directly impact the performance of NLP models.

Bias and Fairness: NLP algorithms use word embeddings, which translate words into a high-dimensional semantic space. These embeddings capture semantic context and relationships but can inherit biases from the data they are trained on, including racial, gender, and occupational biases.

Privacy and Security Concerns: NLP systems frequently handle sensitive information, including personal data and private communications. This raises significant privacy and security concerns and underscores the need for strong data protection measures and compliance with privacy regulations to prevent breaches and misuse.

Hallucinations: NLP models can sometimes generate text that is factually incorrect, nonsensical, or ungrounded in reality, known as hallucinations. These outputs can appear grammatically correct and confidently presented, making them difficult to distinguish from accurate information.

Key Board Risk Oversight Issues for Natural Language Processing

Natural language processing models bring specific challenges due to the intricacies of human language. Important oversight considerations include:

Development and Deployment Guidelines: Ensuring that clear and comprehensive guidelines are established for the development and deployment of NLP systems. These guidelines must address key issues such as bias, fairness, transparency, and explainability, alongside privacy and security. Standards for ethical AI development should also be established, including considerations for the societal impact of NLP systems and their alignment with the company's values.

Data Governance: Implementing robust data governance and privacy practices to protect the confidentiality, integrity, and availability of data used in NLP systems. This includes data access controls, data anonymization, and compliance with relevant data privacy regulations, such as GDPR or CCPA.

Continuous Monitoring and Assessment: Ensuring regular and ongoing monitoring of NLP systems is vital to maintaining their integrity, accuracy, and relevance. Boards should ensure that mechanisms are in place to monitor system outputs for accuracy, detect and mitigate adversarial attacks like data poisoning, and assess the overall performance of the models. Incorporating feedback loops from end users and other stakeholders can also help refine and improve NLP models in real-world contexts.

Regular Audits and Third-Party Evaluations: Ensuring regular audits evaluate the risks associated with NLP systems and ensure compliance with established guidelines and regulations. Boards should mandate both internal and third-party audits that assess model performance, bias detection, data security, and adherence to ethical AI standards. Third-party evaluations can provide an unbiased perspective on the NLP systems' efficacy and fairness.

Ethical and Societal Impact Assessments: Overseeing regular assessments of the ethical and societal impacts of NLP systems. This involves evaluating how these technologies affect different populations and ensuring they do not reinforce harmful biases or contribute to social inequalities. Boards must ensure that NLP systems align with the company's broader ethical standards and social responsibilities.

Vendor and Third-Party Risk Management: Ensuring risk management for third-party NLP vendors. This includes ensuring due diligence is conducted on vendors' ethical standards, data practices, and alignment with the company's AI development guidelines. Managing these relationships carefully is essential to mitigate risks associated with outsourced AI technologies.

Natural Processing Language Decision-Making Paradigm

NLP models operate on a spectrum from probabilistic to deterministic approaches, each with distinct features and governance challenges. Probabilistic models rely on statistical patterns in large text datasets, where outputs are often educated guesses rather than definite answers due to the inherent uncertainty in language. On the other hand, deterministic models use pretrained parameters—weights and biases learned from initial training—that provide a structured understanding of language patterns. However, even these deterministic models can produce varied results, especially when encountering unfamiliar or unexpected data, due to the random elements in the text generation process.

The risk profile changes based on how NLP outputs will be used:

Information Retrieval and Analysis: In tasks such as search, summarization, or sentiment analysis, NLP models face risks related to biased language patterns that may perpetuate stereotypes or disadvantage certain groups. The inherent ambiguity of language can lead to misinterpretation, especially when models struggle to understand context. Additionally, the lack of interpretability in how NLP models derive their outputs can obscure the reasoning behind decisions, raising concerns about fairness and accountability. These risks are particularly pronounced in NLP because language is rich in nuance and context, making errors or biases potentially more impactful.

Actionable Insights and Recommendations: When NLP models are used to provide insights or recommendations—such as analyzing text to inform legal strategies or recommending job candidates based on resume review—the risks are magnified. Biases in the training data can unfairly influence these decisions, leading to suboptimal and discriminatory outcomes.

Direct Interaction and Content Generation: In scenarios where NLP models directly interact with users—like chatbots or virtual assistants—or generate creative content, the risks include the possibility of producing offensive, biased, or harmful language. NLP models may inadvertently reinforce harmful stereotypes or generate toxic language, leading to hostile environments and negative user experiences. Moreover, the ability of NLP models to generate human-like text, rich in content, raises the risk of spreading misinformation, which can erode trust in information sources and influence public opinion. These challenges are particularly acute in NLP due to the dynamic and context-sensitive nature of language.

Organizations can realize the potential of NLP while navigating its unique challenges by addressing these governance questions and implementing corresponding controls. Appendix E offers additional information for governing NLP risks.

Large Language Models: Harnessing the Power of Human Language

Large language models (LLMs) are advanced AI systems capable of processing and generating human language with a high degree of fluency. Unlike traditional AI techniques that primarily rely on numerical data or simple statistical patterns, LLMs and their small language model (SLM) counterparts excel in understanding and handling the subtleties of human communication. This discussion will focus on LLMs but the information applies to SLMs too.

While LLMs fall under the umbrella of NLP, they represent a specific subset of NLP models that are trained on vast amounts of text data. This extensive training allows LLMs to perform NLP tasks with greater accuracy and flexibility compared to traditional models. LLMs are particularly effective in tasks like text classification, language translation, and answering complex questions, making them a powerful tool within the broader field of NLP.

Distinguishing between NLP and LLM may seem difficult, so we include an example to clarify the difference. Consider a customer service chatbot that helps users reset passwords. An NLP-driven chatbot might recognize keywords like "reset" and "password" and then guide the user through a predefined process based on these keywords. If the user asks an unrelated or unexpected question, the chatbot might fail to provide a meaningful response. An LLM-driven chatbot performing the same task could handle the password reset process with similar efficiency but also engage in a more natural dialogue. If the user asks an unrelated question, such as "Can you tell me about your return policy?," the LLM-driven chatbot could seamlessly switch context and provide an appropriate response, demonstrating a higher degree of conversational flexibility.

This added contextual understanding and deeper learning of LLMs make them able to perform a wide range of tasks, including:

Advanced Natural Language Processing: LLMs have significantly improved the accuracy and efficiency of traditional NLP tasks, such as machine translation, text summarization, and question answering. These models excel at understanding context and nuance, which allows them to deliver more accurate translations, concise summaries, and relevant answers to complex queries. However, like all AI models, they can sometimes produce errors or biased outputs based on the data they were trained on.

Automating Text-Based Tasks: LLMs are increasingly used to automate a variety of text-based tasks, including data entry, customer support, and document processing. Their ability to comprehend and generate human-like text makes them valuable for streamlining operations, reducing manual workload, and improving efficiency in customer interactions. Despite their sophisticated capabilities, LLMs may occasionally struggle with understanding subtle nuances or complex contexts, requiring human oversight in critical applications.

Data-Driven Insights and Analysis: LLMs transform how businesses analyze unstructured text data, such as customer feedback, product reviews, and social media posts. By processing large volumes of text, LLMs can uncover hidden patterns, trends, and relationships, providing actionable insights into customer sentiment, brand perception, and market dynamics. While these insights are valuable, they are dependent on the quality and representativeness of the training data, which can introduce biases or inaccuracies in the analysis.

Enhanced Language Understanding: LLMs bring a deeper understanding of language, allowing them to perform tasks that require contextual comprehension, such as recognizing the sentiment behind customer feedback or understanding the intent in user queries. This capability is particularly useful in applications like sentiment analysis, where understanding the subtleties of language is crucial for accurate interpretation.

These advantages of LLMs are being increasingly harnessed in commercial use cases including:

Chatbots for Customer Support: LLMs power chatbots, providing natural language interaction to address customer queries and enhance user experience.[76] Platforms like IBM Watson Assistant[77] and Google Dialogflow[78] enable businesses to create intelligent virtual assistants for customer service and other needs. These platforms are highly effective at handling basic tasks, such as answering questions and resolving issues, while also offering advanced functionalities like lead generation, appointment scheduling, and product recommendations.

Automated Content Generation: LLMs are widely used in content creation for marketing, helping to produce compelling product descriptions, blog posts, and promotional materials. For example, Jasper[79] is an LLM-based writing tool that assists in creating high-quality content by offering suggestions and drafting in various formats. Similarly, Grammarly[80] is an AI-powered writing assistant that checks for grammar mistakes, plagiarism, and style improvements.

Sentiment Analysis: LLMs are employed in sentiment analysis to evaluate the sentiment behind social media posts and online reviews, enabling businesses to understand public opinion and monitor brand perception. Platforms like Reputate[81] use pretrained LLMs or custom-built AI models to analyze sentiment across text, images, and videos, providing insights into customer satisfaction and brand perception.

Legal Document Review: LLMs are increasingly used in the legal industry to assist with document review and analysis. These models can quickly sift through large volumes of legal documents, such as contracts, briefs, and case law, identifying key clauses, flagging potential issues, and extracting relevant information.[82] Platforms like Casetext and Ross Intelligence leverage LLMs to streamline legal research and document drafting.

Virtual Assistants: LLMs are driving a new generation of virtual assistants that enhance productivity by performing tasks such as scheduling meetings, setting reminders, and answering queries. These LLM-powered assistants are becoming valuable tools for professionals, capable of handling an increasing range of tasks. While some are still in development, these assistants have the potential to manage more complex activities, such as data entry and customer support. The effectiveness of these virtual assistants depends on the specific model and the quality of its training data, and their capabilities continue to evolve as technology advances.[83]

Key Board Risk Oversight Considerations for Large Language Models

LLMs and SLMs bring specific governance challenges due to their scale, complexity, and influence on language understanding and generation. While these challenges are common in other AI models, they are especially significant in LLMs and SLMs because of their wide-ranging capabilities. Key governance considerations include:

Hallucinations: Ensuring robust safeguards against the generation of factually incorrect or inappropriate content. Both LLMs and SLMs can generate factually incorrect or inappropriate content, known as hallucinations. While SLMs are often more focused on specific tasks and may have less capacity for complex generative tasks, they still require robust safeguards to ensure accuracy and reliability in their outputs.

Interpretability: Ensuring outputs are interpretable and that advanced Explainable AI (XAI) methods are implemented. This is a challenge for both LLMs and SLMs, though it may be somewhat easier to achieve with SLMs due to their smaller size and simpler architecture.

Evolving Language Use and Cultural Nuances: Ensuring cultural and ethical sensitivity in both LLMs and SMLs. Both can struggle with capturing the subtleties of evolving language use or cultural differences, especially if they are trained on narrow datasets. Ensuring cultural and ethical sensitivity is important for both types of models to avoid outputs that are offensive or misaligned with the intended context.

Continuous Monitoring: Ensuring continuous monitoring systems are implemented. Monitoring is essential to safeguard against risks such as bias, harmful content generation, and privacy.

Transparency and Accountability: Ensuring the establishment of clear feedback channels are established so that concerns are reported and addressed promptly.

Large Language Model Decision-Making Paradigm

LLMs are fundamentally probabilistic models, generating outputs based on learned probability distributions over sequences of words. This probabilistic nature can lead to variability in outputs. Confidence estimation is essential for determining when to trust these outputs. Methods like the CONfidence-Quality-ORDer-preserving alignment approach (CONQORD) help align the model's confidence with the quality of its responses, improving transparency and reliability. However, these models are also prone to producing hallucinations or unexpected responses due to their reliance on statistical likelihoods rather than fixed rules.

LLMs can be configured to produce deterministic outputs, where the same input under identical conditions yields the same result. However, unlike traditional deterministic systems, the determinism in LLMs is influenced by their probabilistic nature, which relies on patterns learned from vast datasets. This means that while outputs can be consistent under fixed settings, they remain subject to variability due to factors like input phrasing, contextual nuances, and hyperparameter choices. As a result, even in deterministic configurations, LLMs might not always produce identical outputs in all scenarios.

The exact mechanisms by which LLMs perform linguistic tasks are not fully understood. As a type of neural network, LLMs are often interpreted through similar theoretical frameworks, but confidence in their outputs is primarily based on empirical performance rather than complete theoretical understanding. The commercial use cases we highlighted demonstrate impressive capabilities, yet the consistent accuracy and reliability of LLMs are still subjects of ongoing research and improvement.

Organizations can harness the power of LLMs and SLMs to drive innovation and efficiency by addressing these governance questions and implementing appropriate controls. Appendix E provides additional information about LLM risk controls.

Generative AI: Unleashing the Power of Creation

Generative AI (GenAI) has emerged as a game-changer by introducing creative generation, significantly expanding the boundaries of what AI can accomplish. Prior to GenAI, traditional AI techniques—such as machine learning, deep learning, and reinforcement learning—focused primarily on predictive tasks, classification, optimization, and pattern recognition. GenAI, however, offers something new: the ability for machines to create original content, simulate possibilities, and engage in more human-like, contextual interactions.

Rooted in traditional machine learning methods, GenAI builds on these foundations to move beyond merely analyzing and predicting from existing data. It employs powerful models like Transformer architectures (such as GPT-3, GPT-4, and Google's Bard), alongside innovative approaches like generative adversarial networks (GANs) and variational autoencoders (VAEs). These technologies enable GenAI to produce a wide range of outputs, from realistic images to fluid, human-like conversations.

But GenAI's impact reaches far beyond language-based interactions. Its capacity for creativity, innovation, and problem-solving is transforming industries globally. In health care, GenAI accelerates medical advancements by generating synthetic medical images, modeling biological interactions, and discovering new drug compounds. GenAI's ability to simulate scenarios and model future possibilities is especially valuable in business strategy, scientific research, and finance. Companies are using GenAI to test assumptions, explore alternative market strategies, and model potential future events, leading to more informed, data-driven decisions. Similarly, researchers in fields like physics and chemistry are leveraging GenAI to simulate experiments, accelerating the pace of discovery, and in some cases reducing the need for costly physical trials.

This ability to simulate, generate, and create on such a large scale makes GenAI one of the most transformative technologies of our time. It is reshaping business strategy, helping organizations develop scenarios, probe assumptions, and automate complex "knowledge work" tasks. Here are some examples:

Drug Discovery and Development: Companies like Insilico Medicine use GenAI to accelerate drug discovery by designing new molecules with desired properties and simulating their interactions with biological targets.[84] Similarly, XtalPi integrates AI, autonomous labs, and domain expertise to discover small-molecule drugs.[85] This approach involves generating and testing target-specific assays and iterating through design-make-test-analyze cycles to find candidates with optimal drug properties.

Design: Wayfair, an online home interior products supplier, uses GenAI through its Decorify tool to help customers redesign their living spaces. The tool uses uploaded photos to offer different design aesthetics, such as bohemian and mid-century modern. For professional design, Autodesk's Fusion 360 integrates GenAI to assist engineers in designing complex products, combining functionalities like CAD, CAM, CAE, and PCB design.[86]

Investment Decisions: BlackRock Systematic uses transformer technology, which is similar to that used in GenAI platforms like ChatGPT, to enhance their investment process.[87] The company is also developing AI "co-pilots" for Aladdin, their flagship investment management platform.[88]

Fashion: The StyleShopper platform leverages GenAI to provide personalized clothing recommendations based on user preferences and style profiles.[89]

Content Creation: Jasper.ai utilizes GenAI to assist writers and content creators in generating various forms of content, such as blog posts, articles, marketing copy, and social media posts.[90]

New Opportunities and Challenges

This technology presents unique opportunities and challenges. The introduction of enterprise-grade GenAI solutions marks a relatively recent evolution in AI offerings, addressing the growing demand for secure, business-oriented tools. These systems ensure that proprietary data remains protected and isolated, conforming to stringent standards such as GDPR, SOC 2, and HIPAA. Enterprise solutions are uniquely designed to integrate seamlessly with corporate systems like enterprise resource planning (ERP) systems, customer relationshionship management (CRM) systems, and data lakes, enabling organizations to leverage GenAI while maintaining control over their data ecosystems. This development reflects the industry's response to corporate needs for privacy, compliance, and operational alignment, making these tools indispensable for handling sensitive information.

In contrast, individual subscriptions to GenAI services typically operate in shared environments with general, but less robust, protections compared to enterprise-grade solutions. These subscriptions may allow input data to be used for training purposes unless explicitly disabled, posing potential risks to sensitive business information. Widely accessible via web and mobile apps, these tools contribute to a "Bring Your Own AI" phenomenon in the workplace. While democratizing access to powerful AI capabilities, this trend introduces significant risks to corporate security and confidentiality if left unmanaged. As employees bring these tools into the workplace, they may unintentionally expose sensitive information, including proprietary data, trade secrets, and other confidential assets. Because these public models operate outside of corporate security controls, they bypass organizational safeguards.

GenAI's transformative power hinges on its ability to produce creative and contextual outputs, but effectively harnessing this capability requires precise prompt engineering. This technique involves crafting well-structured, intentional inputs to guide the model toward desired outputs, whether generating innovative designs, writing, or simulating scenarios. Prompt engineering is particularly critical for mitigating risks inherent in GenAI, such as bias, misinformation, or unoriginal outputs.

Directors need to be aware of the risks associated with using GenAI tools generally, as well as those specific risks that arise from individual licenses or free versions of GenAI tools. These include:

Unoriginality and Plagiarism: GenAI models can produce outputs that are unoriginal or even plagiarized, especially if they are not trained on a dataset of high-quality content that is sufficiently diverse.

Bias and Discrimination: These models can perpetuate biases and stereotypes from the data they are trained on.

Misinformation and Fake Content: GenAI has the potential to generate misleading news, deepfakes, and other deceptive materials.

Intellectual Property and Copyright Concerns: The legal landscape surrounding AI-generated content is still evolving. Issues related to intellectual property rights, such as copyright, patent, and trademark protections, are complex and unsettled.

The risks associated with other creative GenAI activities like scenario analysis, probing assumptions, or modeling scientific or engineering experiments go beyond the concerns of language-based AI:

Modeling Inaccuracies and Bias: GenAI can introduce significant risks when used to simulate complex business scenarios or scientific experiments, particularly if the underlying models are inaccurate, biased, or poorly designed. In addition to flawed data and assumptions, improperly defined constraints, incomplete model architectures, or misaligned objectives can produce misleading or inaccurate outputs.

Overreliance on AI-Generated Scenarios: Overreliance on AI-generated scenarios can lead to significant risks, as these models often fail to capture real-world complexities such as nuanced human behavior, biological systems, or environmental dynamics. When organizations depend too heavily on AI outputs, they risk making flawed decisions, especially if the models overlook rare events, subtle behaviors, or unpredictable variables. Additionally, feedback loops may emerge, where decisions based on flawed AI outputs reinforce incorrect assumptions over time.

Key Board Risk Oversight Issues for Generative AI

Many of the governance topics discussed so far in this book apply to GenAI. Yet because it is new and rapidly advancing, it is worthwhile to draw out some distinctions for board members to help us ask the right questions and ensure the proper risk management frameworks are in place.

Data Governance: Ensuring ongoing monitoring for potential bias, data drift, or security risks. While some organizations still rely on third-party data for training GenAI models, an increasing number are incorporating proprietary data to fine-tune and customize these models for specific business needs. This shift reduces some of the risks associated with third-party datasets but introduces new challenges related to the management, protection, and ethical use of proprietary data. To address these concerns, companies are adopting both third-party data governance frameworks and internal governance protocols to ensure that training data, whether external or proprietary, is reliable, ethically sourced, and sufficiently diverse. Boards should require auditing mechanisms not only for third-party data providers but also for the organization's own data.

Transparency and Explainability: Achieving transparency and explainability in GenAI models is challenging, especially when using third-party models. Contract terms should require transparency regarding the data sources, methodologies, and model design used to train the GenAI. Companies should adopt Explainable AI (XAI) frameworks to ensure that AI outputs are understandable and accessible to nontechnical stakeholders, particularly in regulated industries. Representations and warranties should guarantee full regulatory compliance, and organizations should consider using "glass box" models, where features, parameters, and decision-making pathways are visible and auditable. It is worth noting that the enterprise versions of various GenAI platforms are beginning to incorporate explainability, transparancy and audit features into their models.

Model Design Integrity: Ensuring that GenAI models are built with robust internal integrity, accounting for real-world constraints and ethical considerations. This involves verifying that the model's assumptions, constraints, and parameters are grounded in scientific, physical, or operational realities, particularly in fields like health care, engineering, and environmental science. Safeguards should be in place to regularly test, validate, and recalibrate models based on real-world conditions.

Risk Assessment and Mitigation: Ensuring the implementation of safeguards to prevent the misuse of GenAI such as spreading misinformation, producing misleading scenarios, or generating flawed simulations. Fact-checking mechanisms, model validation, and content moderation should be implemented to ensure the integrity of AI-generated outputs. Clear guidelines around intellectual property rights should be established for AI-generated content, whether it involves text, images, simulations, or designs.

Monitoring and Auditing: In situations where companies may not have direct oversight of employees' use of AI tools on their own devices, the emphasis should be placed on clear policies, ethics frameworks, and proactive education rather than direct auditing alone. Organizations should develop comprehensive policies outlining acceptable use of GenAI and BYOAI apps, with these policies effectively communicated to all employees. Where feasible, automated monitoring tools can help detect unauthorized or noncompliant use of AI tools. Continuous auditing should ensure that usage aligns with internal guidelines and broader regulatory standards.

Generative AI Model Decision-Making Paradigm

GenAI operates on a probabilistic foundation, generating outputs based on learned patterns and their likelihoods, which introduces both creativity and randomness. However, depending on the application, there may be a need for more deterministic outcomes—those that are predictable and repeatable.

Using techniques such as temperature scaling, which adjusts the model's sensitivity to randomness by focusing on higher-probability outputs, and top-k or top-p sampling, which limits the model to select from only the most likely next steps, developers can guide the model's decision making to more deterministic outputs. Additionally, techniques like beam search evaluate multiple possible sequences of outputs and choose the most likely one, while constrained generation applies predefined rules or conditions to ensure outputs meet specific requirements.

This flexibility allows GenAI to blend both probabilistic explorations, which is ideal for creative exploration and innovative content creation, with deterministic precision, crucial in applications like legal document drafting or financial reporting. Directors should understand that with proper governance and controls, GenAI can balance innovation and accuracy, making it both a powerful and manageable tool across a variety of applications. For a more detailed discussion of the risks and considerations associated with GenAI, see Appendix E.

Ensemble Learning

While different types of AI have distinct capabilities and are often employed as standalone systems, the field of artificial intelligence is increasingly embracing ensemble learning. Ensemble learning involves combining the strengths of multiple AI approaches to achieve more robust and accurate results. Ensemble learning can be either homogeneous or multimodal.

Homogeneous Ensemble Learning

Homogeneous ensemble learning involves using multiple instances of the same type of model or algorithm. In this approach, identical or similar models are trained independently on different subsets of the training data, and their outputs are combined to make a final prediction or decision. This technique aims to leverage the strengths of similar models to enhance overall performance, robustness, and generalization.

This method is particularly effective in mitigating overfitting, improving predictive accuracy, and providing a more stable and reliable model. It is important to note that homogeneous ensemble learning typically uses a single data type. Common techniques include bagging (Bootstrap Aggregating) and boosting, which are widely used for their effectiveness in various applications.

For a detailed exploration of five prominent homogeneous ensemble models, please refer to Appendix H.

The advantages of homogeneous ensemble learning compared to single-model approaches are being increasingly harnessed in commercial applications. For example:

Financial Fraud Detection: Capital One leverages a homogeneous ensemble of machine learning models to detect fraudulent transactions in real time, protecting their customers and mitigating financial losses.[91]

Medical Diagnosis Support: GE Healthcare employs ensembles of deep learning models to assist medical professionals in diagnosing diseases and analyzing medical images, improving accuracy and efficiency in health care delivery.[92]

Spam Detection: Google Mail relies on an ensemble of text classification models to identify and filter spam emails, protecting users from unwanted and potentially harmful content.[93]

Key Board Risk Oversight Considerations for Homogeneous Ensembles

Whether homogeneous ensemble learning is inherently more risky than single-model AI from a governance perspective depends on several factors. While it offers potential benefits like improved accuracy and robustness, it also introduces certain complexities that require careful consideration.

Increased Complexity: Ensemble models involve multiple base models, making them more complex and harder to understand and interpret than single-model approaches. The scalability and maintenance of ensemble systems could also be more challenging compared to single models, requiring more sophisticated infrastructure and expertise.

Error Amplification: Homogeneous ensembles can be susceptible to error amplification, where model errors are fed back into the training data, potentially leading to performance degradation over time. This requires robust safeguards and continuous monitoring.

Potential Bias Reinforcement: If not carefully designed, ensemble methodologies can inadvertently reinforce existing biases present in the training data. This requires careful data selection and bias mitigation strategies.

Lack of Explainability: Black-box nature of ensemble models can make it difficult to explain their predictions and decisions, impacting transparency and trust. Explainable AI (XAI) techniques need to be implemented and communicated effectively.

Increased Computational Cost: Ensemble methods often require more computational resources for training and inference compared to single models, which can be a cost factor for organizations.

Organizations can navigate the unique challenges associated with homogeneous ensemble learning by addressing these governance issues and implementing corresponding controls. Appendix E offers additional governance considerations for homogeneous ensemble learning. Appendix G offers additional information on five prominent homogeneous learning ensemble models and their associated advantages, disadvantages and unique risks.

Multimodal Ensemble Learning

Multimodal ensemble learning involves integrating models from different types or core AI techniques within an ensemble. In this approach, diverse models, which may handle distinct types of data or employ different algorithms, are combined to make collective predictions or decisions. The goal is to utilize the complementary strengths of various techniques to enhance the overall performance, robustness, and accuracy of the ensemble.

gAI, particularly GANs, has emerged as an exciting development in multimodal ensembles, inspiring a wave of innovation. By generating realistic synthetic data, GANs can complement other AI techniques by filling gaps in training data or enhancing decision making with novel insights. For example, in a multimodal ensemble designed for a complex task such as image captioning, GANs could generate high-quality images that provide additional context for the NLP models to interpret. Beyond simply generating synthetic data, GenAI has the capacity to create entirely novel scenarios, enriching the diversity and depth of the model's understanding. GANs and other generative techniques can simulate potential outcomes in situations where real-world data is scarce or impossible to obtain, allowing for more comprehensive analysis and decision making.

Multimodal ensembles are particularly useful in scenarios where information from various sources or data types needs to be integrated, such as combining text and image data in NLP or computer vision tasks. By integrating multiple core AI techniques, multimodal ensemble learning provides a more comprehensive and nuanced understanding of complex data.

This synergistic approach enables AI systems to overcome the limitations of individual techniques and achieve superior performance in various applications. For example, combining machine learning with NLP can improve sentiment analysis by utilizing the contextual understanding of language provided by NLP, while GenAI might enhance this by simulating unseen conversational patterns. Similarly, integrating computer vision with machine learning can enhance object detection and recognition by merging visual information with data-driven insights, where GAN-generated synthetic images can be used to bolster training datasets, improving model accuracy and robustness.

Multimodal ensemble learning has a number of advantages over its homogeneous counterpart:

Enhanced Data Integration and Representation: Multimodal ensembles leverage diverse data sources and core AI techniques, capturing richer information than homogeneous ensembles limited to a single data type. This comprehensive integration leads to a more thorough understanding of the problem and can significantly improve model performance.

Improved Generalization and Robustness: By integrating different data perspectives, multimodal ensembles can learn more generalizable patterns and become more robust to noise and variations within individual core AI techniques. This allows them to perform better on unseen data and handle diverse real-world scenarios.

Addressing Multimodal Dependencies and Interactions: In domains where relationships and interactions between different core AI techniques are critical, multimodal ensembles can explicitly capture and learn from these dependencies, leading to more accurate and context-aware predictions. This is particularly relevant for complex problems with inherent interconnectivity between different data types.

These advances and advantages are being increasingly harnessed in complex environments to achieve impressive results. Examples include:

Material Inspection: Multimodal AI integrates advanced computer vision, imaging, and data analysis techniques to revolutionize quality control and inspection processes across various industries. It enables precise surface defect detection, structural and dimensional checking, assembly verification, and packaging and artwork inspection. For instance, AI can detect microscopic defects in materials, ensure precise measurements in products with tight tolerances, confirm assembly accuracy against specifications, and identify cosmetic flaws imperceptible to the human eye. This comprehensive approach significantly enhances accuracy, efficiency, and reliability in quality assurance.

Autonomous Navigation: Tesla's autonomous driving technology utilizes multimodal ensembles that combine sensor data from cameras, LiDAR, and radar to navigate roads safely and efficiently.[94]

Medical Image Segmentation: The NVIDIA Clara AI platform uses multimodal ensembles of deep learning models to segment various medical images, including CT scans and MRIs, for improved diagnosis and treatment planning.[95]

It is important to point out that homogeneous ensemble learning has a number of distinct advantages over multimodal ensembles:

Reduced Complexity: Homogeneous ensembles utilize similar base models, making them inherently simpler to understand, interpret, and debug compared to multimodal ensembles that combine diverse models and data types. This simplifies the development, deployment, and maintenance process.

Enhanced Interpretability: Because homogeneous ensembles rely on similar base models, their predictions can often be traced back to the individual contributions of each base model. This facilitates easier explanation and understanding of decision making compared to the complex and interwoven nature of multimodal ensembles.

Lower Computational Cost: Training and running homogeneous ensembles generally require less computational resources than multimodal ensembles due to their simpler architecture and reliance on similar models. This can be advantageous for resource-constrained environments or applications requiring faster processing times.

Key Board Risk Oversight Considerations for Multimodal Ensembles

Multimodal ensemble learning presents a distinct set of risks and governance challenges compared to single-model AI and even homogeneous ensemble learning. While it offers potential advantages in capturing diverse data types and improving performance, it necessitates heightened vigilance from a governance perspective. Here's why multimodal ensemble learning might be considered riskier:

Increased Complexity: Combining multiple core technique-specific models and integrating different data types significantly increases the overall model complexity. This makes it more challenging to understand, interpret, and debug potential issues.

Data Heterogeneity and Fusion: Integrating diverse data formats and ensuring their consistent representation and fusion can be complex, leading to potential errors and biases. Robust data preprocessing and fusion techniques are critically important.

Model Interdependency and Amplification: Errors in one core technique-specific model can propagate and amplify through the ensemble, impacting overall performance. Assessing interdependencies and implementing safeguards is essential.

Limited Explainability: Understanding how multimodal models arrive at their decisions across diverse data types can be significantly harder compared to single-core technique models, requiring advanced XAI techniques.

Security and Privacy Concerns: Integrating and protecting sensitive data from different core techniques necessitates multifaceted security and privacy protocols, including data anonymization and access controls.

Evolving Data and Learning paradigms: Adapting the ensemble model to new data sources, formats, and evolving learning paradigms requires continuous monitoring, re-evaluation, and potentially retraining, adding to the complexity.

Organizations can navigate the unique challenges associated with multimodal ensemble learning by addressing these governance issues and implementing corresponding controls,. Appendix E offers additional governance considerations for multimodal ensembles. Appendix H highlights five prominent multimodal ensembles.

Summary

In this chapter, we introduced 12 foundational AI techniques, explained their key advantages and limitations, and shared real-world commercial use cases across a variety of industries. We also explored the critical governance considerations and risk management strategies that are essential for responsible AI oversight. Our goal has been to demystify these core AI techniques and spark your curiosity about the incredible possibilities they offer.

While few organizations will apply all of these techniques, having a fundamental understanding of them provides directors with a solid foundation for overseeing AI initiatives and engaging in informed discussions. This knowledge equips leaders to assess the opportunities AI presents, understand its potential risks, and ensure their organizations are well-positioned to leverage AI responsibly and effectively.

We hope this chapter has inspired you to see AI as a powerful tool for innovation, one that requires thoughtful governance and risk management. In the next chapter, we outline a governance framework that boards can adopt and adapt to effect prudent oversight.

CHAPTER 7

A Board Risk Management Framework for AI

AI governance frameworks provide boards with guiding principles and a well-honed process to oversee AI development, deployment, and monitoring, ensuring alignment with the organization's ethical values, risk tolerance, and regulatory compliance. Without such a framework, it is difficult to ensure AI deployments are accurate, safe, ethical, explainable, and transparent.

In this chapter, we outline the elements of a thoughtful governance approach, built on a solid foundation of Responsible AI (RAI) governance principles. This pragmatic approach seeks to build on those governance frameworks already in place and working well in our organizations. We discuss the importance of readiness assessments to evaluate preparedness for AI engagement and examine strategies for integrating governance frameworks into existing structures.

Embracing RAI Governance Principles

Several standard-setting organizations have developed frameworks to assist board and management teams in guiding the responsible development and use of AI models. While these frameworks vary in detail, they share a common core of essential principles. These principles serve as a moral compass, guiding organizations toward the ethical, fair, and transparent use of AI. Boards should ensure these principles are formalized in an AI ethics policy.

>**Human-centered AI:** AI should be designed and used to augment human capabilities, not replace them. Human oversight and accountability must remain central in AI decision-making processes.

Fairness and Nondiscrimination: AI systems should be free from bias and discrimination, ensuring equal treatment and opportunities for all individuals. Regular audits and bias mitigation techniques should be employed to identify and mitigate potential biases.

Transparency and Explainability: AI systems should be transparent in their operation, allowing for an understanding of how decisions are made. Explainable AI techniques should be incorporated to provide insights into algorithmic reasoning and facilitate trust in AI decisions.

Privacy and Security: AI systems should safeguard sensitive personal data, protecting privacy and preventing unauthorized access or misuse. Robust cybersecurity measures and data privacy practices must be implemented to ensure data integrity and confidentiality.

Accountability and Responsibility: Organizations should be accountable for the outcomes of AI systems, establishing clear lines of responsibility and addressing potential harms. Mechanisms for identifying, reporting, and rectifying AI-related incidents should be in place.

Social Responsibility: AI should be developed and deployed with consideration for its broader societal impacts, minimizing potential negative consequences and maximizing positive contributions. Societal impact assessments should be conducted to evaluate the ethical implications of AI applications.

Continuous Improvement: AI governance frameworks should be dynamic and evolving, adapting to emerging technologies, societal norms, and regulatory landscapes. Regular reviews and updates should ensure that AI governance practices remain effective and aligned with evolving AI capabilities.

Well-Defined Operational Boundary Constraints: Clearly defining the operational boundaries for an AI system helps minimize AI risks by restricting the system's scope and capabilities. This can prevent the system from making decisions or taking actions outside its intended purpose, reducing the potential for harm.

Conduct a Readiness Assessment

AI adoption is often described as more of a journey than a destination. This perspective is crucial as integrating AI into company operations is a dynamic and evolving process. Initially, company leadership may not fully grasp AI's potential or its implications for operations, workforce, or strategy. As organizations implement AI, they learn about its capabilities and limitations, refining strategies and applications over time. Typically, AI adoption unfolds in phases, starting with pilot projects and scaling up as the technology proves its value. Each phase provides insights that inform subsequent stages, leading to continuous improvement and deeper understanding of the art of the possible.

To navigate this journey successfully, the board must partner with management to ensure the organization has the proper foundation for AI adoption. This involves conducting a comprehensive readiness assessment to identify strengths, potential gaps, and challenges. The assessment should focus on whether the organization has the necessary infrastructure, talent, and governance structures to support AI, and where adjustments may be needed. The board's role is to oversee this process, ensuring management is not only prepared but also proactive in addressing identified gaps. Key questions in readiness assessments include:

- What resources and capabilities do we already have?
- What gaps need to be filled?
- What obstacles could hinder our progress?

Data Governance

The readiness assessment should begin with an evaluation of data governance maturity, as this is the foundation for building trust in data—critical for confidence in AI outputs. Effective data governance ensures that data is well-managed, secure, and compliant, which fosters trust among those who rely on AI-driven insights. As highlighted in Chapter 5, data is the fuel for AI, and without proper governance structures, even the most advanced AI systems can produce flawed or unreliable results. While all criteria in our readiness assessment are critical to AI success, flawed data governance will compromise any AI initiative from the start.

Talent

The readiness assessment must include a thorough evaluation of whether the organization has the necessary talent to fully leverage AI's transformational potential. This involves identifying key roles—such as data scientists, machine learning and data engineers, UX designers, AI champions, and board members with relevant expertise. The assessment should determine whether we have the right people in place to drive success or if gaps exist. If talent gaps are identified, we need a plan to fill them, either through recruitment or external providers. Given the high demand for AI expertise, securing the right talent is more challenging than ever.

Additionally, the readiness assessment should include a review of the board's skill matrix to determine whether directors with specific AI expertise are necessary, or if expertise in data governance and digital initiatives is sufficient for our strategic goals. This ensures the board is equipped to provide informed oversight and guidance as the organization embarks on its AI journey.

Core System Fitness

An evaluation of our core systems to determine if they are equipped to fully support AI technologies is an important part of a readiness assessment. Many existing systems were not designed to meet the demands of AI, making it crucial to assess the current IT infrastructure, data storage solutions, and computing capabilities. This evaluation should identify critical limitations, such as insufficient scalability, rigid architectures, security vulnerabilities, and lack of adaptability to evolving technologies. Any of these factors can hinder AI implementation. Additionally, the assessment must determine whether our systems can accommodate increasing AI and data privacy compliance requirements. Identify any gaps that could hinder effective AI adoption and develop a plan to address them.

Inventory of AI Uses

The readiness assessment should include a comprehensive catalog of all current AI uses within the company, including third-party solutions. It is critical to understand where and how AI is being utilized, both internally and by external vendors. Vendor management processes should be updated to identify any new AI features introduced by suppliers, as vendors may integrate AI without explicit client awareness. As we strive to strategically leverage AI, our third-party suppliers are doing the same. Therefore, it is essential to establish mechanisms for monitoring and communication with vendors to understand how and when AI is deployed in their solutions and services. Our vetting processes should be adapted to ensure that our vendor's use of AI aligns with our RAI policies.

Market Analysis

The readiness assessment should include a market analysis to understand how competitors are leveraging AI or planning to integrate it. While not every organization may want to be at the cutting edge of AI technology, it is equally important not to fall behind competitors in utilizing this strategic resource. Gaining insight into how competitors are deploying or planning to deploy AI helps us evaluate our position in the market and make informed, forward-thinking decisions about AI investments.

Defensive Posture

An evaluation of how AI might be used against the organization, considering both competitive and security risks, is an important element of a well-rounded readiness assessment. This includes identifying potential vulnerabilities in our AI systems and developing strategies to mitigate these risks. The assessment should consider exposure based on our technological intensity, including the balance between in-house AI development and reliance on third-party solutions. By understanding how competitors or malicious actors could exploit AI, we can proactively strengthen our defenses and ensure resilience in our AI strategy.

Workforce and Cultural Readiness

The readiness assessment should consider AI's impact on employees and corporate culture. AI will inevitably transform roles—creating new opportunities while making others obsolete. Effective change management and strong leadership are crucial to navigating these transitions. To ensure success, AI initiatives should be human-centered, with a clear focus on employees' readiness to adopt and work alongside AI technologies. This includes addressing potential concerns, offering training and support, and prioritizing upskilling throughout the organization.

It is especially important to equip key personnel—such as internal audit staff, compliance teams, and line staff responsible for Sarbanes-Oxley Act (SOX) controls—with the knowledge and skills needed to interface with and drive our AI governance framework. Ensuring that these critical roles are well-versed in AI technologies and governance is essential for maintaining ethical standards and operational effectiveness as AI becomes more integrated into the organization.

Compliance Readiness

Companies must navigate a complex and fragmented regulatory landscape, with significant differences in approach among the European Union, the United States, China, and other jurisdictions. Our readiness assessment should thoroughly evaluate the organization's compliance posture, focusing on awareness, the effectiveness of operating controls, and alignment with applicable laws. The EU's Artificial Intelligence Act classifies AI systems into risk categories, imposing strict compliance requirements for high-risk applications to ensure safety, transparency, and alignment with fundamental rights and EU values. In contrast, the United States lacks a unified federal framework, relying instead on a patchwork of state laws and sector-specific regulations that vary widely in scope, definitions, and enforcement. Meanwhile, China adopts a centralized, prescriptive approach emphasizing national security, ethical AI, and content control. This fragmented landscape demands careful navigation to ensure compliance and mitigate legal risks across jurisdictions.

In this fragmented environment, companies must address several key compliance considerations. Firstly, they should evaluate the regulatory requirements specific to each jurisdiction in which they operate. This includes understanding the differences in data protection laws, such as the California Consumer Privacy Act (CCPA) and Virginia's Consumer Data Protection Act (CDPA), which have distinct provisions for data protection assessments and opt-out rights.

Key questions for compliance readiness should include: Do we have a clear and thorough understanding of the regulatory requirements we must comply with in all jurisdictions where we operate? Are there any specific federal agency guidelines relevant to our industry that we need to adhere to? Have we developed a nuanced understanding of the differing state AI and privacy laws, and are we equipped to address these inconsistencies in our operations? Are we equipped operationally to implement effective processes for consumers to exercise their rights, such as opting out of data-processing activities? Do we have a handle on data-minimization requirements across jurisdictions that restrict the collection, processing, and retention of personal information to what is necessary to complete a defined task? What mechanisms do we have or need to build to keep current with new AI and privacy laws and any federal agency directives that impact our business?

The common elements across AI and privacy laws typically include a focus on transparency, accountability, fairness, and data minimization. However, the specifics of these requirements can differ substantially, creating operational challenges for businesses. Companies must establish clear compliance mechanisms, including regular risk assessments and data protection impact assessments, to navigate these diverse requirements effectively.

Conducting a readiness assessment is an essential first step in preparing the organization for the complexities and opportunities AI brings. This structured process identifies strengths while exposing key gaps in infrastructure, talent, compliance, and governance. Failing to address these gaps early risks derailing AI initiatives before they can deliver value. A comprehensive assessment not only prepares the organization to leverage AI effectively but also provides a strategic plan to address weaknesses and mitigate risks.

Integrate AI Into Governance Frameworks

After conducting a readiness assessment, the second component is to integrate AI considerations into the organization's existing governance frameworks. This approach allows companies to build on established processes, reducing duplication and capitalizing on their existing strengths.

Most mature organizations already have a risk appetite statement that outlines acceptable levels and types of risk. This statement should be expanded to explicitly address AI-related risks, which will help shape enterprise risk management (ERM) strategies, including the measurement, management, and reporting of significant risk exposures. As discussed in Chapter 4, AI introduces new risks that need to be incorporated into these frameworks.

ERM frameworks typically include periodic risk self-assessments conducted by business lines and product areas. It is critically important that these assessments also cover each AI model used within the organization, including third-party solutions. The unique risks introduced by AI—such as model drift, bias, and explainability—must be thoroughly evaluated and managed.

The Three Lines of Defense model, commonly employed in public and private companies, should be adapted to include AI-specific factors at all stages of AI system development, from experimentation and pilot phases to full deployment. Internal audit scopes and critical accounting control mechanisms must also be revised to ensure comprehensive oversight of AI systems. This is particularly important for deterministic AI systems used in control functions such as accounts receivable and payable processing, inventory management, and other key operational areas.

Key Elements of AI Governance Framework

Policy Scope and Objectives

Ensure there is a clearly defined scope for the AI governance policy, specifying the types of AI systems and activities covered. Confirm that the policy objectives align with the organization's RAI ethics policy, forming a solid foundation for all AI-related activities.

Business Strategy and Operating Plans

Guide the integration of AI risk management into the business strategy and operating plans. Ensure that AI initiatives are aligned with strategic objectives and operational processes, supporting overall business goals while managing associated risks. Verify there is clear communication across departments and functions regarding the incorporation of AI considerations into daily decision making and long-term planning. Recognize that organizations are likely to be simultaneously managing a handful of pilot projects, some demonstration projects and some deployments that are actively scaling.

Roles and Responsibilities

Ensure clarity in the definition and assignment of specific roles and responsibilities within the AI governance framework, such as AI governance officers, AI risk managers, data owners, AI ethics experts, and compliance. Clarity in the duties and accountabilities of all stakeholders promotes a structured approach to managing AI risks across the organization.

Risk Appetite

Our risk appetite statement must explicitly address our tolerance for AI-related risks. This sets clear boundaries for AI projects, guiding the development of risk management strategies and ensuring that AI deployments align with the organization's overall risk tolerance. Because of the unique ethical risks introduced by AI, risk appetitie statements should speak to the ethical guardrails that are important to our reputation. A well-crafted risk appetite statement provides a clear and concise framework for decision making, outlining the types and levels of risk the organization is willing to accept to achieve its strategic objectives. It aligns risk-taking with the organization's goals, ensures consistent communication about risk tolerance across all levels, and aids in resource allocation and prioritization. Defining acceptable and unacceptable risks enhances transparency and accountability, enabling better risk management and fostering a culture of informed risk-taking.

Risk Assessments

Given the transformational impact of AI across all aspects of business operations, it is essential to integrate AI risk assessments into existing risk management processes. These assessments should be comprehensive, evaluating specific risks associated with AI systems, including potential biases, errors, and cybersecurity threats in addition to the normal operating and financial risks that are well-managed already. Assessments must be conducted regularly to maintain a thorough understanding of the evolving risk landscape and implementation of effective mitigating controls, ensuring that all potential AI-related exposures are addressed and managed.

The power and transformative impact of AI technologies has, in some cases, rendered traditional risk assessment approaches less effective. As a result, new methodologies have been developed to address the unique risks associated with this powerful technology. These AI risk assessment approaches vary in their strengths and applicability to different core AI techniques. From a boardroom perspective, directors should appreciate the various ways to approach risk assessment and understand the suitability of each approach to the specific AI techniques employed by the organization.

Threat-Based Risk Assessment: This approach identifies and analyzes potential threats that could arise from AI systems. These threats can include bias, discrimination, privacy violations, manipulation, security breaches, and physical harm. This method is particularly well-suited for assessing the risks of AI systems used in sensitive applications, such as facial recognition, autonomous vehicles, social media platforms, and critical infrastructure.[96]

Vulnerability-Based Risk Assessment: This approach focuses on identifying and assessing the vulnerabilities of AI systems. These vulnerabilities can include software bugs, data poisoning attacks, adversarial examples, physical tampering, and supply chain vulnerabilities. This approach is particularly well-suited for assessing the risks of AI systems deployed in complex environments, such as cyber-physical systems, financial markets, and critical infrastructure.[97]

Impact-Based Risk Assessment: This approach focuses on assessing the potential impact of AI systems on individuals, organizations, society, and the environment as a whole. It considers the potential for widespread harm, social implications, economic disruptions, and environmental impacts. This approach is particularly well-suited for assessing the risks of AI systems with the potential for large-scale consequences, such as AI-powered weapons, social scoring systems, self-driving cars, and algorithmic decision-making systems.[98]

Model-Based Risk Assessment: This approach uses statistical models and machine learning techniques to quantify the risk of AI systems. It involves developing models that capture the relationships between AI system inputs, outputs, and potential risks. This approach is particularly well-suited for assessing the risks of AI systems used in high-stakes applications, such as medical diagnosis, financial trading, and self-driving cars.[99]

Qualitative-Based Risk Assessment: This approach identifies potential failure modes in a process or system, analyzes the effects of each failure mode, and assigns a risk priority number to each failure mode. It involves techniques such as failure mode and effects analysis (FMEA), threat modeling, and the Harvard risk framework (HRF). These methods focus on understanding the potential causes, effects, and severity of risks, often using qualitative scales or ratings. The approach is well-suited to applications that involve a wide range of potential risks, including security, bias, fairness, environmental impact, and societal implications, benefiting from the holistic and adaptable nature of qualitative methods. Examples include social media platforms, recommendation engines, and AI-generated content.[100]

Table 7.1 provides a good starting point for understanding the suitability of different risk assessment approaches for various core AI techniques with the most suitable approach listed first. However, it is important to understand that suitability can be subjective and context-dependent. Nonetheless, the general sequence for each technique is based on typical concerns and strengths associated with each risk assessment approach.

Several tools and services are emerging to address the growing need for AI risk assessment. While not all AI governance packages offer

Table 7.1 Suitability of risk assessment approach for core AI techniques

Core AI technique	Suitable risk assessment approaches*
Natural Language Processing	Threat-based, Impact-based, Qualitative-based
Computer Vision	Vulnerability-based, Impact-based, Model-based
Machine Learning	Model-based, Impact-based, Qualitative-based
Robotics	Threat-based, Vulnerability-based, Impact-based, Qualitative-based
Sensor Fusion AI	Vulnerability-based, Impact-based, Model-based, Qualitative-based
Homogeneous Ensembles	Threat-based, Vulnerability-based, Impact-based, Qualitative-based
Multimodal Ensembles	Qualitative-based, Model-based, Threat-based, Vulnerability-based, Impact-based

*Ranked from highly to moderately suitable

comprehensive risk assessment capabilities, some, like those from IBM, Aporia, and Fiddler AI, provide tools that can support organizations in identifying and mitigating potential risks associated with their AI deployments. These tools can be valuable in enhancing overall AI governance practices, but they should be considered supplementary to other efforts and due diligence.

These packages typically include risk identification and assessment tools, which automate the process of identifying and assessing AI-related risks across the AI life cycle. They also offer governance policy management, providing a centralized platform for managing and enforcing AI governance policies and procedures. Additionally, incident management features streamline the reporting, investigating, and remediation of AI incidents. Transparency and explainability tools enhance the clarity of AI systems, enabling a better understanding of decision-making processes. Audit and compliance management capabilities automate audits and reporting to ensure compliance with AI governance policies and regulatory requirements.

By leveraging AI governance packages, organizations can streamline and automate AI risk assessment processes, gain deeper insights into AI-related risks, and strengthen their overall AI governance framework. These tools can also provide assurance to the board that effective controls and risk mitigation strategies are being implemented. However, it is crucial for board members to recognize and address the potential drawbacks of using AI to assess other AI systems. Human oversight, ethical considerations, and continuous adaptation are essential to ensure that AI-driven risk assessments are reliable, unbiased, and aligned with organizational values.

Third-Party AI Systems

Directors should appreciate there is an absence of a universally recognized standard for governing and verifying third-party AI models, applications, APIs, or AI-driven services. This presents significant challenges for organizations. SOC 1 and SOC 2 reports primarily focus on internal controls related to financial reporting and the security, availability, processing integrity, confidentiality, and privacy of customer data, respectively. They do not explicitly include information concerning third-party AI controls, training data validity, or model validation.

While these reports can indirectly touch on aspects relevant to AI, such as data security and processing integrity, they do not provide detailed guidelines or assessments specific to AI systems' unique challenges. For instance, these reports do not typically cover the specific quality and reliability issues associated with AI training data or the methodologies used for model validation. Therefore, organizations relying on third-party AI solutions need to consider additional frameworks and standards specifically designed to address these AI-specific concerns.

Directors should also be aware of the potential compliance liabilities when using third-party AI systems. Even if regulations do not directly hold companies responsible for the actions of third-party vendors, businesses are still accountable for ensuring that these vendors comply with applicable laws. If a third-party AI provider mishandles sensitive data or violates privacy regulations, the company using the AI could face legal consequences, particularly if proper governance oversight is deemed inadequate.

Data Management

Monitor the implementation of robust data management and privacy practices within the existing data governance framework. Verify compliance with relevant regulations in data collection, storage, usage, and disposal, emphasizing the protection of sensitive personal data.

AI Development Life Cycle

Ensure a comprehensive AI development life cycle framework is developed. This provides a structured approach to managing the development, deployment, and maintenance of AI systems. It ensures that AI solutions are aligned with business goals, ethical standards, and regulatory requirements at every stage, from conception to decommissioning.

Model and Training Data Validation

Board oversight must ensure rigorous validation of both AI models and training data as a key component of a well-structured AI governance framework. This validation is crucial for ensuring the accuracy, reliability, and fairness of AI systems. Validating AI models helps confirm that they perform as expected, are free of biases or errors, and make decisions based on accurate and relevant data. Similarly, validating training data ensures that the inputs used to train these models are clean, comprehensive, and representative of real-world scenarios.

AI model validation presents several challenges, particularly when dealing with complex multimodal ensembles and continuously iterating algorithms. For general AI models, validation involves ensuring accurate performance across different datasets and conditions, which can be complicated by issues like data bias, overfitting, and lack of interpretability. Multimodal ensembles, integrating data from various sources (e.g., text, images, audio), add another layer of complexity as each modality may have different characteristics and validation needs, making it difficult to assess the model's overall performance and consistency. Additionally, models that continuously iterate and learn from incoming data, often referred to as "online learning" models, pose unique validation challenges. Their dynamic nature requires ongoing validation processes, continuously checking for shifts in model behavior, performance degradation, and potential biases as new data is ingested. This requires robust monitoring systems and frequent recalibration to ensure that the models remain accurate and fair over time.

Three Lines of Defense

Integrating AI considerations into the Three Lines of Defense model not only ensures comprehensive risk management but also underscores the importance of the human-in-the-loop (HITL) principle. The HITL approach emphasizes the critical role of human oversight in managing and mitigating risks associated with AI systems.

In the first line of defense, operational staff are directly responsible for identifying and managing risks in AI systems. The HITL principle is naturally integrated here, as human operators are crucial for monitoring AI outputs and ensuring that these systems perform as intended. Human oversight helps in recognizing potential issues such as data biases or algorithmic errors that might not be apparent through automated processes alone. This active human involvement is vital for ensuring that AI systems are aligned with the organization's goals and ethical standards, and for intervening when anomalies or unexpected behaviors are detected.

The second line of defense, consisting of risk management and compliance functions, plays a key role in overseeing the implementation of AI systems. Here, the HITL principle is crucial in developing and enforcing standards and controls. Human decision makers interpret and apply ethical guidelines, assess compliance with regulatory frameworks, and manage the risks associated with third-party AI providers. This oversight is essential for maintaining accountability and transparency in AI operations, particularly when it comes to sensitive areas like data privacy and fairness.

The third line of defense involves internal audits that provide independent assurance of the effectiveness of the controls and processes established by the first and second lines. As of this writing, there is no comprehensive, universally accepted standard specifically dedicated to the internal audit of AI systems. The absence of a comprehensive standard means that internal auditors often rely on a combination of existing IT audit standards, risk management and AI governance frameworks, and AI-specific guidelines to conduct their assessments. This can lead to inconsistencies and gaps in how AI systems are evaluated. However, an external audit adds another layer of review helping to ensure that AI applications have appropriate oversight mechanisms and that any decision-making processes involving AI are subject to review and intervention where necessary.

The successful integration of AI into the Three Lines of Defense model demands upskilling and continuous learning for all affected employees. Training programs should cover the fundamentals of AI, the specific risks associated with AI technologies, and the ethical and legal considerations of AI use. Equipping employees with this knowledge helps organizations ensure that all team members are prepared to effectively conduct their oversight roles.

Incident Response

Effective incident response planning for AI systems is essential to maintain system integrity and mitigate risks such as unexpected behavior, data breaches, or system failures. Boards must ensure organizations have robust plans specifically tailored to the complexities of AI technologies in use. This process begins with establishing clear protocols for identifying, managing, and mitigating incidents. It involves defining specific roles and responsibilities for team members and ensuring that they are prepared to respond swiftly when an incident occurs. Regular training and simulations help maintain this state of readiness.

To effectively detect and respond to incidents, organizations should employ AI monitoring tools that can identify anomalies and potential issues early. Such tools can provide real-time alerts, enabling proactive intervention before minor issues escalate into major disruptions. Whenever an incident is detected, a structured approach to investigation and resolution is important. This includes clear communication protocols to ensure all stakeholders are informed and a response is coordinated. Essential to the response plan are rollback capabilities and kill switches, which allow the organization to revert to previous system states or halt operations to contain the incident and reduce potential damage.

In the event of a critical AI incident, it is crucial for organizations to have a clear escalation process in place. This ensures that incidents are promptly elevated to the appropriate level of authority within the company, allowing for a swift and effective response. When an incident is deemed critical, immediate communication with senior management and relevant departments is necessary. This includes IT, legal, compliance, and public relations teams, depending on the nature of the incident. The escalation process should include predefined criteria for what constitutes a critical incident, such as potential regulatory breaches, significant data loss, customer harm, or threats to operational continuity.

Furthermore, in situations where the incident results in harm—whether to individuals, customers, or the public—there may be a need for disclosure. This is especially true if the harm involves breaches of personal data, financial loss, or any other significant negative impact. Disclosure requirements are often mandated by law, particularly in the case of data breaches, under regulations such as the General Data Protection Regulation (GDPR) in Europe or similar laws in other jurisdictions. Beyond legal requirements, ethical considerations also play a role. Organizations may choose to disclose information to affected parties and the public, even when not required to do so, in order to maintain transparency and trust.

Incident response plans must be regularly reviewed and updated to address evolving risks and incorporate lessons learned from past incidents. This continuous improvement is critical in adapting to new threats and maintaining the effectiveness of the response strategy. Board oversight plays a vital role in this process, ensuring accountability and providing a strategic perspective on managing AI-related risks within the organization.

Privacy and AI Regulatory Compliance

As discussed in the readiness assessment, organizations face increasing challenges in establishing mechanisms and protocols to comply with the diverse regulatory frameworks applicable to their AI systems and practices. The complexity is heightened by differing standards across jurisdictions and often conflicting regulations, particularly in the fragmented state-by-state landscape in the United States. It is essential for organizations to stay informed about evolving regulations and adapt their internal policies and procedures accordingly. Regular audits and legal reviews are necessary to ensure compliance and effectively navigate these complex regulatory environments.

The adoption of AI, whether developed in-house or sourced from third parties, introduces a growing set of compliance obligations. Data privacy regulations, such as GDPR and various U.S. federal and state laws (e.g., CCPA, HIPAA), impose stringent requirements on how AI systems handle sensitive information. Boards must ensure that AI systems adhere to these frameworks by implementing robust data security measures, including encryption and access controls. Additionally, it is important to closely follow guidance from federal regulatory agencies like the FTC and SEC, particularly concerning issues like algorithmic bias and potential discrimination in AI-driven decisions. The rapidly evolving AI compliance landscape requires a structured process for keeping up with the latest guidance and regulatory changes.

To support these efforts, an increasing number of automated tools, such as Drata and Vanta, offer frameworks like the NIST AI Risk Managewment Framework to assess, authorize, and monitor AI systems, ensuring they meet security and regulatory standards. Whether an organization chooses to automate aspects of compliance monitoring and documentation or not, it is imperative that boards establish a clear governance framework for AI compliance. By prioritizing compliance and responsible AI practices, boards can guide their companies toward leveraging the transformative potential of AI while effectively mitigating associated risks.

Assurance and AI Audits

Despite the rapid deployment of AI across various critical company functions, the practice of auditing these systems has not kept pace, leaving companies uncertain about how to design and implement effective controls and raising concerns about reliability and compliance with regulations like the Sarbanes-Oxley Act (SOX). While there is no universally accepted standard specifically for AI audits, the ISO/IEC 42001 standard, introduced in 2023, provides guidelines for establishing, implementing, maintaining, and continuously improving an Artificial Intelligence Management System (AIMS). This standard serves as a foundational guideline, helping organizations manage AI-related risks, including ethical considerations and compliance issues, with a focus on security, safety, fairness, transparency, and data quality.

Traditional auditors, typically trained as CPAs, are well-equipped to audit deterministic AI systems used in financial functions, such as accounts receivable (AR), accounts payable (AP), and revenue recognition. However, many AI systems, especially those involving machine learning, present challenges that extend beyond traditional auditing expertise. These systems require auditors to have specialized knowledge in algorithms, data quality, model interpretability, and ethical issues such as bias and fairness. The dynamic nature of AI systems, which evolve over time with new data, adds further complexity, necessitating an understanding of life cycle management, including updates and retraining processes.

Therefore, effective AI audits require an interdisciplinary approach, involving collaboration between auditors and specialists in AI, data science, and ethics. This approach ensures comprehensive evaluations that address both technical and nontechnical aspects of AI systems. To address these challenges, the auditing community, including organizations like the Institute of Internal Auditors (IIA) and NIST, is focusing on specialized training and developing frameworks to equip auditors with the necessary skills. Conducting AI audits is essential for organizational oversight, enabling companies to leverage the benefits of AI responsibly and ethically while mitigating potential harms.

Liability Insurance for AI

Companies typically seek insurance to shield themselves from business risks. However, current Directors and Officers (D&O) and Errors and Omissions (E&O) policies were primarily designed in a pre-AI era. This raises a crucial question: do these existing insurance policies effectively safeguard companies and their directors against AI-related liabilities, such as those arising from discriminatory algorithms or patent infringement by faulty algorithms? The uncertainty extends to how insurance programs address AI's impact on business valuation, licensing deals, and other areas of concern for boards and directors.

The effectiveness of specific insurance products, such as rep and warranty insurance or tail coverage, in protecting boards and sellers from AI-related exposures is still unclear. These uncertainties compel boards to stay well-informed about the evolving landscape of insurance markets related to AI. Directors must grasp the nuances of existing liability insurance coverage, including exclusions and limitations, and engage in conversations with insurance risk professionals to address any gray areas. It is imperative to ensure that errors and omissions coverage explicitly covers AI-related areas. Given that insurance policies may have exclusions or limitations pertaining to AI-specific areas, directors need to ensure existing policies are meticulously reviewed and consider obtaining additional coverage if deemed necessary.

Oversight Strategy

Establishing a clear oversight strategy for AI initiatives early on is an important third aspect of an AI governance framework. This ensures alignment with strategic goals, regulatory compliance, and responsible and ethical implementation. Early decisions on oversight help set clear accountability, streamline decision-making processes, and mitigate risks associated with AI deployment. Since a company's AI journey often begins with small experiments and pilot projects that scale up as the technology proves its value, the governance framework must be adaptable to this iterative and experimental nature.

AI's profound potential to transform business operations makes it closely tied to strategic planning. Unlike narrower domains like cybersecurity, AI impacts the core of what an organization does and how it does it. AI can drive innovation, reinvent business models, and open new avenues for competitive advantage, making it a central element of strategic planning. Therefore, it is essential for boards and top management to deeply consider how AI could reshape their organization, asking fundamental questions like: If we were to start this company today with the power of AI, would we build it the same way? What would we do differently?

Situationally Tailored Oversight

An organization's oversight strategy should be customized to fit its unique situation. For tech-heavy companies developing proprietary models and deploying AI in multiple applications, a rigorous oversight approach is essential. Even organizations not directly involved in AI development will encounter AI through third-party software and services. In these cases, oversight should focus on vendor management and ensuring awareness of all instances of third-party AI usage. Companies that rely on third-party models with user-tunable parameters must monitor these parameters and ensure that third-party AI models comply with ethical and legal standards.

The question of whether every board needs AI expertise is increasingly relevant as AI becomes integral to business strategy and operations. The answer depends on the company's context. For tech-heavy companies, having board members with significant experience in AI deployment, data governance, and digital execution may be necessary. Such organizations may require several directors with deep relevant expertise to guide company strategies effectively. Conversely, organizations that primarily rely on third-party solutions and APIs may benefit more from board members with strong vendor management and data analytics skills. The board's skill matrix should reflect the company's unique circumstances and strategy.

Establishing a clear oversight strategy for AI initiatives early on is crucial for aligning with strategic goals, ensuring regulatory compliance, and promoting responsible implementation. Early decisions on oversight help set clear accountability, streamline decision-making processes, and mitigate risks associated with AI deployment. As organizations typically start their AI journey with small experiments and pilot projects, scaling up as the technology proves its value, the governance framework must be adaptable to accommodate this iterative and experimental nature.

Cultivating AI Governance Expertise

Building on the need for specialized skills in AI, data governance, and digital execution within the board, it is essential that all board members, regardless of their specific expertise, have a working understanding of AI's capabilities, risks, and governance considerations. This understanding is essential for fulfilling their oversight responsibilities, which include the duty of care, the duty of loyalty, the duty to monitor, and the duty to disclose.

Boards must actively participate in shaping the organization's AI strategy, ensuring that AI initiatives align with the company's values and mission. They must also ensure that potential risks associated with AI development and deployment are identified and mitigated. To effectively fulfill this expanded role, boards need to cultivate a strong foundation of AI governance expertise, starting with AI literacy in the boardroom. Directors must understand the fundamentals of AI technologies, their capabilities, and their limitations. Additionally, they need to grasp the principles that underpin responsible AI development and deployment and stay informed about the latest advancements in AI technologies, regulatory developments, and societal expectations regarding AI governance.

Strategies for Cultivating AI Governance Expertise at the Board Level

Continuous Learning and Education: Offer tailored training and education programs to enhance board members' understanding of AI technologies, AI governance principles, and emerging AI risks.

External Expertise: Engage external experts in AI governance, academia, external auditors, and workforce development to provide insights and perspectives on emerging frameworks, best practices, and the evolving AI landscape.

Board Composition Refresh: Consider updating the board with directors who possess strong AI expertise or experience in industries that are leading in AI adoption.

Open Dialogue and Debate: Foster a culture of open dialogue and debate within the boardroom regarding AI governance issues. Encourage the exchange of ideas and the identification of potential risks and opportunities.

Regular Assessments and Reviews: Conduct regular assessments and reviews of the board's AI governance expertise to ensure it remains relevant and effective in addressing evolving AI challenges and societal expectations.

Rethinking Committee Structures

Building on the discussion of boardroom expertise, a key question arises: which committee is best suited to oversee AI governance, and how should a board make this decision? Traditionally, the audit committee might oversee such responsibilities due to its focus on risk assessment and internal controls. However, the complexities of AI, including issues like bias, discrimination, privacy, and security, may require a broader perspective.

A risk management committee, with its expertise in risk identification, assessment, and mitigation, could be well-suited for AI governance. Alternatively, a technology committee might be ideal for organizations with a strong focus on technological innovation, as it brings an understanding of AI systems, data issues, and emerging technologies. In some cases, a dedicated AI and data governance committee, comprising experts in AI, ethics, law, and risk management, might be necessary for specialized oversight. An important new contribution to AI governance is the National Association of Corporate Directors' (NACD) Blue Ribbon Report on Technology Leadership in the Boardroom and should be a must-read for directors.

Regardless of the structure chosen, it is important to clearly define AI governance responsibilities and establish a robust framework for communication, collaboration, and escalation.

Key Considerations for Committee Structures

Boards should consider several factors when deciding whether to restructure or reassign responsibilities in light of AI:

The Organization's size, Complexity, and AI Maturity Level:
Larger, more complex organizations with a higher level of AI adoption may require a more dedicated approach to AI governance, potentially calling for a specialized committee. A specialized committee is warranted in larger and more complex organizations with significant potential to be impacted by AI, both positively and negatively. Additionally, organizations with a

higher level of AI maturity are likely to have more AI initiatives in place, warranting a more sophisticated governance structure to manage risk and ensure alignment with the organization's overall strategy.

The Organization's Risk Appetite and Tolerance for AI-Related Risks: Boards with a lower risk appetite for AI risk may be more cautious about deploying AI systems, especially in areas where there could be significant potential harm if the AI system malfunctions or makes mistakes. They may also be more likely to require extensive testing and validation of AI systems before deploying them. Boards with a higher risk appetite for AI risk are more likely to be willing to take on some level of risk in order to reap the potential benefits of AI. They may be more willing to experiment with AI in new or emerging areas, and they may be less concerned about the possibility of setbacks or failures.

Industry and Regulatory Environment: In industries with strict regulations or where reputational risks are significant, a rigorous approach to AI governance is necessary. For example, sectors like health care and finance are subject to specific guidelines and regulations, such as those issued by the FDA or the Financial Industry Regulatory Authority (FINRA), which require careful oversight.

Whether the Organization Is an AI Developer or Is Licensing Third-Party Solutions: Organizations actively developing their own AI operate at a higher level of risk and complexity compared to those using third-party AI solutions. They require a more robust and nuanced oversight approach. While both AI-developing and AI-licensing organizations have inherent risks, the nature of AI oversight differs. Developing AI systems requires deeper technical expertise on the board, potentially warranting a dedicated committee or members with specialized AI expertise. Those organizations that license third-party solutions that allow for user-tuned parameters, such as a credit scoring model, warrant rigorous vendor selection processes, thorough risk assessments of the specific AI offering, careful oversight of how parameters are set and tuned, and continuous monitoring to ensure compliance with ethical and legal considerations.

The Potential for Business Model Disruption: While the disruptive potential of AI is often exaggerated, boards should adopt a proactive and vigilant stance toward potential disruptions to their core business from AI initiatives outside of the company. By considering the potential for business model disruption from outside the company, boards can design a committee structure that is proactive, risk-aware, and responsive to the evolving AI landscape.

The Organization's Existing Committee Structures and the Availability of Expertise: Boards should evaluate the expertise and experience of existing committees, determining if additional training or recruitment is necessary. While not every board member needs deep technical expertise in AI, a fundamental understanding of AI concepts, potential applications, and associated risks is increasingly expected. This knowledge is crucial for effectively overseeing AI initiatives, ensuring responsible adoption, and mitigating potential risks to the organization's reputation and financial stability.

Strategies for Building AI Expertise Within the Ranks of Management

While board-level expertise is essential, it is equally important for boards to ensure that there is sufficient AI, digital and data governance expertise within the organization's management team. This includes:

AI Governance Training for Management: Management should undergo training and education programs to deepen their understanding of AI governance principles, risk assessment methodologies, and the importance of embedding responsible AI practices into decision-making processes. It is important that those responsible for SOX internal controls and the organization's three lines of defense must be equipped to assess the implications and risks associated with AI, digital technologies, and data governance. This ensures they can effectively vet these technologies, identify potential vulnerabilities, and uphold the organization's compliance and ethical standards.

AI Governance Roles and Responsibilities: Clearly define AI governance roles and responsibilities within the organization, ensuring there is a dedicated team or individuals responsible for overseeing AI initiatives and ensuring compliance with AI governance policies.

Recruiting to Fill Critical Gaps: Following the readiness assessment, which identified specific expertise gaps in AI, digital technologies, and data governance, a targeted recruitment strategy should be implemented to address these needs. This includes seeking candidates with a strong technical background and experience in the relevant areas identified. Given the surge in AI interest, finding such specialized talent can be challenging.

Cross-Functional Collaboration: Encourage collaboration between AI teams, legal, risk management, and other relevant departments to integrate AI governance considerations into all aspects of AI development and deployment.

Regular Communication and Feedback: Ensure clear communication channels and feedback loops are established between the board and management to address AI governance concerns promptly and ensure that AI initiatives align with the board's oversight responsibilities.

Continuous Improvement of AI Governance Practices: Foster a culture of continuous improvement in AI governance, encouraging the organization to learn from experiences, adapt to evolving risks, and refine its AI governance framework accordingly.

Boards should ensure that all critical elements outlined above are thoroughly addressed within the organization's governance structure. This includes verifying that key aspects such as risk management, data privacy, model validation, monitoring, incident response, and compliance with regulatory frameworks are effectively integrated and working. It is essential that the board or an appropriate committee has clear visibility into the performance and effectiveness of these elements and actively engages with management to address any issues that arise. This proactive approach ensures that our organizations are well-prepared to navigate the complex and rapidly evolving landscape of AI, safeguarding both operational integrity and our ethical standards.

Decisioning Framework

A fourth aspect of a well-defined AI governance framework is how we decide on AI priorities. Organizations must establish a robust decision framework for evaluating and selecting AI initiatives for funding. Given the considerable capital investment and significant demands on staff time and organizational resources required for AI initiatives, it is crucial to prioritize projects that align with the organization's strategic objectives and offer the greatest potential for transformative impact.

While it is important to encourage and incentivize bottom-up sourcing of potential AI applications—drawing on the insights and creativity of employees at all levels—the ultimate decision about which initiatives to fund must be made from the top down. This ensures that resources are allocated to projects that are strategically aligned and have the highest potential for value creation.

The vast array of potential AI use cases demands a sorting mechanism to identify and prioritize high-impact applications. While each organization will craft an evaluation framework tailored to its unique circumstance, evaluation criteria to be weighed might include strategic alignment, expected impact and value, data availability, technical infrastructure and expertise, workforce impact, regulatory and compliance risks, risk management, scalability, and stakeholder support.

It is vital to establish clear objectives and desired outcomes for each AI initiative from the outset. This clarity enables organizations to measure the effectiveness of AI deployments post-implementation, assessing whether the anticipated advantages and benefits have been realized. The decision-making framework should consider the degree of clarity regarding expected outcomes and impacts. However, it is important to recognize that demanding sharp, clear benefit statements may sometimes limit innovation and exploration, especially in a dynamic and evolving field like AI. AI initiatives often involve a journey of discovery, where the full potential and benefits may not be immediately apparent.

Regardless, AI projects at the forefront of innovation and exploration can still be guided by clear benefit statements. For example, setting broad objectives focused on exploration, such as investigating the potential of AI for customer service improvements, allows for flexibility in discovering various applications. Milestones can be established to assess feasibility, integration, and early learning, ensuring that projects have defined checkpoints without restricting innovation. This approach helps organizations balance the need for exploration with accountability, ensuring that AI initiatives can progress and adapt as new insights emerge.

By establishing a mix of well-defined and flexible criteria, organizations can make strategic resource decisions for AI that encourage both calculated risks and innovative exploration, aligning with long-term business goals while remaining open to unexpected opportunities.

Tracking Mechanisms

The fifth component of a well-defined AI governance framework is tracking mechanisms. It is not uncommon for organizations to have multiple AI initiatives at various stages, from experiments to scaled deployments, so it is essential for the board to have a comprehensive understanding of the progress, potential benefits, and overall value of these projects.

Regular Progress Reports and Dashboards

Best practices for AI initiatives include implementing regular reporting mechanisms to track progress, often using dashboards that provide real-time data and analytics on milestone attainment or key performance indicators (KPIs). While directors may already be familiar with financial and customer satisfaction KPIs, AI introduces a range of new, critical metrics that may be less familiar but are essential for understanding whether AI projects are on track. Among these are statistical measures, including accuracy, precision, recall, and F1 scores.

- **Accuracy** shows how often a model makes correct predictions, which is important for evaluating performance in areas like risk assessment or customer segmentation. However, accuracy alone doesn't always provide a complete picture.
- **Precision** (or specificity) tells us how many of the predicted positive results are actually correct.
- **Recall** (or sensitivity) measures how many actual positive cases the model successfully identifies.
- **F1 scores** combine both precision and recall, giving a more balanced view of the model's effectiveness. This is especially useful in fields like health care or fraud detection, where both false positives and false negatives can have serious consequences.

Directors don't need to deeply understand specific statistical KPIs, but they do need to be confident that the right metrics are being tracked and managed by qualified experts within the organization. Directors should focus on ensuring that appropriate KPIs are in place to monitor AI performance and risks, that capable teams are overseeing these metrics, and that clear, transparent processes exist for reporting issues like model drift or ethical concerns to leadership. In addition to tracking KPIs, directors should ensure that AI aligns with the organization's strategic objectives, ethical principles, and compliance requirements, with accountability mechanisms that ensure timely and decisive action when necessary.

Phased Evaluation and Milestone Reviews: AI initiatives can often be evaluated at key milestones. For experimental or pilot phases, the focus may be on proof-of-concept success, technical feasibility, and initial ROI assessments. As projects move toward scaling, reviews should include more comprehensive evaluations of business impact, operational integration, and scalability. This phased approach allows the board to make informed decisions about whether to continue, scale, or pivot projects.

- **Cross-Functional Oversight and Governance:** AI initiatives typically span multiple functions within an organization, such as IT, data science, compliance, and business units. Cross-functional oversight serves as a tracking mechanism by ensuring that AI initiatives are monitored and evaluated from multiple perspectives within the organization. This team's role is to assess the alignment of AI projects with both technical capabilities and business goals, ensuring that the initiatives are progressing as intended and meeting their objectives.

- **Benchmarking and External Validation:** Top companies often benchmark their AI initiatives against industry standards and best practices. Organizations like Gartner, Forrester, and McKinsey regularly publish reports on AI trends, benchmarks, and best practices. These reports serve as valuable reference points for companies to compare their performance and stay updated on industry standards. Many firms also seek external validation, such as audits or certifications, to ensure that their AI systems meet high standards of quality and compliance. This provides an objective measure of progress and credibility to stakeholders.

- **Continuous Learning and Adaptation:** AI is a rapidly evolving field. Boards should encourage a culture of continuous learning and adaptation, where feedback from AI deployments is regularly used to refine models, processes, and strategies. This helps ensure that the organization stays ahead of technological advancements and market trends.

- **Investment Analysis and ROI Tracking:** Finally, boards need to continuously evaluate the financial performance of AI initiatives. This involves tracking ROI and comparing it against initial projections. Key questions include whether the initiatives are delivering the anticipated value and if additional investments are justified. If projects are not meeting expectations, it may be necessary to reassess or redirect resources.

The purpose of tracking mechanisms is to provide a continuous flow of information, enabling the board and management to maintain an ongoing overview of AI initiatives. This helps in identifying potential issues early and making real-time adjustments to ensure projects stay aligned with organizational goals.

Reporting and Feedback Mechanisms

The final component of a well-defined governance framework is the information the board receives about AI outcomes. Reporting and feedback mechanisms play an essential role in board governance by providing structured and periodic communication of results and insights about AI initiatives. These mechanisms are essential for translating the detailed data collected through ongoing tracking mechanisms into comprehensive, high-level summaries that the board of directors and other key stakeholders can use to make informed decisions.

One key aspect of these mechanisms is the preparation of board reports. Board reports are comprehensive documents prepared for board meetings that provide an in-depth summary of the progress, challenges, and outcomes of AI initiatives. They typically include detailed analyses of KPIs, risk assessments, and the financial implications of the projects. By presenting this information in a structured format, board reports enable directors to understand the current state of AI initiatives, assess whether they are meeting strategic objectives, and evaluate their potential return on investment. This detailed insight is crucial for the board to fulfill its oversight responsibilities and ensure that resources are being used effectively.

Executive summaries are another critical component of reporting and feedback mechanisms. These concise overviews are provided to senior leadership and often to the board committee with specific oversight responsibility, and offer a snapshot of the most important achievements, strategic implications, and any significant issues that require immediate attention. Executive summaries distill complex information into a more digestible format, making it easier for senior leaders to quickly grasp the key points and implications of AI initiatives. This helps streamline decision-making processes, ensuring that leadership can swiftly address any urgent concerns or capitalize on emerging opportunities.

Feedback sessions, which are meetings or discussions involving stakeholders such as project teams, management, and the board, provide a platform for reviewing the outcomes of AI initiatives. These sessions are interactive, allowing the board to ask questions, seek clarification, and provide guidance based on the information presented. Such engagements are essential for aligning the understanding of AI projects across different levels of the organization, ensuring that all stakeholders are on the same page regarding project status, challenges, and next steps. Feedback sessions also allow the board to offer strategic input, helping to shape the direction of ongoing and future AI initiatives.

The primary purpose of reporting and feedback mechanisms is to provide a high-level overview and analysis of the outcomes of AI initiatives, focusing on strategic assessment and accountability. Unlike tracking mechanisms, which provide real-time updates and granular data for operational management, reporting and feedback mechanisms are periodic and designed for strategic oversight. They enable the board to assess the overall impact of AI projects, ensuring that they align with the organization's long-term goals and strategic priorities. By focusing on the broader implications and results of AI initiatives, these mechanisms help boards to hold management accountable and to ensure that projects deliver the expected value.

Summary

In this chapter, we explored the essential principles of Responsible AI (RAI) governance and how boards can ensure effective oversight of AI initiatives. We introduced six components of a well-defined AI governance framework:

- Conduct a readiness assessment to evaluate an organization's preparedness, ensuring it has the necessary people, processes, and systems in place.
- Weave AI considerations into existing enterprise risk governance frameworks and activities.
- Define an oversight strategy that aligns with the organization's AI maturity and level of sophistication ensuring that governance practices are purpose fit, with the right board expertise to match this strategy.
- Develop a decision-making framework to identify and prioritize high-impact AI initiatives.
- Develop tracking mechanisms to monitor milestone attainment and report on outcomes.
- Establish monitoring and feedback mechanisms to ensure AI models are performing as expected.

This AI governance framework provides boards with a structured approach to oversee AI initiatives effectively. By ensuring preparedness, aligning oversight with AI maturity, and implementing robust tracking and feedback mechanisms, organizations can mitigate risks, optimize AI performance, and ensure that AI investments are delivering the intended results responsibly and transparently.

CHAPTER 8

A Board Director Call to Action

Emerging Boardroom Considerations

Throughout this book we have spotlighted unsettled issues that are still being worked out related to AI. Here we pull them together and provide additional insight into these matters that require ongoing monitoring.

Evolving Case Law and Regulation

Boards should stay informed about emerging case law and its implications for risk management and organizational liability. A significant unsettled issue is how existing copyright laws apply to AI-generated content. Questions continue to arise about who owns the rights to content created by AI and whether using copyrighted material to train AI models constitutes infringement. See the discussion on *Intellectual Property* below for additional considerations on this topic.

Determining liability when AI systems cause harm or make erroneous decisions is a significant legal challenge. This includes questions about who is responsible—the developer, the deployer, or the AI itself.

The use of AI raises concerns about potential antitrust violations, such as collusion facilitated by AI systems, which may require new regulatory approaches.

The use of AI to generate content and moderate online platforms raises questions about free speech rights and the extent to which AI-generated content is protected under the First Amendment.

AI's use of vast amounts of personal data raises significant concerns about compliance with privacy laws like GDPR or CCPA. Boards must assess whether AI systems are collecting, processing, and storing data in compliance with these regulations, and what liabilities may arise from breaches or misuse.

Intellectual Property Considerations

AI, particularly generative AI, introduces several unsettled intellectual property (IP) risks that organizations must navigate. These risks encompass both the protection of an organization's own IP and the potential infringement on third-party IP rights.

A primary question is who owns the rights to AI-generated content. Traditional IP laws typically require human authorship for copyright protection, but AI-generated works challenge this notion. Some jurisdictions, like China, recognize copyright for AI-generated content with human involvement, while others are still debating the issue.

AI systems rely heavily on data for training, and questions about data ownership can arise, particularly when using third-party datasets. Directors need to be vigilant about whether the organization has clear rights to use the data and whether it has the proper licenses or permissions in place to avoid legal disputes. AI models are often trained on large datasets that may include copyrighted material. This raises concerns about whether using such data without explicit permission constitutes infringement. The lack of clear guidelines on what constitutes fair use in this context adds to the uncertainty.

The outputs of AI models can inadvertently replicate or derive from copyrighted works, leading to potential infringement claims. It remains unclear how similar an AI-generated output must be to an existing work to be considered infringing, and this is likely to be clarified through future litigation or legislation.

AI's role in innovation raises questions about patent rights, particularly whether AI can be named as an inventor. Current patent laws generally require a human inventor, leading to potential challenges in securing patents for AI-driven innovations.

When AI models generate code, there is a risk that the generated code may inadvertently include elements from licensed software, potentially violating licensing agreements. This is particularly concern-ing with copyleft licenses, which may impose open-source requirements on derivative works. A copyleft license is a type of open-source license that allows software or creative works to be freely used, modified, and distributed but requires that any derivative works or redistributed versions be licensed under the same terms. This ensures that the work and any modifications remain open and freely available to the public.

Evolving Regulatory Landscape

The regulatory environment around AI is rapidly developing, with governments worldwide introducing new laws and guidelines. Boards must ensure that their organizations comply with these evolving regulations, which often encompass data protection, ethical use of AI, and transparency. Staying abreast of these changes is crucial to avoid legal penalties and reputational damage.

Insurance and Liability

The evolving insurance market, particularly in areas like Directors and Officers (D&O) insurance, Errors and Omissions (E&O), and specialized policies like Representations and Warranties and tail coverage, is another unsettled area.

The central question is how insurance policies will respond to liability for decisions made by AI systems. Traditional insurance policies may not explicitly cover AI-related risks, leading to uncertainties about what is insurable. This extends to how current policies such as cyber insurance or product liability insurance apply to AI-related incidents.

The potential for significant losses due to algorithmic failures remains an unsettled area. The potential consequences—ranging from personal injury, property damage, business interruption, and professio-nal liability to medical malpractice—require boards to monitor policy changes and exclusions to ensure that their organization's are adequately covered.[101]

AI Audits and Standards

There is a growing recognition of the need for standardized auditing frameworks for AI systems. While organizations like the National Institute of Standards and Technology (NIST) and the Institute of Internal Auditors are developing guidelines, no single, comprehensive standard has yet been established. Boards should advocate for and oversee the implementation of robust AI audit practices within their organizations, ensuring that these systems are fair, transparent, and accountable.[102]

Security and Privacy Risks

The rise of sophisticated cyberattacks, including the malicious use of AI for creating deepfakes and disinformation, poses new security threats. These risks can have far-reaching impacts, from data breaches to manipulating public opinion. Boards must prioritize robust cybersecurity measures and ensure that their AI systems are resilient against such threats.

The Changing Role of Boards in the AI Era

The rapid growth of AI requires boards to significantly adapt their oversight responsibilities. Beyond gaining expertise and establishing governance frameworks, boards have a fiduciary duty to actively monitor how AI is used in their organizations. This includes ensuring AI is used ethically, aligns with corporate values, and contributes to long-term value. Boards must also assess AI's impact on performance, risk, strategy, and purpose. Directors are required to stay informed, particularly with transformative technologies like AI, and failure to monitor AI-related risks could result in liability for negligence.

A Boardroom Imperative

Corporate boards have a responsibility to understand the impact of AI on their organizations. We must actively monitor the competitive landscape to identify opportunities and threats posed by AI, including how competitors use it for advantage and potential industry disruptions. Boards also need to ensure sound governance processes for the responsible and ethical use of AI.

Early investment in AI is becoming a key driver of competitive advantage. By embracing AI technologies, organizations can automate tasks, optimize operations, and enhance customer experiences, gaining a market edge. This investment in AI—whether in talent, infrastructure, or algorithms—positions companies to lead their industries and safeguard against competitive threats.

However, AI brings risks that boards must manage thoughtfully. As AI reshapes industries and challenges traditional business models, it is crucial for boards to ensure that AI is used ethically, transparently, and in alignment with long-term goals. Boards must oversee AI's use across performance, strategy, risk management, and corporate purpose, ensuring responsible practices and accountability in this rapidly evolving landscape. AI governance requires a nuanced approach tailored to the unique risks of each deployment, given the diverse methodologies used in modern AI systems.

Throughout this book, we've gained a clear understanding of our critical role in overseeing responsible AI adoption. We have deepened our knowledge of AI's complexities, from its core techniques to its risks, and have equipped ourselves with the tools to lead with both care and foresight. With greater awareness of the importance of data governance, ethical AI practices, and strong risk management, we are now positioned to guide AI innovation effectively and prudently.

Appendix A

Board Oversight Checklist for AI

Inventory and Mapping: Ensure a comprehensive list of all AI systems in use (internal, third-party, and embedded) is maintained. Clearly identify the purpose, use case(s) data used, and KPIs being used to monitor the effectiveness of each system.

Model Identification: Identify the core AI type for each deployment (e.g., machine learning, NLP, computer vision) and whether the model tends toward deterministic or probabilistic outcomes. Understand the process and frequency for updating each model.

Stage of AI Deployment: Ensure that AI systems are clearly categorized by their stage of deployment—whether in experiment, pilot, or scaling. Validate that appropriate governance, monitoring, and risk management processes are applied at each stage, including clear criteria for moving between stages.

AI Development Life Cycle: Ensure oversight of the entire AI development life cycle, from initial concept and design to testing, deployment, and maintenance. Validate that clear governance processes are in place for each stage, with appropriate checkpoints and reviews to ensure continued alignment with business objectives and compliance.

Data Governance Maturity: Assess the maturity of data governance structures and policies, ensuring data quality, integrity, security, and compliance with regulations. Effective data governance is foundational for successful AI initiatives.

Training Data Oversight: Verify that the training data used in AI models is properly vetted for quality, bias, and representativeness. Ensure that mechanisms are in place to assess data sources, compliance with privacy regulations, and adequacy for the model's intended purpose.

Core System Fitness: Evaluate the readiness of core systems to support AI, including IT infrastructure, data storage solutions, and computing capabilities. Identify limitations such as scalability, rigid architectures, and potential security vulnerabilities. Develop a plan to address any gaps.

Talent and Skills: Assess whether the organization has the necessary talent, including data scientists, ML and data engineers, UX designers, AI champions, and board members with relevant expertise. Identify skill gaps and strategies to fill them, either through recruitment or external providers. Include the board's skill matrix in this assessment to determine any missing skill sets in the boardroom.

Market and Competitive Analysis: Ensure a market analysis is conducted to understand competitors' AI strategies. Assess the organization's position relative to competitors to enable informed decisions about AI investments.

Defensive Posture: Ensure an evaluation is conducted on ways AI might be used against the organization, considering both competitive and security risks.

Workforce and Cultural Readiness: Assess AI's impact on employees and corporate culture. Develop strategies for effective change management and training to support AI adoption.

Compliance Readiness: Ensure understanding and compliance with specific jurisdictional requirements, including data protection and privacy laws for in-house and third-party solutions. Establish mechanisms to keep current with new laws and directives.

Strategic Review of AI Threats and Vulnerabilities: Ensure thorough risk assessments are conducted for each deployed model, addressing biases, privacy, security, transparency, intellectual property concerns, and compliance.

Governance Framework: Establish a comprehensive governance framework, including risk identification, assessment, mitigation, monitoring, and review. Ensure vendor management and third-party oversight are included in the framework.

Ethics and Responsibility: Develop an AI employee code of conduct emphasizing responsible and ethical use. Ensure regular ethics training for all employees, including the board.

Audit and Control: Ensure regular audits of AI systems are conducted to ensure adherence to governance policies. Establish a cross-functional oversight body for ethical AI development. Ensure that staff responsible for the three lines of defense have appropriate skills for AI responsibilities.

Readiness and Resilience: Review insurance coverage for AI-related liabilities and develop crisis management plans for AI-related incidents. Ensure protections are in place for AI-related intellectual property.

External Engagement: Ensure a communication strategy is in place for disclosing AI use responsibly to investors, regulators, and other relevant constituents.

Appendix B

Checklist for Third-Party AI Adoption

Risk Assessment and Mapping

- **Inventory and Mapping**: Ensure a comprehensive inventory of all AI deployments embedded in third-party software, services, and APIs. Verify the core AI type and decision-making paradigm for each has been identified and that KPIs have been established and are being monitored.
- **Comprehensive Risk Assessment**: Verify that thorough risk assessments for each third-party AI solution have been conducted, considering risks such as biases, hallucinations, explainability, data integrity, and compliance. Ensure the provenance, quality, and biases of training data have been scrutinized.
- **Model Validation and Documentation**: Ensure the vendor's model validation processes align with industry standards. Verify that AI-related and data governance risks are mapped to the board-approved risk management framework and integrated into regular risk reporting mechanisms.

Three Lines of Defense

- **First Line**: Verify that AI risk awareness and controls are integrated into operational processes, including SOX controls.
- **Second Line**: Ensure internal audit scope includes AI-driven processes, focusing on privacy, ethics, bias, data integrity, and appropriate KPIs for each model.

- **Third Line**: Ensure external auditors review third-party model validation and provide assurance of compliance with risk management standards.

Vendor Due Diligence and Contractual Safeguards

- **Due Diligence**: Ensure thorough due diligence has been conducted on third-party AI vendors, evaluating their development practices, governance policies, and history of addressing ethical concerns and bias mitigation.
- **Contractual Safeguards**: Ensure contracts with third-party AI providers clearly define data usage, confidentiality, security measures, compliance with privacy and data transfer laws, and audit provisions. Verify contracts cover data retention, subprocessors, liability, indemnification, and API security requirements, particularly for high-risk AI systems.

Monitoring and Auditing

- **Continuous Monitoring**: Ensure systems are in place to continuously monitor the performance of third-party AI, including accuracy, bias, drift, and unintended consequences. Verify model validation results are regularly reviewed, and ensure the board receives appropriate performance reporting.
- **SOC Assessments**: Validate that SOC 1 and/or SOC 2 assessments have been reviewed for the robustness of financial controls and third-party internal controls for managing AI risks.

Transparency and Explainability

- **Explainability**: Demand clear explanations of how third-party AI models operate, including decision-making processes, potential biases, mitigation strategies, and limitations.

- **Stakeholder Communication**: Ensure transparency by openly communicating the purpose, benefits, risks, and mitigation strategies of third-party AI solutions to stakeholders. Verify that mechanisms for reporting concerns and gathering feedback are in place.

Human Oversight and Accountability

- **Human Oversight**: Establish clear mechanisms for human oversight and intervention in critical decision-making processes powered by third-party AI.
- **Accountability**: Ensure that responsibility and accountability are clearly defined for potential AI failures or unintended consequences, both within the organization and with third-party providers.

Disclosure and Regulatory Compliance

- **Disclosure Responsibilities**: Ensure that AI deployments are mapped to relevant regulatory and compliance requirements, including the identification of material risks and necessary disclosures.
- **Regulatory Awareness**: Ensure mechanisms are in place to maintain awareness of evolving AI regulations and to adapt governance practices as needed.

Continuous Improvement and Learning

- **Continuous Learning**: Foster a culture of continuous improvement and learning regarding AI governance. Encourage the sharing of best practices and lessons learned from third-party AI adoption with peer organizations.
- **Board and Executive Training**: Ensure ongoing training and development for board members and executives on responsible AI governance and best practices.

Appendix C

Board Director Checklist for AI Data Governance

Data Inventory and Mapping

- **Comprehensive Inventory**: Verify that the organization maintains a comprehensive inventory of all data collected, stored, and used, with ongoing monitoring.
- **Data Categorization**: Verify that data types and sources are clearly identified and categorized.
- **Data Lineage**: Confirm that data lineage processes are documented and traceable with regular assessments in place to ensure data is tracked through its life cycle.
- **Data Classification**: Confirm data is categorized and classified based on sensitivity, purpose, and relevant regulations.
- **Data Ownership and Access**: Ensure data ownership and access rights are clearly defined and documented.

Data Quality and Integrity

- **Standards for Data Quality**: Verify that defined standards for data quality and integrity are in place across the organization.
- **Data Accuracy and Completeness**: Ensure processes are established to maintain data accuracy, completeness, and consistency.
- **Data Cleansing Procedures**: Confirm that data cleansing and validation procedures are regularly conducted.

Data Security and Privacy

- **Data Security Measures**: Ensure robust data security measures are in place to protect against unauthorized access, breaches, and loss.
- **Regulatory Compliance**: Validate compliance with relevant data privacy regulations and ethical guidelines.
- **Anonymization Procedures**: Ensure clear policies for data anonymization and de-identification are implemented.

Data Governance Framework

- **Governance Framework**: Ensure a defined data governance framework with clear roles and responsibilities exists.
- **Data Policies**: Ensure policies are in place for data access, retention, and disposal.
- **Monitoring and Enforcement**: Confirm there is a mechanism for ongoing monitoring and enforcement of data governance practices.

Data for AI Development and Deployment

- **Ethical Data Acquisition**: Ensure data acquisition methods are ethical and transparent.
- **Bias Mitigation**: Verify processes for identifying and mitigating potential bias in data collection are in place.
- **Labeling Processes**: Ensure labeling processes are well-defined, reliable, and minimize human error and bias.
- **Quality of Labeled Data**: Confirm procedures exist for evaluating the quality and representativeness of labeled data.

Data Use in AI Models

- **Guidelines for AI Data**: Verify that guidelines are in place for the types and amount of data used for AI training.

- **Ethical Data Usage**: Ensure that ethical guidelines are in place for the use of data, especially in AI applications, with clear accountability for data misuse.
- **Data Drift Awareness**: Ensure the organization monitors the potential for data drift and model degradation over time.
- **Ongoing Data Monitoring**: Confirm mechanisms are in place for continuous data monitoring and feedback loops to improve AI performance.

Data Sharing and Collaboration

- **Third-Party Data Sharing Policies**: Ensure clear policies for data sharing with third-party vendors or collaborators are established.
- **Data Minimization**: Verify data minimization practices are employed to limit the amount of data shared to what is absolutely necessary.
- **Compliance in Data Sharing**: Ensure mechanisms are in place to ensure compliance with data privacy regulations during data sharing.

Board Oversight and Accountability

- **Regular Reporting**: Verify the board receives regular reports on data management practices, including risks and challenges.
- **Metrics and KPIs**: Ensure metrics and KPIs are defined to measure the effectiveness of data governance.
- **Bias Mitigation Reports**: Confirm the board is informed about potential data biases and their mitigation strategies.

Independent Audits and Reviews

- **Regular Audits**: Ensure regular independent audits are conducted to assess the effectiveness of data governance practices.

- **AI Model Audits**: Verify AI models and algorithms are subjected to independent audits for bias and fairness.
- **Policy Review**: Ensure the board reviews and approves data-related policies and procedures.

Appendix D

Board Governance Checklist for Third-Party Data in AI

Data Sourcing and Due Diligence

- **Third-Party Data Inventory**: Ensure that a comprehensive inventory of all third-party data sources is maintained, including details on the provider, types of data sourced, and the intended use.
- **Data Provider Reputation**: Ensure thorough due diligence is conducted on third-party data providers to assess their credibility, data quality standards, and adherence to ethical and legal guidelines.
- **Compliance With Regulatory Requirements**: Confirm that the third-party data provider complies with all relevant privacy regulations (e.g., GDPR, CCPA) and ethical sourcing practices.

Data Quality and Integrity

- **Data Quality Assessment**: Ensure processes are in place to assess the quality, accuracy, completeness, and timeliness of third-party data before it is used.
- **Bias and Representativeness**: Verify that third-party data has been scrutinized for potential biases and assessed for its representativeness, particularly if it will be used for AI model training or decision making.
- **Data Integrity Agreements**: Ensure contracts with third-party providers include provisions for maintaining data integrity, with guarantees for regular updates and error correction.

Data Use and Ethical Considerations

- **Data Usage Permissions**: Verify that proper permissions are obtained from third-party providers for how their data can be used (e.g., model training, analysis, redistribution), ensuring there are no restrictions that could impact compliance or operations.
- **Ethical Use of Third-Party Data**: Ensure that third-party data is ethically sourced, with clear documentation of its origins and verification that the data was collected in compliance with legal and ethical standards.

Third-Party Data for Proprietary Models

- **Model Compatibility**: Confirm that third-party data is compatible with the organization's proprietary models and can be effectively integrated without compromising performance or introducing risks (e.g., bias, inaccuracy).
- **Data Traceability and Provenance**: Ensure mechanisms are in place to track the provenance of third-party data used in proprietary models, including its source, transformations, and usage.
- **Data Labeling and Augmentation**: Verify that third-party data is appropriately labeled or augmented to meet the needs of proprietary AI models, with processes in place to evaluate its quality and relevance.

Third-Party Data for External Models

- **Model Accuracy and Fitness**: When using third-party data to feed external models (those provided by vendors), ensure that the data aligns with the quality standards required for those models to function correctly.
- **Data Security and Privacy Protections**: Ensure that third-party data providers have implemented robust security measures and comply with privacy protections to safeguard

sensitive data, especially when shared with external AI vendors.

- **Vendor Data Monitoring**: Verify that third-party vendors continuously monitor the data they use in their models to prevent data drift, bias, or model degradation over time.

Contractual Safeguards for Third-Party Data

- **Data Ownership and IP Rights**: Ensure that contracts clearly define data ownership and intellectual property rights, including ownership of any insights, models, algorithms, or outputs created using third-party data. Confirm that there are no restrictions that limit the organization's ability to own, modify, or commercialize these outputs and that any licensing terms grant the organization full rights over the resulting intellectual property.
- **Liability and Indemnification**: Confirm that contracts include liability clauses to cover risks associated with the use of third-party data, such as inaccuracies, biases, or breaches.
- **Audit and Compliance**: Ensure that contracts provide the right to audit third-party data providers to verify compliance with data quality, security, and privacy standards.
- **Data Retention and Disposal**: Verify that contracts clearly outline the retention period for third-party data and specify the process for securely disposing data at the end of its life cycle. Ensure that any necessary documentation or records related to data destruction are retained for audit purposes.

Regulatory Compliance and Risk Management

- **Data Localization Requirements**: Verify that third-party data complies with any data localization laws or cross-border data transfer regulations.
- **Risk of Data Breaches**: Ensure third-party data providers have robust breach response protocols and that your

organization is protected from liability in case of a data breach involving third-party data.

- **Regulatory Alignment**: Verify that third-party data use complies with applicable regulations, including data retention, reporting obligations, and any jurisdiction-specific requirements.

Board Oversight and Reporting

- **Regular Risk Assessments**: Ensure the board receives regular risk assessments on the use of third-party data, including potential risks related to quality, bias, and regulatory compliance.
- **Ongoing Reporting**: Verify that the organization maintains ongoing reporting to the board on the effectiveness of third-party data sourcing and governance practices.
- **Third-Party Data Audits**: Ensure regular audits are conducted on third-party data providers to assess their adherence to contractual obligations, data quality standards, and regulatory requirements.

Appendix E

Governance Questions for Core AI Techniques

The question and interpretive guide format introduced in this appendix is designed to help directors with specific AI oversight duties fulfill their obligations. Additionally, practitioners including risk management professionals, corporate secretaries, and general counsels will find the discussion of risks and associated controls to be instructive. It is important to remember that this information is a general overview and should not be interpreted as a definitive assessment of risk for any specific AI model. The questions are intended to assist board directors in ascertaining that the appropriate control framework is in place and is functioning as intended. The interpretative guide provides directors with details of the control framework that management should have in place when deploying each core AI technique.

Symbolic Learning

Symbolic learning is an approach to artificial intelligence that uses explicit, human-readable symbols and rules to represent knowledge and logic, allowing machines to perform reasoning and problem-solving tasks in a way that mimics human cognitive processes. It relies on predefined rules and structured knowledge bases to interpret and manipulate data, making it particularly suited for tasks requiring logical reasoning and decision making. This table provides a practical guide to understanding symbolic learning risks and appropriate controls.

Table E.1 Symbolic AI governance questions and interpretive guide

Knowledge Base Maintenance: How is it updated?	Ensure structured updates and validation processes, especially for deterministic AI systems where inaccuracies can lead to significant errors.
Rule Conflicts and Ambiguities: How are they resolved?	Ensure a governance mechanism is established for transparent decision making to address discrepancies in rule interpretation.
Domain Expertise Integration: How is it incorporated?	Ensure collaboration between AI developers and domain experts for continuous feedback and incorporation of evolving expertise.
Consistency Measures: How is consistency ensured?	Ensure version controls, validation, and regular audits are in place to prevent inconsistencies over time.
Accountability and Auditing: How is the system audited?	Ensure an auditing framework for the decision-making process has been established, promoting accountability and traceability in rule execution.
Decision-Making Traceability: How is it tracked?	Ensure logging and tracking mechanisms have been established to capture rationale behind rule-based decisions for transparency.
Unintended Consequences: How are they addressed?	Ensure a response plan and learning mechanisms have been developed to update rules based on unintended consequences.
External Changes: How are they incorporated?	Ensure there is a process to monitor external changes (regulations, industry shifts) and establish a process for swift knowledge base updates.
Expert Judgment and Rule Revision: How is it incorporated?	Ensure cross-functional collaboration exists between AI developers and domain experts to capture nuanced human insights for rule revision.
Stakeholder Involvement: How are stakeholders involved?	Foster stakeholder engagement in rule definition and validation to address diverse perspectives and ensure inclusivity.

Supervised Learning

Supervised learning is a machine learning technique that trains algorithms on labeled data to make predictions or classifications. This table provides a practical guide to understanding supervised learning risks and appropriate controls.

Table E.2 Supervised learning governance questions and interpretive guide

Bias Mitigation in Training Data: How is it addressed?	Ensure tailored bias detection and mitigation strategies are implemented. Regularly audit and update datasets to address potential bias impacts.
Label Accuracy: How is it ensured?	Ensure data quality assurance processes and validation checks have been established to verify and maintain label accuracy.
Privacy Concerns in Labeling: How are they addressed?	Ensure privacy-preserving techniques like anonymization or differential privacy for labeling personal data are being employed. Have protocols to protect individual privacy.
Model Fairness: How is it ensured across demographics?	Ensure fairness-aware algorithms and metrics to assess and mitigate biases in predictions are being used. Implement fairness-enhancing techniques during training and evaluation.
Model Generalization: What validation processes are used?	Ensure robust validation and cross-validation are in place to ensure the model generalizes across diverse datasets. Regularly assess performance on unseen data to avoid overfitting.
Model Interpretability and Explainability: How are they ensured?	Ensure interpretability techniques tailored for supervised learning models are in place. Utilize model-agnostic methods or interpretable architectures to enhance explainability.
Data Quality in Online Learning: How is it ensured?	Ensure protocols for continuous monitoring of data quality and real-time correction of issues in dynamic online learning scenarios have been established.
Adversarial Attack Detection and Mitigation: How are they performed?	Ensure defenses against adversarial attacks suited for supervised learning models are being used. This may include adversarial training, input perturbation detection, and regular security audits.
Model Update Rollback: How is it handled in case of issues?	Ensure rollback mechanisms for model updates are in place in case of unintended consequences or performance degradation. Ensure a rapid response plan to revert to a previous model version if needed.
Model Robustness Against Noisy Labels: How is it ensured?	Ensure techniques to handle and mitigate the impact of noisy labels in the training data are adopted. This may include outlier detection, data augmentation, or robust training strategies.

Unsupervised Learning

Unsupervised learning is a machine learning technique that allows algorithms to discover patterns and structures within unlabeled data. This table provides a practical guide to understanding unsupervised learning risks and appropriate controls.

Table E.3: Unsupervised learning governance questions and interpretive guide

Anomaly Detection: How is it handled?	Ensure robust unsupervised anomaly detection mechanisms are in place. Algorithms should be regularly updated and refined to identify unusual patterns or outliers.
Clustering Interpretability: How is it ensured?	Ensure interpretability frameworks are developed for clustering results, utilizing visualization techniques and metrics for understanding and validation.
Privacy Concerns in Feature Learning: How are they addressed?	Ensure privacy-preserving techniques are implemented such as federated learning or secure multiparty computation are implemented to protect sensitive information during model training.
Validation of Discovered Patterns: What processes are used?	Ensure validation procedures are established using domain expertise and external datasets to assess the quality and relevance of discovered patterns.
Model Robustness Against Outliers: How is it ensured?	Ensure techniques such as robust clustering algorithms or outlier rejection mechanisms are implemented to enhance model robustness against noisy or outlying data.
Validation of Latent Representations: How is it done?	Ensure validation protocols are in place to ensure the utility of latent representations for downstream tasks, evaluating them through tasks like classification or retrieval.
Fairness in Outputs: What measures ensure it?	Ensure fairness-aware algorithms and metrics are used to assess and mitigate biases in clustering results or learned embeddings across different groups.
Hyperparameter Tuning: How is it done?	Ensure a tuning strategy has been established that accounts for unsupervised learning challenges, considering methods like unsupervised-specific optimization or automated search.
Unintended Biases: How are they addressed?	Ensure bias detection and mitigation techniques specific to unsupervised outputs are being used, regularly assessing and addressing biases that may emerge without labeled examples.
Model Stability: How is it ensured?	Ensure strategies for model stability are in place, particularly in scenarios with changing data distributions. Implement mechanisms for continuous monitoring and adaptation.

Reinforcement learning

Reinforcement learning (RL) is a machine learning technique where agents learn to make decisions by interacting with an environment and receiving rewards or penalties. This table provides a practical guide to understanding reinforcement learning risks and appropriate controls.

Table E.4 Reinforcement learning governance questions and interpretive guide

Exploration-Exploitation Balance: How is it ensured?	Ensure mechanisms for balanced exploration and exploitation are in place. Design policies that enable the model to learn while utilizing existing knowledge, avoiding overreliance on either.
Reward Function Definition and Evaluation: How are they handled?	Ensure a governance framework for defining and evaluating reward functions is established. Ensure alignment with ethics and business objectives, preventing unintended consequences.
Model Robustness in Dynamic Environments: How is it ensured?	Ensure strategies for robust models in dynamic environments are developed. Implement continuous monitoring and adaptation mechanisms to handle changing scenarios.
Safe Exploration in Real-World Applications: What mechanisms ensure it?	Ensure safety mechanisms are implemented for responsible exploration in real-world applications. Incorporate constraints and safeguards to prevent harmful actions during learning.
Ethics Embedding in Reinforcement Learning Policies: How is it achieved?	Ensure ethical considerations are embedded into reinforcement learning policies. Establish guidelines and constraints that prioritize ethical behavior, avoiding reinforcement of harmful actions or biases.
Explainability in Reinforcement Learning Decisions: What measures ensure it?	Ensure mechanisms are implemented for explainable reinforcement learning decisions. Utilize techniques like state-action explanations or model-agnostic interpretability methods to enhance transparency.
Transfer Learning Controls to Avoid Unintended Biases: How are they implemented?	Ensure controls are in place to manage transfer learning in reinforcement learning. Ensure responsible knowledge transfer across environments, avoiding unintended biases or negative impacts.
Model Update Rollback for Unintended Consequences: How is it handled?	Ensure a rollback mechanism is established for model updates in case of unintended consequences. Develop a rapid response plan to revert to a previous model version if needed.

(continued)

Table E.4 (Continued)

Human Values in Reward Design: How are they incorporated?	Ensure human values are integrated into the design of reward functions. Establish protocols for involving domain experts and stakeholders to ensure alignment with ethical and societal values.
Fairness in Reinforcement Learning Policies: How is it ensured?	Ensure fairness-aware reinforcement learning algorithms are in place. Regularly assess and mitigate biases in the learned policies to ensure fair and equitable decision making.

Deep Learning

Deep learning is a subset of machine learning that utilizes artificial neural networks with multiple layers to automatically learn and extract complex patterns from large amounts of data. This table provides a practical guide to understanding deep learning risks and appropriate controls.

Table E.5 Deep learning governance questions and interpretive guide

Model Complexity and Under-standability: How is it achieved?	Ensure interpretability strategies such as layer-wise relevance propagation or attention mechanisms are implemented to understand the model's decision-making process.
Data Privacy in Deep Learning: What measures are in place?	Ensure privacy-preserving mechanisms such as federated learning or differential privacy are established to protect individual privacy during model training.
Hyperparameter Tuning Optimization: How is it handled?	Ensure governance controls are in place for tuning. Establish protocols for responsible tuning to avoid overfitting and ensure model generalization across diverse datasets.
Adversarial Attack Detection and Mitigation: What methods are used?	Ensure defenses such as adversarial training, input preprocessing, or robust optimization are used to enhance model resilience against targeted attacks.
Transfer Learning Controls to Avoid Unintended Biases: How are they implemented?	Ensure governance mechanisms are in place for transfer learning. Ensure responsible knowledge transfer across domains, avoiding unintended biases or negative impacts.
Model Robustness to Noisy Data: What measures ensure it?	Ensure techniques such as dropout regularization or robust training strategies are used to handle variations in training data and enhance model robustness.

(continued)

Table E.5 (Continued)

Model Update Rollback for Unintended Consequences: How is it handled?	Ensure a rollback mechanism and response plan is in place to revert to a previous model version if unintended consequences occur.
Fairness in Deep Learning Model Outputs: How is it ensured?	Ensure fairness-aware algorithms and metrics are implemented. Regularly assess and mitigate biases in the learned representations to ensure fair and equitable decision making.
Communicating Model Uncertainties in Decision Making: How is it done?	Ensure techniques such as uncertainty estimation or probabilistic models are used to convey the confidence level of model outputs in decision-making processes.
Model Life Cycle Management for Accountability: How is it controlled?	Ensure a comprehensive life cycle management framework with documentation, version control, and monitoring processes to ensure accountability and traceability throughout the model's lifespan is implemented.

Computer Vision

Computer vision is a field of artificial intelligence that enables machines to interpret and understand visual information from the world, such as images or videos, by processing and analyzing visual data. This table provides a practical guide to understanding computer vision risks and appropriate controls.

Table E.6 Computer vision governance questions and interpretive guide

Visual Bias Detection and Mitigation in Training Data: How is it handled?	Ensure comprehensive strategies for detecting and mitigating biases in image datasets are implemented. Regularly evaluate data for diverse and representative visual content.
Privacy Safeguards for Image Data: What measures are in place?	Ensure privacy-preserving measures are in place for image data used in computer vision models. Consider techniques such as federated learning or on-device processing to protect individual privacy.
Model Explainability in Image Recognition Outputs: How is it ensured?	Ensure explainability techniques are implemented into models. Utilize methods such as attention visualization or saliency maps to enhance interpretability and transparency of image recognition results.

(continued)

Table E.6 (Continued)

Fairness in Computer Vision Outputs Across Groups: What measures ensure it?	Ensure fairness-aware algorithms and metrics are implemented for computer vision outputs. Regularly assess and mitigate biases that may arise across different demographic groups in image recognition results.
Transfer Learning Controls to Avoid Unintended Biases: How are they implemented?	Ensure governance mechanisms for transfer learning are developed in computer vision. Ensure responsible knowledge transfer across visual domains, avoiding unintended biases or negative impacts.
Adversarial Attack Detection and Mitigation in Image Recognition Models: How is it done?	Ensure defenses against adversarial attacks specific to image recognition models are implemented. Explore techniques such as adversarial training, input preprocessing, or robust optimization to enhance model resilience.
Robustness to Noisy or Low-Quality Image Data: What steps are taken?	Ensure techniques are implemented to enhance model robustness to noisy or low-quality image data. Explore methods such as data augmentation, denoising, or robust training strategies to handle variations in image quality.
Model Update Rollback for Unintended Consequences in Image Recognition: How is it handled?	Ensure a rollback mechanism for model updates in image recognition is established in case of unintended consequences. Develop a rapid response plan to revert to a previous model version if needed.
Continuous Monitoring for Visual Bias and Model Performance: How is it implemented?	Ensure continuous monitoring processes to track visual bias and model performance in real time are implemented, including feedback loops and response mechanisms to address issues promptly.
Ethical Use of Computer Vision in Sensitive Contexts: What steps ensure it?	Establish ethical guidelines for the use of CV in sensitive contexts such as surveillance. Implement mechanisms to prevent misuse and regularly update policies to align with evolving ethical standards.

Sensor Fusion

Sensor fusion harnesses the power of multiple sensor inputs to create a comprehensive and accurate perception of the environment. This table provides a practical guide to understanding sensor fusion risks and appropriate controls.

Table E.7 Sensor fusion governance questions and interpretive guide

Sensor Calibration and Accuracy Across Modalities: How is it ensured?	Ensure rigorous calibration processes are implemented for sensors involved in fusion. Regularly validate and adjust sensor accuracy to maintain consistency across different modalities.
Sensor Data Synchronization in Real Time: What measures ensure it?	Ensure mechanisms for real-time synchronization of sensor data are established. Implement timestamping and alignment procedures to ensure temporal coherence for accurate fusion.
Redundancy Handling for Robustness: How is it done?	Ensure protocols for handling redundancy in sensor data are established. Implement fusion algorithms that leverage redundant information for robust decision making in case of sensor failures.
Privacy Safeguards for Sensor Data Fusion: What are they?	Ensure privacy-preserving measures are utilized for sensor data fusion, especially in sensitive environments. Utilize encryption, anonymization, or edge processing to protect individual privacy.
Sensor Fusion Model Explainability for Decision Transparency: How is it achieved?	Incorporate explainability techniques into sensor fusion models. Utilize methods such as feature importance analysis or model-agnostic interpretability to enhance transparency in decision making.
Consistency in Sensor Fusion Outputs Over Time: What measures ensure it?	Establish processes to monitor and maintain consistency in sensor fusion outputs over time. Regularly update the fusion model to adapt to changing sensor characteristics and environmental conditions.
Addressing Adverse Environmental Conditions in Fusion Algorithms: How is it done?	Ensure strategies have been developed to handle adverse environmental conditions such as weather, humidity, electromagnetic fields, and others. Implement algorithms that adapt to challenging environmental factors and ensure reliable performance.
Fairness in Sensor Fusion Outputs Across Sensor Types: What steps ensure it?	Ensure algorithms that consider fairness during fusion are implemented to address sensor-specific biases such as weighting of sensor data based on reliability or using domain-adversarial training. Additionally, use fairness metrics such as statistical parity or equalized odds to assess and refine the fusion process.
Model Update Rollback for Unintended Consequences in Sensor Fusion: How is it handled?	Ensure a rollback mechanism for model updates is established in Sensor Fusion in case of unintended consequences. Develop a rapid response plan to revert to a previous model version if needed.
Continuous Monitoring for Sensor Health and Fusion Model Performance: How is it implemented?	Ensure continuous monitoring processes are implemented to track sensor health and fusion model performance in real time. Set up feedback loops and response mechanisms to address issues promptly.

Natural Language Processing

Natural language processing (NLP) unlocks the power of language for machines. This table provides a practical guide to understanding NLP risks and appropriate controls.

Table E.8 Natural language processing governance questions and interpretive guide

Bias Mitigation in NLP Training Data: How is it addressed?	Ensure diverse data selection, bias detection, and mitigation strategies are implemented. Regularly assess and adjust datasets for fair and unbiased language model behavior.
Ethical Use of NLP in Language Generation: What measures ensure it?	Establish ethical guidelines for language generation. Implement mechanisms to prevent harmful content and update policies with evolving ethical standards.
Explainability in NLP Model Outputs: How is it achieved?	Ensure explainability techniques such as attention visualization or interpretability tools are incorporated. Enhance transparency in language model decision-making processes.
Privacy Safeguards for User Interactions: What are they?	Ensure privacy-preserving measures are in place. Ensure responsible handling of sensitive information and consider options such as anonymization or differential privacy.
Adversarial Attack Detection and Mitigation in NLP Models: How is it done?	Ensure defenses against adversarial attacks specific to NLP models are in place. Implement techniques such as adversarial training, input preprocessing, or robust optimization.
Debiasing Effectiveness Measurement: How do you ensure it?	Ensure fairness-aware algorithms and metrics for NLP model outputs are implemented. Regularly assess and mitigate biases to ensure fair and equitable language model decision making.
Transfer Learning Controls to Avoid Unintended Biases: How are they implemented?	Ensure governance mechanisms for transfer learning in NLP , such as freezing layers or learning rate tuning. Ensure responsible knowledge transfer across linguistic domains, avoiding unintended biases or negative impacts.
Model Robustness to Linguistic Variations: What measures ensure it?	Ensure techniques to enhance model robustness to variations in linguistic patterns have been implemented. Explore methods such as data augmentation, linguistic diversity in training data, or robust training strategies.

(continued)

Table E.8 (Continued)

Model Update Rollback for Unintended Consequences: How is it handled?	Ensure a rollback mechanism for model updates in NLP is established in case of unintended consequences. Develop a rapid response plan to revert to a previous model version if needed.
Content Moderation Protocols for NLP Applications: What are they?	Ensure content moderation mechanisms to filter out inappropriate or harmful content generated by NLP models are implemented. Utilize a combination of automated tools and human review for responsible language model outputs.

Large Language Models

Large language models (LLMs) are advanced AI models designed to understand and process natural language by leveraging vast amounts of text data and sophisticated algorithms. They excel at tasks such as language comprehension, translation, summarization, and answering questions by analyzing context and patterns within the language. This table provides a practical guide to understanding LLM risks and appropriate controls.

Table E.9 Large language model governance questions and interpretive guide

Bias Mitigation in Training Data: How is it addressed?	Ensure comprehensive bias detection and mitigation strategies are in place. Regularly audit and update datasets to ensure fair and inclusive model behavior.
Ethical Use of Language Models: What measures exist?	Ensure ethical guidelines are established for model use. Implement mechanisms to prevent harmful or inappropriate content generation and update policies regularly.
Explainability of Language Model Outputs: How is it achieved?	Ensure explainability techniques are in place. Utilize methods such as attention visualization or generation of explanations to enhance transparency and understanding of model decisions.
Privacy Safeguards for User Interactions: What are they?	Ensure privacy-preserving measures are implemented. Ensure responsible handling of sensitive information and consider options such as anonymization or differential privacy.
Control of Model Fine-Tuning: How is it managed?	Ensure governance mechanisms are established for fine-tuning. Ensure controls are implemented and thorough testing conducted before deploying updated models.

(continued)

Table E.9 (Continued)

Detection and Mitigation of Adversarial Attacks: How are they handled?	Ensure language-model-specific defenses are in place. Ensure techniques for detecting and mitigating adversarial inputs are implemented to enhance model robustness.
Inclusivity in Language Model Training: How is it ensured?	Take proactive steps toward inclusivity. Ensure diverse datasets are utilized, involve a wide range of contributors, and regularly assess performance across different demographic groups.
Content Moderation in User-Generated Interactions: How is it handled?	Ensure moderation mechanisms are implemented. Utilize a combination of automated tools and human review to ensure responsible content generation.
Consistency of Language Model Outputs Over Time: How is it maintained?	Ensure processes for monitoring and maintaining consistency are established. Regularly update the model to adapt to language shifts while ensuring reliable and consistent behavior.
Continuous Monitoring of Language Model Behavior: How is it implemented?	Ensure continuous monitoring processes are implemented. Set up feedback loops and response mechanisms to address issues promptly and maintain responsible behavior.

Generative AI

Generative AI (gAI) refers to models that create new content—such as text, images, or audio—based on patterns learned from existing data. These models, including advanced versions of LLMs, can generate coherent and contextually relevant outputs, often used in creative applications, content generation, and automated design. This table provides a practical guide to understanding gAI risks and appropriate controls.

Table E.10 Generative AI governance questions and interpretive guide

Originality, Copyright, and Scenario Integrity: How to prevent plagiarism and ensure novel scenario generation?	Ensure data diversity controls are implemented, incentivize exploration and novelty in both language generation and scenario creation, and use adversarial training to discourage copying.
Bias, Fairness, and Inclusivity: How to avoid perpetuating stereotypes, discrimination, or exclusion in generated content and scenarios?	Ensure diverse training data is used, bias detection and mitigation techniques are employed, and human oversight is applied to both language and scenario-based outputs.
Responsible Use and Ethical Outputs: How to avoid harmful, unethical, or unintended consequences from AI-generated content and scenarios?	Establish clear ethical guidelines, ensure continuous monitoring with human oversight, and implement safeguards against harmful or irresponsible content and scenario generation.
Transparency and Explainability: How to understand and explain decision-making processes for both content and scenario creation?	Ensure model training, parameters, and outputs—whether language or scenario-based—are well documented and provide tools for visualization and interpretation.
Security, Confidentiality, and Scenario Sensitivity: How to protect sensitive information and confidential scenarios?	Implement robust cybersecurity measures, including access controls, data encryption, vulnerability assessments, and safeguards for confidential or strategic scenario generation.
Employee Usage Management: How to ensure adherence to policies when using AI for both content generation and scenario planning?	Establish clear policies and procedures, provide training on responsible AI usage, and monitor for potential misuse in both language and scenario creation contexts.
Workforce Impact and Scenario Displacement: How to assess job displacement, new skill requirements, and scenario-based decision-making impacts?	Conduct workforce impact assessments, engage with employees, and develop retraining and upskilling strategies, particularly when scenario-based AI tools are introduced.
Intellectual Property and Scenario Ownership: How to protect innovations and ensure fair attribution for AI-generated content and scenarios?	Establish guidelines for ownership and licensing of AI-generated content and scenarios and implement mechanisms to track and protect intellectual property rights.
Regulatory Compliance and Ethical Standards: How to align AI-generated content and scenarios with industry and legal requirements?	Implement mechanisms to stay updated on evolving regulations and ethical standards for both AI-generated content and scenario use, and conduct regular compliance assessments.
Responsible AI Culture: How to promote transparency, accountability, and ethical considerations within the organization, especially when creating scenarios or content?	Establish an AI ethics committee, encourage open dialogue and collaboration, and embed ethical principles into organizational culture and decision-making processes, including scenario-based use.

Homogeneous Ensemble Learning

Homogeneous ensemble learning, where multiple models of the same type are combined to create a stronger, more accurate predictive system, offers immense potential for various applications. This table provides a practical guide to understanding homogenous ensemble AI risks and appropriate controls.

Table E.11 Homogenous ensemble learning governance questions and interpretive guide

Diversity and Independence: How to avoid bias and echo chambers?	Ensure the criteria for diverse base models (training data, architectures, hyperparameters) are carefully defined. Regularly monitor for potential bias or correlation, and mitigate via diverse model selection.
Error Amplification Mitigation: How to prevent performance degradation?	Ensure the susceptibility of the chosen ensemble technique is assessed. Implement safeguards such as data sanitization, outlier detection, and diverse model selection to prevent feedback loops and ensure long-term accuracy.
Explainability and Transparency: How to avoid the black box problem?	Ensure XAI techniques such as SHAP or LIME are used to understand individual base model contributions. Communicate limitations and uncertainties of model output to stakeholders.
Generalizability and Overfitting: How to ensure good performance on unseen data?	Ensure techniques such as regularization, early stopping, or cross-validation are implemented to control complexity and prevent overfitting. Regularly evaluate performance on unseen data to assess generalizability.
Model Drift Monitoring and Response: How to address changes in data or real-world scenarios?	Ensure continuous monitoring systems to track model performance and data distribution changes are in place. Ensure development of a clear process for retraining or updating the ensemble model when drift is detected.

Multimodal Ensemble Learning

Multimodal ensemble AI combines different AI techniques and different types of data—such as text, images, and audio—to create a unified prediction or decision, leveraging the strengths of each modality to improve overall performance and robustness. This approach enhances the model's ability to understand complex, real-world scenarios by integrating diverse sources of information. This table provides a practical guide to understanding multimodal ensemble AI risks and appropriate controls.

Table E.12 Multimodal ensemble learning governance questions and interpretive guide

Consistent Representation and Integration: How to address biases and inconsistencies?	Ensure robust data preprocessing and fusion techniques (normalization, alignment, dimensionality reduction) are implemented. Ensure data quality and potential biases across modalities are regularly assessed.
Interdependency Management: How to prevent error propagation and performance degradation?	Ensure intermodel dependencies and their impact have been assessed. Ensure safeguards such as local error correction or robust aggregation techniques are implemented to mitigate error amplification.
Explainability and Transparency: How to understand how diverse data contributes to decisions?	Ensure advanced XAI techniques for multimodal data (attention mechanisms, counterfactual explanations) are utilized. Ensure visualization tools and communication strategies are developed for clear explanations to stakeholders.
Security and Privacy Protection: How to ensure robust protection for sensitive data?	Ensure multilayered security measures (encryption, access control, data anonymization) are implemented and data usage and access logs are monitored for potential vulnerabilities.
Adaptability to New Data Sources and Changes: How to handle evolving data landscapes?	Ensure flexible and modular architectures are utilized for easy incorporation of new data types. Ensure continuous learning mechanisms are implemented. Ensure the data landscape is monitored for potential changes requiring model adaptation or retraining.

Appendix F

Root Causes of Bias in AI Models

Directors should recognize that bias in AI models is a complex issue that can stem from biased data, algorithms, metrics, or deployment practices. The main root causes of bias and the corresponding mitigation strategies are previewed below.

Biased Data

Selection Bias: Occurs when the data chosen for training or evaluation doesn't reflect the real-world population, leading to skewed model performance and unfair outcomes. Nonrepresentative training data can result in models that perform poorly for specific segments of the target population. For example, biased sampling methods, such as relying solely on volunteer datasets or easily accessible demographics, can distort the data's distribution and perpetuate existing biases. Mitigation involves ensuring representative and diverse sampling.

Historical Bias: Even perfectly measured and sampled data may contain embedded historical biases that reflect past societal inequities. This can encapsulate unfair stereotypes in how AI classifies, recommends, or judges people, perpetuating discrimination and undermining fairness. For example, word embeddings capture the meanings and relationships between words, where words with similar meanings are grouped closer together in the embedding space. Training data with more instances of "doctor" referring to men than women can cause the word embedding for "doctor" to be closer to words associated with masculinity. This can lead to biased results in downstream tasks, such as predicting the gender of a doctor based on medical text. Mitigation includes re-evaluating and cleaning historical data.

Representation Bias: Occurs when the data used to train models doesn't accurately reflect the real world, leading to unfair and inaccurate results. This bias happens when the development sample underrepresents certain groups or characteristics within the larger use population. Models trained on skewed data fail to generalize well for underrepresented groups, potentially leading to discriminatory or inaccurate outcomes. Mitigation strategies involve augmenting datasets to better represent all segments of the population.

Data Bias: Predictable Versus Masked

- **Deterministic Models**: Biased data translates directly into predictable and systematic outcomes. For example, a loan approval model trained on biased data reflecting past discrimination against certain demographics might consistently disadvantage those groups, creating a clear and predictable pattern of bias. Mitigation requires robust data sanitation with careful audits and bias correction techniques.
- **Probabilistic Models**: Bias introduces a layer of uncertainty that can mask or amplify data bias depending on the model and data distribution. For instance, a credit scoring model with biased data might show a wider range of probability scores for certain groups, highlighting potential bias, but could also obscure precise effects due to inherent uncertainty. Mitigation involves uncertainty quantification and data quality measures to interpret and manage risk effectively.

Biased Algorithms

Algorithms are crafted with specific objectives in mind, but these goals can inadvertently prioritize certain outcomes over others. Moreover, seemingly neutral choices about which data points matter can have profound consequences.

Measurement Bias: Arises when features and labels chosen, collected, or computed for a prediction problem misrepresent the underlying constructs they aim to approximate. These constructs, often abstract concepts like "creditworthiness" or "successful student," require proxy features as stand-ins. These proxies may capture only a narrow facet or introduce systematic errors. Further, features or labels may be collected or generated in ways that differ systematically for different groups within the population, skewing the model's understanding of the target construct and leading to biased predictions. For example, using GPA as the sole proxy for "successful student" overlooks diverse measures such as resilience, adaptability, or contributions beyond grades, potentially disadvantaging students from certain backgrounds. Mitigation includes using multiple proxies and ensuring comprehensive feature selection.

Learning Bias: Manifests in various ways, from model design choices favoring certain data patterns to optimization methods overlooking outliers or underrepresented groups. For example, the trade-off between privacy and fairness is evident in differential private training, which improves data privacy but can lead to skewed results for underrepresented groups. Mitigation involves balancing fairness with other objectives such as privacy and ensuring fair and equitable outcomes.

Aggregation Bias: Arises when a single model is applied to data containing distinct underlying groups or example types that require nuanced handling. For instance, a sentiment analysis model trained on all customer reviews might misinterpret sarcasm as genuine anger, failing to grasp the cultural context and tone within specific communities. Similarly, a medical diagnosis model trained primarily on data from affluent regions could overlook the unique health care needs of rural populations, leading to misdiagnoses and inequitable care. Mitigation includes using tailored models for distinct data segments.

Algorithmic Bias: Encoded Versus Distributed

- **Deterministic Models**: Biases encoded in the algorithm directly translate into unintended or implicit biases in the outputs. For example, a facial recognition algorithm biased toward lighter skin tones might misidentify people of color more often, creating a clear and visible bias. Mitigation requires fairness-aware algorithm design and thorough reviews to identify and address potential biases.

- **Probabilistic Models**: Bias can be distributed across the probability distribution of outcomes. For example, a language model trained on biased text data might generate discriminatory outputs with higher confidence for certain groups. While the bias is still present, its impact is spread across a range of possibilities, making it less visible but potentially more pronounced. Mitigation focuses on fairness in probability distributions and algorithm design to ensure equitable outcomes.

Biased Metrics

Metrics are vital data points that quantify a model's performance, assess its strengths and weaknesses, diagnose errors, and guide optimization efforts. However, their selection can inadvertently cast biased shadows, steering models toward skewed outcomes and potentially unfair consequences.

Evaluation Bias: Arises when benchmark data fails to represent the real world, leading to skewed performance assessments. Models trained on their training data are often assessed against external datasets such as UCI benchmarks or other standards. Misrepresentative benchmarks foster models that excel on a narrow slice of data, leaving the broader population poorly served. The problem is compounded by metric choices: aggregate measures might hide subgroup underperformance while focusing solely on one type of metric (like accuracy) can obscure disparities in others (like false negatives). Mitigation includes using diverse benchmarks and ensuring metrics capture subgroup performance.

Metrics Bias: Masked Accuracy Versus Misleading Uncertainty

- **Deterministic Models**: Biased metrics can mask unfair outcomes by focusing solely on accuracy and ignoring potential disparities in error rates. For example, judging a recidivism prediction model solely on accuracy might neglect its disproportionate impact on certain groups. Mitigation involves using fairness-aware metrics alongside traditional metrics to ensure inclusive evaluation.
- **Probabilistic Models**: Rely heavily on metrics for uncertainty quantification. Biases in these metrics can distort the interpretation of confidence scores and lead to misinformed decisions. For instance, using accuracy as the sole metric for a medical diagnosis model with biased data could mask false positives for underrepresented groups, resulting in serious health implications. Mitigation requires transparency in communicating uncertainty levels alongside fairness-aware metrics to manage risk effectively.

Biased Deployment

Developers may repurpose AI models for new tasks, driven by curiosity, efficiency, or time/resource pressures, but venturing off-label can lead to performance dips, hidden biases, and ethical quandaries. Quantifying the exact prevalence of off-label use is tricky, as developers might not always disclose or even be aware of it themselves. One study found that over 40 percent of machine learning models in health care were used for tasks not originally intended.

> **Biased Deployment**: Arises when there is a mismatch between the problem a model is intended to solve and the way it is actually used. For example, a health care risk assessment model applied solely to low-income communities could exacerbate existing health disparities. Mitigation involves ensuring appropriate use and considering deployment contexts.

Deployment Bias: Contextual Impact Versus Adaptive Interventions

- **Deterministic Models**: Biased contexts lead to fixed unequal outcomes without inherent flexibility. Mitigation requires human-in-the-loop safeguards and active monitoring for biased outcomes.

- **Probabilistic Models**: Offer more opportunities for adaptive interventions based on the range of predicted probabilities. For instance, a health care risk assessment model with a probabilistic approach could adjust its decision making based on specific contexts and individual characteristics, potentially mitigating biased deployment impacts. Mitigation involves leveraging model flexibility and real-time feedback mechanisms.

Understanding these root causes is the first step toward effective mitigation governance. Recognizing the diverse causes of bias is essential for prudent oversight.

Appendix G

Five Prominent Homogeneous Ensemble Learning Models

Random Forest

Primarily used for supervised learning tasks, where the model learns from labeled examples to predict future outcomes. They are trained on data with known input and output pairs, allowing them to generalize and make predictions on unseen data.

Underlying AI Type: Supervised learning.

Application: Classification and regression tasks.

Advantages: High accuracy, robust to outliers and noise, easily interpretable, and good for high-dimensional data.

Disadvantages: Black box nature can be computationally expensive to train, and overfitting can occur.

Risk Management: Model explainability and interpretability need to be addressed to mitigate bias and fairness concerns.

XGBoost

Falls under supervised learning but utilizes boosting, a specific learning technique. Boosting algorithms iteratively build an ensemble of models, focusing on improving the performance of previously misclassified examples.

Underlying AI Type: Supervised learning (with elements of boosting).

Application: Regression and ranking tasks, often used for boosting decision trees.

Advantages: Extremely fast and efficient, handles missing data well, and highly accurate.

Disadvantages: Black box nature, requires careful hyperparameter tuning, and can overfit easily.

Risk Management: Monitoring overfitting and ensuring responsible AI development practices are crucial.

Gradient Boosting Machine (GBM)

Employs supervised learning with a boosting approach. It sequentially adds models to the ensemble, focusing on reducing the overall error of the ensemble on the training data.

Underlying AI Type: Supervised learning (with elements of boosting).

Application: Regression and classification tasks.

Advantages: High accuracy, handles complex nonlinear relationships, and can be used with different loss functions.

Disadvantages: Black box nature, susceptible to overfitting, and requires careful hyperparameter tuning.

Risk Management: Emphasizing model fairness, explainability, and addressing potential biases during development and deployment.

Stacked Ensemble

Combines different supervised learning models. Each individual model is trained on the original dataset, and then a second model (meta-learner) is trained on the predictions of the first-level models.

Underlying AI Types: Supervised learning (various models).

Application: Combining multiple models for improved accuracy and robustness.

Advantages: Highly accurate, reduces overfitting, and leverages the strengths of different models.

Disadvantages: Can be complex to design and train, requires significant computational resources.

Risk Management: Monitoring model performance and ensuring each individual model is well-governed.

Bayesian Model Averaging (BMA)

Leverages supervised learning models, but it specifically requires models capable of providing probabilistic predictions. This allows BMA to weight the predictions based on their individual uncertainties, leading to more robust predictions.

Underlying AI Types: Supervised learning (various models with probabilistic outputs).

Application: Combining multiple models with probabilistic predictions.

Advantages: Improves model uncertainty estimation and provides more robust predictions.

Disadvantages: Computationally expensive, requires strong priors, and can be sensitive to model quality.

Risk Management: Ensuring proper prior selection and addressing potential biases within individual models.

Appendix H

Five Prominent Multimodal Ensemble Learning Models

Multimodal Generative Models (e.g., GPT, DALL·E)

Generative AI plays a key role in multimodal configurations, enabling models to create content from multiple types of data, such as text and images. GPT-4, for instance, can generate text from prompts, while DALL·E generates images from text descriptions. These models are widely used due to their versatility and ability to blend different data types.

> **Underlying AI Types**: Generative AI + NLP + computer vision.
> **Application**: Image generation from text, video summarization, multimodal content creation, and cross-modal search.
> **Advantages**: Highly flexible across domains, strong in creative content generation, and robust in handling cross-modal relationships.
> **Disadvantages**: Computationally expensive and resource-intensive, and results can be biased without careful data management.
> **Risk Management**: Ensuring diversity in training data to mitigate bias, fostering transparency in model outputs, and balancing creativity with control.

Vision-Language Models (e.g., CLIP, Flamingo)

Vision-language models like CLIP and Flamingo are designed to bridge the gap between image and text data. These models excel at understanding and generating content that combines visual and textual inputs, enabling tasks such as visual question answering and image retrieval. CLIP combines vision and language understanding, allowing models to interpret images based on textual input, making it useful for tasks such as image captioning, creative content generation, and cross-modal understanding.

Underlying AI Types: Supervised learning + generative AI + computer vision.

Application: Visual question answering, multimodal search, image generation from text, and captioning.

Advantages: Strong cross-modal understanding, robust for real-time multimodal tasks, and versatile for a variety of applications.

Disadvantages: Models can be computationally demanding and require vast amounts of training data to perform well across domains.

Risk Management: Regular audits for bias in training data, ensuring interpretability by revealing how models link text and images, and enforcing data privacy measures.

Multimodal Transformers (e.g., ViLT, LXMERT)

Multimodal transformers such as ViLT and LXMERT leverage transformer architectures to fuse text, image, and sometimes audio data. These models are optimized for tasks such as image captioning, visual question answering, and video summarization, enabling deep cross-modal understanding by processing multiple data streams in parallel. Their architecture allows them to model complex relationships between different modalities.

Underlying AI Types: Supervised learning + NLP + computer vision.

Application: Image captioning, visual question answering, video summarization, and content recommendation.

Advantages: High interpretability of attention mechanisms, scalable to large datasets, and effective at capturing relationships across data types.

Disadvantages: Sensitive to hyperparameter tuning, computationally expensive, and can suffer from overfitting without proper regularization.

Risk Management: Managing computational cost through efficient training strategies, tuning hyperparameters carefully, and mitigating bias in multimodal datasets.

Multimodal Variational Autoencoders

Variational autoencoders (VAEs) have found success in unsupervised multimodal learning, where they help in discovering latent factors that unify diverse data types. VAEs are used in tasks such as anomaly detection, multimodal clustering, and dimensionality reduction, allowing the identification of hidden relationships across text, images, and audio.

Underlying AI Types: Unsupervised learning + generative AI + NLP + computer vision.

Application: Multimodal clustering, anomaly detection, latent representation learning, and topic modeling.

Advantages: Identifies hidden relationships between data modalities, reduces dimensionality of complex data, and useful for unsupervised tasks.

Disadvantages: Interpretability can be challenging, and the model requires careful selection of latent dimensions to produce meaningful outputs.

Risk Management: Ensuring fair representation of data in latent space, promoting transparency in model outputs, and safeguarding data security and privacy.

Multimodal Attention Networks (e.g., FLAVA)

Attention-based multimodal models, like FLAVA, focus on selecting the most relevant information across multiple data types. By applying attention mechanisms, these models can efficiently process and synthesize data from modalities such as text, images, and audio. FLAVA is particularly effective in applications where the system needs to reason across modalities, such as visual question answering and multimodal reasoning.

Underlying AI Types: Supervised learning + attention mechanisms + generative AI.

Application: Multimodal reasoning, visual question answering, cross-modal content generation, and sentiment analysis.

Advantages: High interpretability due to attention layers, efficient at synthesizing multimodal information, and flexible across tasks.

Disadvantages: Training can be computationally expensive, and attention mechanisms can sometimes overfit to irrelevant features.

Risk Management: Monitoring for overfitting, ensuring fairness in attention weights, and regularly auditing the data for bias and privacy concerns.

Glossary of AI Terminology

Adaptation Mechanisms Techniques and strategies that enable artificial intelligence systems to adjust or modify their behavior in response to changes in the environment, input data, or task requirements. These mechanisms are important for ensuring that AI systems can operate effectively and robustly in dynamic and evolving conditions.

Adversarial Example Defense Strategies and techniques employed to enhance the robustness of machine learning models against adversarial attacks. Adversarial examples are inputs deliberately crafted to mislead or deceive machine learning models, leading them to make incorrect predictions or classifications. Defenses against adversarial examples aim to mitigate the impact of these crafted inputs and improve the model's resilience.

Adversarial Training A technique used in machine learning to improve the robustness and resilience of a model against adversarial attacks. Adversarial attacks involve making small, carefully crafted modifications to input data with the goal of deceiving the model and causing it to make incorrect predictions.

Agents Particularly in reinforcement learning, an algorithm that makes decisions by interacting with its environment, learning from feedback in the form of rewards or penalties, and adjusting their actions to maximize long-term rewards. Key aspects of agents include perception, decision making, action, goal orientation, and autonomy.

Alignment Controls Mechanisms and strategies designed to ensure that an AI system's behavior, decisions, and outcomes remain consistent with human values, goals, and ethical standards throughout its development and deployment.

Anonymization The process of transforming or modifying personal or sensitive information in a way that prevents the identification of individuals while still maintaining the usability and integrity of the data. The primary goal of anonymization is to protect privacy by making it difficult or impossible to link specific data points to identifiable individuals.

APIs (Application Programming Interfaces) Sets of rules and protocols that allow different software applications to communicate and interact with each other, enabling data exchange or functionality sharing between systems. They serve as bridges between applications, making it easier for developers to integrate different services or systems without needing to understand the internal workings of each.

Attention Mechanisms A set of techniques used in machine learning models, particularly in natural language processing (NLP) and computer vision, to selectively focus on specific parts of input data when making predictions. These mechanisms enable models to assign varying degrees of importance or attention to different elements in the input sequence, allowing the model to adaptively weigh the relevance of each part.

Attention Visualization The process of visually representing and interpreting the attention mechanisms employed by certain machine learning models, particularly those used in natural language processing (NLP) and computer vision tasks.

Bias The unfair skew in how AI systems are developed or how they make decisions, often reflecting societal biases present in the training data or the design choices made by developers. This can result in AI models making discriminatory decisions or reinforcing harmful stereotypes. Bias can arise from underrepresented or misrepresented data or from algorithms that favor certain outcomes, even if the data isn't overtly biased. Additionally, the way AI is used in real-world applications can further amplify these biases.

Bagging (Bootstrap Aggregating) An ensemble learning technique that aims to improve the stability and performance of machine learning models. It involves training multiple instances of the same learning algorithm on different subsets of the training data, created through bootstrapping (random sampling with replacement). The final prediction or decision is then often determined by averaging (for regression) or voting (for classification) over the predictions or decisions made by each individual model.

Bagging helps reduce overfitting and variance, enhancing the overall robustness and accuracy of the ensemble model. Random Forests, a popular ensemble method, employs bagging with decision trees as base learners.

Bayesian Network A model that visually shows how different events or variables are connected and influence each other. It helps in making predictions by using probabilities to represent the relationships between these variables, making it easier to understand how one factor affects another.

Beam Search A search algorithm used in generative AI that evaluates and keeps multiple possible output sequences at each step, ultimately selecting the most likely sequence based on overall probability, improving accuracy and consistency in the generated output.

Boosting An ensemble learning technique that combines multiple weak learners to create a strong learner. The algorithm works iteratively, assigning more weight to misclassified instances in each round to focus on the harder-to-learn examples. By sequentially training weak models and adjusting their weights, boosting aims to improve overall accuracy and performance, making it particularly effective in handling complex and challenging datasets. AdaBoost and Gradient Boosting are common boosting algorithms used in various machine learning applications.

Brittleness The tendency of some AI models to perform poorly or break down when faced with situations outside of their training data or expected operating conditions. These situations can range from minor changes, such as unexpected input formats or slight variations in data patterns, to major changes, like real-world complexities not represented in the training data.

Classification The process of assigning a category label to a data point, often based on its latent representation in deep learning models. This is achieved by training a model on a labeled dataset, where each data point has a known category. The model learns the relationship between these representations and the category labels, allowing it to predict the category of new, unseen data points.

CCPA or The California Consumer Privacy Act The CCPA is a privacy law granting California residents significant control over their personal information collected by businesses. While not explicitly focused on AI, the CCPA has important implications for both users and developers of AI technologies operating in California or handling data from California residents. The CCPA broadly defines personal information to include identifiers like names and addresses, as well as inferred data, such as browsing history and online activity, that can be linked to individuals. This means that data used in AI models involving California residents may fall under the CCPA's regulatory scope.

Clustering-Based Anomaly A technique that groups data points into clusters and identifies instances that do not conform to the patterns of normal clusters as potential anomalies or outliers. This approach assumes that normal data points form dense clusters, while anomalies are found in less dense regions or as isolated points.

Collaborative Filtering Algorithms A class of recommendation systems in AI that make predictions about a user's preferences or interests by leveraging information from the preferences and behaviors of a group of users. Instead of relying on explicit knowledge about items or users, collaborative filtering methods focus on identifying patterns and similarities in user behavior to provide personalized recommendations.

CONfidence-Quality-ORDer-Preserving Alignment (CON-QORD) A method designed to improve the reliability of LLMs by matching their confidence levels to the quality of their responses. Using reinforcement learning, the model is trained to express higher confidence in better-quality answers. This alignment helps users know when to trust the model's responses and when to seek external information, which enhances the transparency and trustworthiness of the LLM's outputs.

Conflict Resolution The process of managing and resolving conflicts or inconsistencies that may arise in the knowledge or decision-making processes of an AI system. These conflicts can occur when there are contradictory pieces of information, conflicting goals, or ambiguous situations within the system.

Content Moderation The use of artificial intelligence and machine learning technologies to monitor, analyze, and control user-generated content on digital platforms to ensure it complies with community guidelines, legal requirements, and ethical standards. The goal of content moderation is to identify and filter out inappropriate, harmful, or offensive content, promoting a safe and respectful online environment.

Constrained Decoding A technique used in language generation models to control and guide the output by imposing specific restrictions or constraints during the decoding process. This ensures that the generated text adheres to desired characteristics, such as lexical, syntactic, semantic, style, and length constraints.

Constrained Generation A technique in generative AI that imposes specific rules or conditions during the generation process to ensure outputs meet predefined requirements, such as adhering to structure, avoiding certain words, or following a particular style.

Convolutional Neural Networks (CNNs or ConvNets) A class of deep neural networks designed specifically for tasks related to computer vision, image recognition, and visual processing. CNNs are characterized by their ability to automatically learn hierarchical representations of features from input images through the use of convolutional layers. These networks have been highly successful in various image-related tasks, such as image classification, object detection, and image segmentation.

Core Technique A fundamental approach used by an AI model to acquire knowledge and improve its performance. It defines how the model interacts with data and learns from its experiences.

Cross-Validation A statistical technique used in AI and machine learning to assess the performance and generalizability of a predictive model. The primary goal of cross-validation is to provide a more accurate and reliable estimate of a model's performance on unseen data than a single train-test split would offer.

Counterfactual Explanations A technique in explainable AI that aims to understand and communicate the reasoning behind an AI model's decision by identifying the smallest, most realistic changes to the input features that would have led to a different outcome.

Data Augmentation The process of artificially expanding a dataset by applying various transformations to the existing data. The objective is to increase the diversity and quantity of the training data available for machine learning models. By introducing variations and perturbations to the original dataset, data augmentation helps improve the robustness and generalizability of the models.

Data Hygiene The ongoing practices and procedures that ensure the quality, accuracy, consistency, and integrity of data used in AI systems. It involves a set of principles and best practices that aim to maintain clean, reliable, and trustworthy data throughout the entire AI development life cycle.

Data Pipelines A well-designed and reliable system for efficiently moving, transforming, and processing data from various sources to its destination, all while ensuring data quality, consistency, and accuracy.

Data Scrubbing Also referred to as data cleaning or data cleansing, is the process of identifying and correcting errors, inconsistencies, and other issues within a dataset to improve its quality and reliability. This is a crucial step in preparing data for use in AI and machine learning since the quality of the data directly impacts the performance and trustworthiness of AI models.

Decision-Making Paradigm The framework or approach an AI system uses to process information and make choices. It shapes how the system evaluates data and determines the best course of action, influencing the methods and algorithms applied to reach decisions.

Deepfakes Synthetic media created using AI to convincingly manipulate audio, video, or images by altering a person's likeness. This technology allows a person's face, voice, or actions to be realistically imposed onto someone else in a video, audio, or image, making it appear as though they said or did things they never actually did.

Deep Learning A subset of machine learning techniques based on artificial neural networks, particularly deep neural networks. Deep learning models are designed to automatically learn hierarchical representations of data through the use of multiple layers, allowing them to capture intricate patterns and features. These models have demonstrated remarkable success in a wide range of tasks, including image and speech recognition, natural language processing, and complex decision making.

Denoising The process of removing or reducing noise from data, which is unwanted or irrelevant information that can interfere with the accurate interpretation or analysis of the data. In various AI applications, denoising techniques are employed to enhance the quality of input data, leading to improved performance in tasks such as image recognition, speech processing, and signal analysis.

Deterministic A decision-making paradigm based on fixed rules and logic. Given the same input, a deterministic system will always produce the same output.

Differential Privacy A concept and framework that aims to provide strong privacy protection for individuals in datasets. The goal is to allow useful information to be extracted from the dataset while minimizing the risk of identifying or exposing sensitive information about any individual.

Drift The gradual or sudden changes in the distribution of input data or the underlying relationships between features and labels over time. This can create a mismatch between the training environment and the real-world deployment, potentially compromising the performance of machine learning models.

Dropout Regularization Dropout regularization is a technique used to prevent overfitting and improve the generalization performance of neural networks. It works by randomly dropping out (ignoring) a certain percentage of neurons in a layer during the training process. This forces the network to learn more robust features and prevents it from becoming too reliant on any individual neurons.

Edge Processing Also known as edge AI, this term refers to the deployment of AI algorithms and models directly on devices at the edge of a network, rather than on centralized cloud servers. This approach enables faster, more efficient, and secure real-time processing closer to where data is generated, and often includes offline capabilities.

Ensemble Learning A machine learning technique that combines multiple models to improve predictive performance. In homogeneous ensembles, multiple instances of the same model type) are combined, while heterogeneous (or multimodal) ensembles integrate different types of models to leverage the strengths of each technique for improved accuracy and robustness.

Evolutionary Algorithms A class of AI algorithms inspired by the principles of natural evolution, such as selection, mutation, and reproduction. They mimic the way nature evolves species over generations to solve complex optimization and search problems.

Expert Systems AI applications that emulate the decision-making ability of a human expert in a particular domain by utilizing a knowledge base of explicit rules and heuristics, allowing them to provide informed solutions or advice within that specific area of expertise.

Explainable AI (XAI) A field of research that focuses on making AI systems more explainable to humans. XAI aims to develop methods and techniques that allow humans to understand how AI systems make decisions and to identify potential biases or errors in these decisions. There are many different approaches to XAI, but they can generally be divided into two categories: Posthoc explanation techniques and explainable AI techniques. Posthoc explanation techniques explain the output of an AI system after it has been trained. These techniques can be used to generate explanations for individual decisions or to provide general insights into how the AI system works. Explainable AI techniques build explainability into the AI system itself. These techniques can be used to make AI systems more transparent and understandable from the start. Even when using explainable AI techniques, understanding how some models work can remain a mystery.

Explainability Frameworks Software tools and libraries designed to implement various techniques for explaining and interpreting the decisions and predictions made by AI models. They play an important role in making AI more transparent, trustworthy, and accountable. Many frameworks are designed to work with various types of AI models, including decision trees, neural networks, and more. Popular explainability frameworks include: LIME (Local Interpretable Model-Agnostic Explanations), SHAP (SHapley Additive exPlanations), AIX360 (AI Explainability 360 from IBM), What-If Tool (from Google), InterpretML (from Microsoft), DARTS (Deep Learning interpretability for Activation Ranking Techniques), DeepLIFT, and Skater.

Exploration-Exploitation Balance The strategic allocation of resources or actions to explore new possibilities (exploration) while also exploiting existing knowledge or strategies (exploitation). This concept is particularly relevant in the context of reinforcement learning and decision making, where an agent or system must navigate an environment, learn from experiences, and make choices to achieve its goals.

Exploration Techniques Techniques used to push the boundaries of learning and discovery to guide an AI system toward new and potentially better solutions, fueling its growth and adaptability. Important exploration techniques include:

Multiarmed bandit: Inspired by the classic bandit problem in gambling, this technique allows an AI agent to choose between multiple options (arms) with unknown rewards. By balancing the exploitation of the seemingly best option with the exploration of other arms, the agent learns which option offers the highest long-term reward.

Epsilon-greedy: This simple yet effective technique involves choosing the currently best option (exploitation) with a certain probability (1-epsilon) and exploring other options (randomly) with the probability epsilon. The epsilon value controls the balance between exploitation and exploration, with higher assigned values for epsilon encouraging more exploration.

Boltzmann exploration: This technique utilizes a probability distribution based on the current option's values and a temperature parameter. Higher temperatures encourage exploration by assigning higher probabilities to less-explored options, while lower temperatures favor exploitation.

Upper confidence bound (UCB): This technique estimates the upper bound of each option's value based on observed rewards and confidence intervals. It prioritizes options with high upper bounds, balancing exploration with ensuring that exploration leads to potentially better options.

Curiosity-driven learning: This technique equips an AI agent with an internal curiosity drive that motivates it to seek out novel and informative information. By prioritizing actions that reduce uncertainty or surprise, the agent actively explores its environment and learns new things.

Thompson sampling: This technique involves treating each option as a random variable with a probability distribution based on observed rewards. It then samples from these distributions to make decisions, favoring options with higher probabilities of good outcomes while still encouraging exploration.

Active learning: This technique involves an AI agent actively requesting information or feedback from the user or environment to guide its exploration. By focusing on informative data points, the agent can learn efficiently and avoid wasting resources on irrelevant information.

Fairness-Aware Algorithms Techniques and approaches designed to address and mitigate biases and discrimination in machine learning models. These algorithms aim to ensure that AI systems treat individuals or groups fairly and impartially, avoiding unjust or discriminatory outcomes. Fairness awareness is a crucial aspect of responsible and ethical AI development, particularly in applications where the impact of AI outputs on different demographic groups can be significant.

Fairness-Enhancing Techniques Methods and approaches designed to address and mitigate biases, discrimination, and unfairness in machine learning models and algorithms. These techniques aim to ensure that AI systems treat individuals or groups fairly, without perpetuating or amplifying existing social, gender, racial, or other biases present in the training data.

Federated Learning A machine learning approach that enables training models across multiple decentralized devices or servers holding local data samples, without exchanging the data itself. Instead of centralizing the data on a single server for training, federated learning allows model training to occur locally on individual devices, and only the model updates or aggregated information is shared with a central server.

Feedback Loops Situations where the output or consequences of a system's actions are fed back into the system, influencing its future behavior. In the context of machine learning and AI systems, feedback loops can occur when the predictions or recommendations made by the system influence user behavior, and the resulting user actions are then used as input to refine and update the system. These loops can amplify biases, reinforce existing patterns, or lead to unintended consequences, emphasizing the importance of careful design and monitoring in AI applications.

Fusion Algorithms Techniques that combine or integrate information from multiple sources or modalities to make more informed and accurate decisions. These algorithms are particularly valuable in scenarios where different data types or modalities provide complementary information and combining them enhances the overall performance of a system.

GDPR or The General Data Protection Regulation A legal framework enacted by the European Union (EU) that regulates how personal data is collected, used, and protected within the EU and by EU businesses operating globally.

Generative Adversarial Networks (GANs) A class of artificial intelligence models consisting of a generator and a discriminator network that are trained simultaneously through adversarial training. The generator aims to create realistic data, such as images, while the discriminator's role is to distinguish between genuine and generated data, resulting in a competitive process that enhances the generator's ability to produce increasingly realistic outputs. GANs have found widespread use in image generation, style transfer, and various other tasks in the field of generative modeling.

Graphics Processing Unit (GPU) A specialized electronic circuit designed to accelerate the rendering of graphics and visual images. While originally designed for graphics-intensive tasks like gaming and video editing, GPUs have become increasingly important for a wide range of computing applications, including AI, machine learning, scientific computing, and cryptocurrency mining.

Grammar-Based Models Use formal grammars, such as context-free grammars, to define rules and structures for generating syntactically correct and coherent outputs, commonly in the form of text or code. These models ensure adherence to predefined syntax, making them suitable for applications in natural language generation and code synthesis where structured and grammatically accurate content is essential.

Generalization The ability of a trained model to perform well on new, unseen data that is not part of the training dataset. It reflects the model's capability to learn and understand the underlying patterns and relationships in the data, allowing it to make accurate predictions or classifications on instances it has not encountered during the training phase.

Hallucinations In language models, factually incorrect or nonsensical text outputs, often appearing deceptively plausible and posing challenges in areas like misinformation and bias amplification. In robotics, it refers to situations where robots perceive or act based on incorrect information. Faulty sensor readings, outdated internal models, or environmental interference can all contribute to these misinterpretations. While the concept of robotic hallucinations is gaining traction, research in this area is still in its early stages. There's no single, universally accepted definition, and concrete examples are relatively rare.

Hierarchical Clustering A method of organizing and grouping data points into a hierarchy of clusters. Unlike other clustering techniques, hierarchical clustering creates a tree-like structure that represents the relationships between clusters at different levels of granularity. This technique is widely used in various fields, including machine learning, biology, and data analysis.

HIPAA or The Health Insurance Portability and Accountability Act (HIPAA) A U.S. law that sets national standards for protecting Protected Health Information (PHI). PHI refers to any individually identifiable information related to a person's past, present, or future physical or mental health condition, the provision of health care services to the individual, or payment for the provision of health care services.

Human-in-the-loop (HITL) A collaborative and interactive approach where human expertise and judgment are integrated into the machine learning or artificial intelligence system's workflow. In a human-in-the-loop system, humans and machines work together, with humans contributing to various stages of the AI process, such as data annotation, model training, validation, and decision making.

Hyperparameters The configuration settings that are external to the model and are not learned from the training data. These parameters are set prior to the training process and influence the behavior and performance of the machine learning model. Unlike the parameters of the model itself, which are learned during training, hyperparameters are set by the user or data scientist based on prior knowledge, experimentation, or optimization.

Input Perturbation Detection The identification and analysis of changes or manipulations made to input data in a system, particularly in the context of artificial intelligence and machine learning. The goal of input perturbation detection is to recognize alterations to the input that may impact the performance or behavior of the system.

Input Preprocessing The steps and techniques applied to raw input data before it is fed into a machine learning model for training or inference. The goal of input preprocessing is to transform and prepare the data in a way that makes it suitable for the specific requirements of the model, improving the model's performance, convergence, and generalization.

k-Means Clustering An unsupervised machine learning algorithm used for partitioning a dataset into K distinct, nonoverlapping subsets (clusters). The goal of k-means clustering is to group similar data points together and assign them to the same cluster while keeping different clusters as distinct as possible.

k-Nearest Neighbors (k-NN) A supervised machine learning algorithm used for classification and regression. It assigns a label or value to a data point based on the majority class or average of its k nearest neighbors. The algorithm is simple and effective, often using distance metrics like Euclidean distance, and works well when the decision boundary is complex or unclear.

Knowledge Base The central component that stores and organizes the knowledge and information
used by a symbolic learning artificial intelligence system. This knowledge is typically represented in a symbolic or declarative form, allowing the system to perform various reasoning and problem-solving tasks.

Knowledge Representation Languages Formal systems used to represent information about the world in a format that a computer can utilize to perform various tasks such as reasoning, problem-solving, and decision making. These languages are designed to express knowledge in a structured and organized manner, allowing machines to understand and manipulate the information.

Labeled Data A dataset in which each example is paired with a corresponding annotation or tag, indicating the correct output or category, serving as training input for supervised machine learning algorithms to learn and generalize patterns.

Language Model Outputs The generated text or responses produced by a natural language processing (NLP) model, often known as a language model. These outputs are the model's predictions or responses based on the input it receives. Language models are designed to understand and generate human-like text, making them useful for various NLP tasks, including text generation, translation, summarization, and more.

Language Model Specific Defense (LMSD) A set of techniques designed to protect language models from adversarial attacks and ensure their reliability, fairness, and robustness. These defenses address vulnerabilities unique to language models, which are often exploited to manipulate their outputs, generate harmful content, or leak sensitive information.

Latency The delay or time lag between the initiation of a process or operation and its completion. It is a measure of the time it takes for a system, model, or algorithm to respond to a stimulus or input. In the context of artificial intelligence, latency is a critical factor that influences the responsiveness and performance of AI applications.

Latent Representations Hidden or underlying structures within the data that capture essential features or patterns. These representations are learned by machine learning models during the training process and are often characterized by reduced dimensionality compared to the original data. Latent representations aim to capture relevant information in a more compact and meaningful form, facilitating tasks such as feature learning, data compression, and generation.

Layer-Wise Relevance Propagation (LRP) A technique used for interpreting and understanding the predictions made by deep neural networks. It is a method for attributing the prediction of a neural network back to the input features, providing insights into the contribution of each input feature to the model's output. LRP is commonly employed in tasks where interpretability is crucial, such as image recognition or natural language processing.

Learned Embeddings Also known as dense representations, these are numerical representations of data points generated by machine learning models. These representations capture the underlying relationships and semantic meaning of the data, allowing models to perform tasks more efficiently and effectively. This allows them to adapt to the specific data they are trained on, capturing subtle nuances and relationships that might be missed by hand-crafted features.

Linear Dimensionality Reduction (LDR) A method that reduces the number of variables in a dataset by simplifying it to fewer dimensions while keeping the key information. It is important because it makes data easier to work with and speeds up analysis without losing what's most valuable.

Memorization A model's ability to simply remember and reproduce specific patterns it has observed in its training data without truly understanding the underlying relationships or principles.

Metadata The descriptive information or data that provides context, meaning, and additional details about other data. This includes data descriptions, data source, feature information, annotations and labels, preprocessing history, quality and confidence ratings, versioning, and other tags or descriptors. In the context of artificial intelligence and machine learning, metadata plays a crucial role in understanding, organizing, and managing various aspects of the data used for training models or making predictions.

Missing at Random (MAR) A type of missing data pattern where the probability of a data point being missing depends on other observed variables in the dataset, but not on the missing value itself. This means that while missingness is not completely random, it can be explained by the information that is present in the dataset.

Missing Completely at Random (MCAR) A type of missing data pattern where the absence of values in a dataset is completely unrelated to any observed or unobserved variables. It means the probability of a data point being missing is the same for all observations, regardless of their values or any other factors.

Missing Not at Random (MNAR) A type of missing data pattern where the probability of a data point being missing depends on the missing value itself, even after accounting for other observed variables in the dataset. It is the most challenging type of missing data to handle because it introduces potentially unresolvable bias into analyses.

Modality The type of data or input that an AI system is designed to process and understand. It is the way information is presented or expressed, and different AI models have varying capabilities to handle different modalities. Common AI modalities include:

Text: AI systems that work with text can analyze, generate, translate, and understand written language, used for tasks such as language translation, text summarization, chatbots, and question answering.

Speech: AI models that process speech can recognize and interpret spoken language, enabling voice-controlled interfaces, speech-to-text transcription, and virtual assistants.

Vision: AI systems that handle visual data can analyze and interpret images and videos, enabling object recognition, facial recognition, image classification, and self-driving cars.

Audio: AI models that work with audio can recognize and process sounds, used for music generation, sound classification, and noise reduction.

Sensory: AI systems that integrate sensor data can understand physical environments, used for robotics, autonomous navigation, and health monitoring.

Model Architecture The structural design of a machine learning model, outlining its components, their arrangement, and how they interact with each other to process information and make predictions. This is the blueprint or the "brain structure" of the AI model. Model architectures are often composed of fundamental building blocks like layers, neurons, activation functions, and connections.

Model Rollback The practice of reverting a machine learning model to a previous version or state. Rollback is an important risk mitigation strategy in model deployment and management, allowing for recovery from degradation issues like deteriorated performance, unexpected errors or biases, and integration problems, compatibility issues, or other deployment-related challenges.

NIST AI Risk Management Framework (AI RMF) A set of guidelines developed by the National Institute of Standards and Technology to help organizations manage the risks associated with the development, deployment, and use of artificial intelligence systems, ensuring they are reliable, ethical, and secure.

Noisy Data Data that contains errors, inconsistencies, or other forms of corruption that make it inaccurate or misleading.

Noisy Labels Errors or inaccuracies present in the labeled training data used to train a machine learning model. These errors can arise due to various reasons, such as human annotator mistakes, mislabeled instances, or inconsistencies in the labeling process. Noisy labels can significantly impact the performance of a machine learning model, as it learns from incorrect or misleading information during the training phase.

Novelty Incentives Mechanisms or approaches that encourage the generation, exploration, or adoption of novel or unconventional ideas, solutions, or patterns within artificial intelligence systems. These incentives are designed to foster creativity, diversity, and innovation in AI research, development, and applications.

On-Device Processing The execution of artificial intelligence algorithms and models directly on the device or hardware where the data is generated or resides, rather than relying on external servers or cloud-based resources. This approach brings computational tasks, such as machine learning inference, data processing, and decision making, closer to the source of data, offering benefits in terms of privacy, latency, and efficiency.

Outlier Detection Also known as anomaly detection, this refers to the identification of data points or instances that deviate significantly from the expected or normal behavior within a dataset. Outliers are observations that are rare, unusual, or distinct from the majority of the data and may indicate errors, anomalies, or important but uncommon patterns.

Outlier Rejection Mechanism A set of techniques or procedures designed to identify and exclude outliers from a dataset or a model's training process. Outliers are data points that deviate significantly from the typical patterns in the data and may negatively impact the performance or accuracy of machine learning models. The goal of an outlier rejection mechanism is to improve the robustness and reliability of the model by mitigating the influence of these extreme or anomalous data points.

Overfitting Describes a situation when a model learns the training data too well, capturing not just the underlying patterns but also the noise or random fluctuations present in the data. As a result, the model performs exceptionally well on the training dataset but fails to generalize effectively to new, unseen data.

Pretrained Parameters Numerical values that have already been learned and stored within a machine learning model, often through extensive training on a large dataset. These parameters encode the model's knowledge and understanding of the patterns and relationships it has observed in the data.

Principal Component Analysis (PCA) A dimensionality reduction technique that transforms a large set of correlated variables into a smaller set of uncorrelated variables, called principal components, which capture the most important information or variance in the data. PCA is important because it simplifies complex data by reducing the number of variables, making it easier to analyze and process, while still keeping the most important information.

Probabilistic A decision-making approach that incorporates uncertainty and probability into the reasoning process. The paradigm excels in situations with incomplete, missing, or noisy data, as it can quantify and manage uncertainty. Probabilistic systems can adapt to new information and learn from experience, making them suitable for dynamic environments.

Random Forest An ensemble learning method that constructs a multitude of decision trees during training and outputs the class that is the mode of the classes (classification) or the mean prediction (regression) of the individual trees. It operates by training each tree on a random subset of the training data and introducing randomness in the feature selection process, promoting robustness and mitigating overfitting. Random Forests are versatile and widely used for tasks such as classification, regression, and feature importance estimation.

Random Noise Unpredictable and irregular variations or disturbances in data, introducing randomness that can affect the performance and reliability of algorithms.

Recurrent Neural Networks (RNNs) A class of artificial neural networks specifically designed to handle sequential data, where the order of information matters. They excel at tasks that involve understanding and processing patterns in sequences, such as text, time series data, audio, and video.

Regularization Techniques used to prevent overfitting and improve the generalization performance of machine learning models. Examples of regularization techniques include Lasso and Ridge Regressions, Dropout Layers, and Early Stopping. Regularization is an important tool in AI for building more generalizable, robust, and interpretable models.

Retrieval Finding similar data points based on their latent representations. This is often used in tasks like recommender systems, where the system retrieves items similar to ones the user has interacted with in the past. Similarly, retrieval can be used in image search engines to find images similar to a query image.

Reward Design The process of defining the rewards or reinforcement signals in reinforcement learning algorithms. The reward function is crucial in shaping the agent's behavior and guiding the learning process.

Robust Optimization Techniques that aim to produce models or solutions that are resilient and perform well under uncertain or varying conditions. The goal of robust optimization is to create models that can generalize effectively across different scenarios, handle variations in input data, and maintain satisfactory performance in the presence of uncertainties, noise, or adversarial inputs.

Rules-Based Systems A type of AI application that makes decisions or performs actions based on a set of explicitly defined rules and conditions, typically represented in the form of "if-then" statements, allowing for logical reasoning and automation in various problem-solving domains.

Rules Definition A formal statement that specifies a relationship, condition, or logical implication between different elements in the knowledge base. These rules are a fundamental part of the representation of knowledge in symbolic or declarative form. The purpose of rule definitions is to guide the reasoning and decision-making processes of the artificial intelligence system.

Saliency Maps The visual representations that highlight the most important regions or features of an input data point, such as an image, with respect to a particular model's prediction. Saliency maps help interpret and understand the decision-making process of machine learning models, particularly in tasks like image classification or object detection. They provide insights into which parts of the input contribute most to the model's output.

Sample Efficient Algorithms A class of algorithms that can achieve high performance with relatively small amounts of training data. This makes them particularly valuable in scenarios where data is scarce and expensive to collect. These algorithms achieve efficiency through various techniques, including transfer learning, meta-learning, Bayesian optimization, active learning, synthetic data generation, data augmentation, and regularization. By reducing reliance on large datasets, they accelerate research, development, and deployment of AI systems, enhance model generalization, and promote responsible AI development, making them crucial for addressing real-world challenges and enabling wider AI adoption across industries and domains.

Secure Multiparty Computation (SMPC) A cryptographic technique that enables multiple parties to jointly compute a function over their inputs while keeping those inputs private. In other words, SMPC allows parties to collaborate on computations without revealing their individual data to each other. This is particularly useful in scenarios where privacy and confidentiality of data are critical concerns.

Semistructured Data Information that does not fit neatly into traditional structured databases but contains some level of organization, often using tags, keys, or other markers, allowing for a balance between flexibility and organization in data processing and analysis.

Signal-to-Noise Ratio (SNR) A measure of the relative strength of meaningful information (signal) compared to irrelevant or unwanted data (noise) within a dataset or system. This is an important concept for evaluating data quality, model performance, and the ability to extract meaningful insights from data.

Singular Value Decomposition (SVD) A mathematical technique used in linear algebra and machine learning for decomposing a matrix into three other matrixes, with the aim of capturing the inherent structures and patterns within the original matrix. In the context of AI and machine learning, SVD is often employed for dimensionality reduction, feature extraction, and collaborative filtering in recommendation systems.

Sparsity This occurs when the available data for training an AI model is scarce, incomplete, or scattered. Model sparsity refers to the presence of a large number of zero or near-zero values within the model's parameters (weights and biases).

State-Action Explanations The process of providing insights or justifications for the decisions made by an AI system, particularly in the context of reinforcement learning or decision-making algorithms. In reinforcement learning, an agent makes decisions by selecting actions based on the current state of the environment.

Stochasticity Incorporating the element of randomness or uncertainty into algorithms and models. It introduces controlled randomness, allowing AI systems to explore a broader range of solutions beyond deterministic ones. Stochastic algorithms can improve performance by learning from diverse situations, making models more flexible and adaptable to new data or environments. This randomness also helps them handle noise and uncertainty better, reducing the risk of overfitting to specific training data.

Structured Data Information that is organized and presented in a highly formatted manner, typically tabular or relational, with a clear and predefined schema, making it easily analyzable and suitable for systematic processing by machine learning algorithms.

Temperature Scaling A technique used in generative AI to control the randomness of the model's outputs by adjusting the model's output probability distribution, making it more or less confident in selecting certain tokens (words, images, etc.) during generation.

Temporal Coherence The consistency or smooth transition of information over time in the context of temporal data or sequences. It is a concept commonly encountered in tasks involving time-series data, video processing, natural language processing, and other domains where the order or sequence of information is crucial for understanding and analysis. In applications involving multiple events or processes over time, temporal coherence ensures that events are synchronized in a way that aligns with the logical progression of the underlying process.

Test and Learn An iterative and experimental approach to developing and refining machine learning models, algorithms, or systems. This approach involves designing experiments, conducting tests, and learning from the outcomes to make informed decisions and improvements. The goal is to iteratively refine the model's performance, adapt to changing conditions, and enhance overall effectiveness.

Top-K Sampling A technique that limits a generative AI model's choices to the k most probable tokens, ensuring more controlled and relevant outputs by reducing randomness.

Top-P Sampling (also known as nucleus sampling) is a technique that limits a generative AI model's choices to the smallest set of tokens whose cumulative probability exceeds a certain threshold p, allowing for more flexible control over randomness while still focusing on likely outputs.

Transfer Learning A machine learning paradigm where a model trained on one task is adapted or fine-tuned to perform a second related task. Instead of training a model from scratch for each specific task, transfer learning leverages knowledge gained from solving a source task to improve performance on a target task. This approach is particularly useful when the target task has limited labeled data, as the model can benefit from the knowledge acquired during the training on the source task.

Transformer A type of neural network architecture that has revolutionized natural language processing (NLP) and is increasingly used in other AI domains. These models excel at handling sequential data, such as text and time series, by effectively capturing long-range dependencies and contextual relationships within the data.

Uncertainty Modeling The practice of quantifying and representing the degree of uncertainty or doubt associated with a model's predictions or outputs. This is an important aspect of building more robust, reliable, and trustworthy AI systems, especially when dealing with real-world scenarios characterized by noise, ambiguity, and incomplete information.

Uncertainty Quantification (UQ) The practice of measuring and characterizing the degree of uncertainty associated with the predictions or outputs of an AI model. It is the specific aspect of uncertainty modeling that focuses on measuring and expressing the degree of uncertainty in a quantitative way. It involves assigning numerical values or probabilities to represent the uncertainty associated with a model's predictions. Common methods include confidence intervals, standard deviations, entropy, or Bayesian posterior distributions.

Unlabeled Data A dataset that lacks explicit annotations or tags, providing raw and unstructured information without predefined categories or target outputs, often requiring unsupervised learning techniques to discover patterns and relationships within the data.

Unstructured Data Information that lacks a predefined data model or organized format, often in the form of text, images, or audio, presenting challenges for traditional data processing methods and requiring advanced techniques such as natural language processing or computer vision for meaningful analysis.

Variational Autoencoders (VAEs) A type of AI model that generates realistic data by using a probabilistic approach. It works by learning to compress data into a simplified form (latent space) and then reconstruct it, using two networks: an encoder and a decoder. VAEs are useful for tasks like image generation, data compression, and learning meaningful data representations, and they are commonly used in unsupervised learning.

Visualization Techniques The methods and tools used to visually represent and communicate complex patterns, relationships, and insights derived from AI models or data. Visualization plays an important role in making AI results more interpretable, accessible, and actionable for both technical and nontechnical stakeholders.

XAI See explainable AI.

References

1   Son, H. 2017. *JPMorgan Software Does in Seconds What Took Lawyers 360,000 Hours.* Bloomberg.

2   Canaday, H. November 1, 2022. Aviation Week. "EasyJet Reaps Big Gains From Early Predictive Maintenance Efforts."

3   Uber Freight. September 28, 2023. "Uber Freight Doubles Down on Enterprise Technology, Unveils Next Generation Product Roadmap With AI-Powered Logistics." *PR Newswire.*

4   Prosus. 2023. "Prosus 2023 Annual Report." 82. www.prosus.com/~/media/Files/P/Prosus-CORP/investors/full-year-results-2023/result-report-events/prosus-annual-report-2023.pdf.

5   Statista.com. 2024. "Artificial Intelligence—Worldwide." Statista Market Insights.

6   Day, J. February 29, 2024. NGDATA. "Rewired and Running Ahead: Digital and AI Leaders Are Leaving the Rest Behind. www.ngdata.com/rewired-and-running-ahead-digital-and-ai-leaders-are-leaving-the-rest-behind/.

7   National Association of Corporate Directors (NACD). 2018. "The Report of the NACD Blue Ribbon Commission on Adaptive Governance: Board Oversight of Disruptive Risks."

8   Smaje, K. and R. Zemmel. January 9, 2024. McKinsey & Co. "Ten Unsung Digital and AI Ideas Shaping Business. www.mckinsey.com/capabilities/mckinsey-digital/our-insights/ten-unsung-digital-and-ai-ideas-shaping-business#innovators.

9   Edelman, D. and V. Sharma. November 2, 2023. "It's Time for Boards to Take AI Seriously. *Harvard Business Review.*

10 IBM. May 16, 2024. "IBM Study: As CEOs Race Towards Gen AI Adoption, Questions Around Workforce and Culture Persist." *PR Newswire.* NY, New York: Armonk.

11 Deloitte & Society for Corporate Governance. June 9, 2023. "Artificial intelligence: An Emerging Oversight Responsibility for Audit Committees?" www2.deloitte.com/us/en/pages/center-for-board-effectiveness/articles/artificial-intelligence-an-emerging-oversight-responsibility-for-audit-committees.html.

12 Nagrani, M. March 24, 2024. "Companies Are About to Waste Billions on AI—Here's How Not to Become One of Them."

13   Renieris, E.M., D. Kiron, and S. Mills. June 2023. "Building Robust RAI Programs as Third-Party AI Tools Proliferate." *MIT Sloan Management Review and Boston Consulting Group.*

14   Knowledge Sourcing Intelligence. n.d. "AI Solutions Market." www. knowledge-sourcing.com/report/ai-solutions-market.

15   Raji, I., A. Smart, R. White, et al. 2020. "Closing the AI Accountability Gap: Defining an End-to-End Framework for Internal Algorithmic Auditing." In *FAT '20: Proceedings of the 2023 ACM Conference on Fairness, Accountability, and Transparency,* 3344. Association for Computing Machinery.

16   Babic, B., I.G. Cohen, T. Evgeniou, and S. Gerke. January–February, 2021. "When Machine Learning Goes off the Rails: A Guide to Managing the Risks." *Harvard Business Review.* https://hbr.org/2021/01/when-machine-learning-goes-off-the-rails.

17   Naraine, R. May 17, 2024. "User Outcry as Slack Scrapes Customer Data for AI Model Training." *SecurityWeek.*

18   Leidinger, A. and R. Rogers. 2023. "Which Stereotypes Are Moderated and Under-Moderated in Search Engine Autocompletion?" In *FAccT '23: Proceedings of the 2023 ACM Conference on Fairness, Accountability, and Transparency,* 1049—1061. Association for Computing Machinery.

19   Dastin, J. October 10, 2018. Amazon scraps secret AI recruiting tool that showed bias against women. Reuters.

20   Angwin, J. and G. Wells. September 13, 2022. "The Facebook Files: Instagram's Harmful Effects on Teens Documented by Internal Research." The Wall Street Journal. www.forbes.com/sites/jemimamcevoy/2021/09/14/facebook-internal-research-found-instagram-can-be-very-harmful-to-young-girls-report-says/.

21   Senju, H. March 3, 2022. "The Three Main Challenges of AI Safety." Forbes Technology Council. www.forbes.com/sites/forbestechcouncil/2022/03/03/the-three-main-challenges-of-ai-safety/.

22   Ramlochan, S. October 23, 2023. "The Black Box Problem: Opaque Inner Workings of Large Language Models." Prompt Engineering Institute. www.promptengineering.org/the-black-box-problem-opaque-inner-workings-of-large-language-models/.

23   Hendrycks, D., T. Woodside, and M. Mazeika. October 9, 2023. "An Overview of Catastrophic AI Risks." Center for AI Safety. www.alignmentforum.org/posts/wpsGprQCRffRKG92v/catastrophic-risks-from-ai-4-organizational-risks.

24   Kasy, M. and R. Abebe. 2021. "Fairness, Equality, and Power in Algorithmic Decision-Making." In *FAcct'21: Proceedings of the 2021 ACM Conference on Fairness, Accountability, and Transparency.* 576–586.

25   McDade, A. and S. Sundar. May 19, 2023. "BT Is Cutting 55,000 Jobs. Its CEO Says AI Could Replace 10,000 of Those by 2030." *Business Insider*. www.businessinsider.com/bt-ceo-ai-replace-10000-jobs-job-cuts-2023-5.

26   Yagoda, M. February 23, 2024. "Airline Held Liable for Its Chatbot Giving Passenger Bad Advice—What This Means for Travellers." *BBC*.

27   Mehta, I. and I. Lunden. May 17, 2024. "Slack Under Attack Over Sneaky AI Training Policy." TechCrunch.

28   Buchanan, B.G. and E.H. Shortliffe. 1984. *Rule-Based Expert Systems: The MYCIN Experiments of the Stanford Heuristic Programming Project*. Addison-Wesley.

29   Zhang, X., Y. Xu, J. Wang, and H. Huang. 2023. "Explainable Fraud Detection With Deep Symbolic Classification." https://arxiv.org/abs/2312.00586.

30   Kasiri, H. and M. Kashanizadeh. 2022. "Integrating Symbolic Learning and Machine Learning for Intelligent CAD Systems." In *Emerging Research in Computing, Information, Communication and Applications*, 127–140. Springer Nature.

31   Nkambou, R., R. Mizoguchi, and J. Bourdeau. 2012. "A Framework for Symbolic AI-Based Adaptive Educational Systems." *International Journal of Artificial Intelligence in Education* 22(4): 514–546.

32   Thomas, L.C., D.B. Edelman, and J.N. Crook. 2002. *Credit scoring and Its Applications*. SIAM.

33   Linden, G., B. Smith, and J. York. 2003. "Amazon.com Recommendations: Item-to-item Collaborative Filtering." IEEE Internet Computing.

34   Sahami, M., S. Dumais, D. Heckerman, and E. Horvitz. 1998. "A Bayesian Approach to Filtering Junk E-mail. In *Learning for Text Categorization: Papers from the AAAI Workshop* (Vol. 62).

35   Dal Pozzolo, A., G. Boracchi, O. Caelen, C. Alippi, and G. Bontempi. 2015. "Credit Card Fraud Detection: A Realistic Modeling and a Novel Learning Strategy." *IEEE Transactions on Neural Networks and Learning Systems*.

36   Obermeyer, Z. and E.J. Emanuel. 2016. "Predicting the Future—Big Data, Machine Learning, and Clinical Medicine." *The New England Journal of Medicine*.

37   Jain, A.K., M.N. Murty, and P.J. Flynn. 1999. "Data Clustering: A Review." *ACM Computing Surveys (CSUR)* 31(3): 264–323.

38   Chandola, V., A. Banerjee, and V. Kumar. 2009. "Anomaly Detection: A Survey." *ACM Computing Surveys (CSUR)* 41(3): 15.

39   Ricci, F., L. Rokach, and B. Shapira. 2015. *Recommender Systems Handbook*. Springer.

40   Lee, L.H. and K.H. Kang. 2001. "A Hybrid Approach to Supply Chain Management." *Computers & Operations Research* 28(11–12): 1141–1154.

41   Huang, Z., C. Chen, and Y. Yu. 2021. "Supply Chain Demand Forecasting Uusing Machine Learning: A Comprehensive Literature Review." *Journal of Big Data* 9(1): 1–32.

42   Manning, C.D., P. Raghavan, and H. Schütze. 2008. *Introduction to Information Retrieval*. Cambridge University Press.

43   Jain, A.K., M. Murthy, and P.J. Flynn. 1999. "Data Clustering: A Review." *ACM Computing Surveys (CSUR)* 31(3): 261–326.

44   Booth, A., P. Choudhury, K. Karoui, and A. Kirilenko. 2017. "Machine Learning and the Cross-Section of Expected Returns." *Journal of Financial Economics* 126(1): 171–199.

45   Li, Y., L. Yang, and S. Xu. 2018. "Deep Reinforcement Learning in Portfolio Management." *Quantitative Finance* 18(8): 1273–1285.

46   Chen, M., R. Kishore, Y. Zhang, C. Ma, B. M. Hodge, and Z. Y. Dong. (2019). "A Survey and Taxonomy on Energy Management of Data Centers and Clouds." *IEEE Transactions on Sustainable Computing* 4(1): 37–58.

47   Cai, M., C. Zhang, J. Wu, B. Wang, and Z. Zhang. 2017. "A Deep Reinforcement Learning Approach to Energy-Efficient and Privacy-Aware Indoor Temperature Regulation for Internet of Things." *IEEE Transactions on Industrial Informatics* 14(10): 4624–4632.

48   Feng, L., K. Zhang, and D. Zhang. 2021. "Application of Reinforcement Learning in Smart Grid Control: A Survey." *IEEE Transactions on Smart Grid* 12(6): 4556–4565.

49   Zeng, W., T. Wang, L. Yu, and X. Bu. 2019. "Reinforcement Learning in Supply Chain Operations: A Survey." Computers & Operations Research 98: 194–206.

50   Sutton, R.S. and A.G. Barto. 2018. Reinforcement Learning: An Introduction, 2nd ed. *Cambridge University Press*.

51   Chen, Y., Y. Dong, and C. Wang. 2018. "A Deep Reinforcement Learning Approach to Dynamic Pricing." In *Proceedings of the 24th ACM SIGKDD International Conference on Knowledge Discovery and Data Mining* (2442–2451).

52   Chen, H. and J. Sheldon. 2016. "An Empirical Study of Surge Pricing in the Uber Network." In *Proceedings of the 2016 ACM Conference on Economics and Computation*, (133–142). ACM.

53   Schulman, J., S. Levine, P. Abbeel, M. Jordan, and P. Moritz. 2015. "Trust Region Policy Optimization." In *Proceedings of the 32nd International Conference on Machine Learning*, Vol. 37, 1889–1897.

54   Rajeswaran, A., V. Gupta, J. Tenenbaum, and S. Levine. 2022. "Human-Level Robotic Manipulation." *Science* 377(6605): 39–46.

55 Nieto, M., C. Huang, L. Wang, and S. Escalera. 2019. "Deep Learning for Privacy-Preserving Face Recognition: An Experimental Evaluation of Adversarial Learning and Differential Privacy." In *Proceedings of the 27th ACM International Conference on Information and Knowledge Management (CIKM) 2018*, 2077–2080. ACM.

56 Agrawal, A., R. Chhatrapati, and V. Bhatnagar. 2022. "Leveraging AI in the Food and Beverage Industry: A Review of Current Trends and Applications." In *AI for the Food Industry*, 19–44. Springer, Cham.

57 Litjens, G., T. Kooi, B.E. Bejnordi, A.A. Setio, F. Ciompi, M. Ghafoorian, and C.J. Sánchez. 2017. "A Survey on Deep Learning in Medical Image Analysis." *Medical Image Analysis* 42: 60–88.

58 Li, Z., Z. Wu, and X. Wang. 2018. "Deep Learning for Maritime Route Planning: A Review." *IEEE Access* 6: 59347–59360.

59 Digital Diagnostics. n.d. "IDx-DR: Diabetic Retinopathy Screening for Primary Care." https://blogs.nvidia.com/blog/digital-diagnostics-idx-dr.

60 Siemens.com. 2023. "Siemens Smart Traffic Lights: Improving Traffic Efficiency and Safety."

61 Schroff, F., D. Kalenichenko, and J. Philbin. 2015. "FaceNet: A Unified Embedding for Face Recognition and Clustering. In *Proceedings of the IEEE Conference on Computer Vision and Pattern Recognition*, 815–823.

62 Cognex Corporation. 2023. "Machine Vision for Manufacturers." www.cognex.com/products/machine-vision.

63 Omron Automation & Safety. 2023. "Machine Vision Systems." www.ia.omron.com/products/category/sensors/vision-sensors_machine-vision-systems.

64 Dworski, B. October 6, 2022. *PaymentsDive*. "Checkout-Free Technology Spreads at Airports." www.paymentsdive.com.

65 Waymo.com. 2023. "Waymo: Advancing the Science of Self-Driving."

66 Amodei, D., Q. Zhu, S. Szegedy, S. Kosaraju, F. Iandola, Q. Shan, and Y.H. Ng. 2022. "Neural Networks for Real-Time Control in Robotics." *Nature* 599(7885): 603–612.

67 Tovar, L.M. and M. Guizani. 2021. "Sensor Fusion in Formula One Racing: A Review." *IEEE Sensors Journal* 21(11): 13175–13186.

68 JohnsonControls.com. 2023. "Johnson Controls Smart Buildings: Sensor Fusion for Building Optimization and Occupant Comfort."

69 AgFunder.com. 2018. "John Deere Embraces Computer Vision for Precision Agriculture."

70 Metz, R. August 8, 2024. "Move Over, LLMs. Small AI Models Are the Next Big Thing." *BNN Bloomberg*.

71 translate.google.com. 2023. "Google Translate: Real-Time Translation for the World."

72   duolingo.com. 2023. "Duolingo: Learn a Language for Free."

73   Talafha, M., A. Aljohar, and O. Zaidan. 2021. "Semantic Scholar: Semantic Search for Scholarly Literature." In *Proceedings of the 26th ACM Conference on Information and Knowledge Management (CIKM)*, 3935–3942.

74   meltwater.com. 2023. "Meltwater: Media Intelligence Platform for Brands, Agencies, & PR Pros."

75   Schneider Electric, se.com. 2023. "Schneider Electric EcoStruxure: Open, IoT-Enabled Architecture With NLP-Powered Virtual Assistant."

76   Wilson, S.E., S.J. Grieve, and P. Cairns. 2021. "Chatbots for Customer Support: Enhancing User Experience Through Natural Language Interaction." *International Journal of Human-Computer Studies* 147: 1–13.

77   IBM. n.d. "IBM Watson Assistant." www.ibm.com/products/watson-assistant.

78   Google Cloud. n.d. "Dialogflow." https://cloud.google.com/dialogflow.

79   Jasper. n.d. "Jasper: The AI Writing Assistant That Helps You Write Better, Faster, and Mmore Creatively." www.jasper.ai.

80   Grammarly. n.d. "Grammarly: Your Writing Assistant." www.grammarly.com.

81   Repustate. n.d. "Sentiment Analysis." www.repustate.com/blog/sentiment-analysis-platform.

82   Marcus, J. 2022. "Legal Writing in the Age of Artificial Intelligence." *Stanford Law Review* 74: 931.

83   Bostrom, N. and J. Sullins. 2022. "The Impact of Large Language Models on the Legal Profession." *Jurimetrics: The Journal of Law, Science, and Technology* 62(4): 1–25.

84   Insilico Medicine. n.d. "Insilico Medicine: Accelerating Drug Discovery With Generative AI." https://insilico.com.

85   XtalPi. n.d. "XtalPi: Revolutionizing Materials Science With Generative AI." www.XtalPi.com.

86   Autodesk Fusion 360. n.d. "Fusion 360: 3D CAD, CAM, and CAE Software for Product Design and Engineering." www.autodesk.com/products/fusion-360.

87   *South China Morning Post*. October 17, 2023. "BlackRock: AI Tools Like ChatGPT Are a 'Revolution' in Investment Analysis, Able to Pull Nuance From Vast Data Sets."

88   Normanton, T. January 12, 2024. WatersTechnology. "BlackRock Developing AI Copilots for Aladdin." www.waterstechnology.com/trading-tech/7951617/blackrock-developing-ai-copilots-for-aladdin.

89   StyleShopper. n.d. "StyleShopper: Personalize Your Style With AI." https://medium.com/master-of-code-global/how-to-develop-a-personal-shopper-app-powered-by-data-intelligence-and-humans-4dc8787a957.

90   Jasper.ai. n.d. "Jasper AI: The World's Most Advanced Writing Assistant." www.jasper.ai/.

91   Sharma, A. and F. Iorio. October, 2019. "Ensemble Learning for Anomaly Detection in Financial Transactions." In *2019 IEEE International Conference on Big Data (Big Data)*, 4357–4364. IEEE.

92   Litjens, G., T. Kooi, B.E. Bejnordi, A.A.E. Setio, F. Ciompi, M. Ghafoorian, and B. van Ginneken. 2017. "A Survey on Deep Learning in Medical Image Analysis." *Medical Image Analysis* 42: 60–88.

93   Drucker, H., R.E. Schapire, and P. Wu. 1998. "Boosting: Foundations and Algorithms." *Microsoft Research Technical Report* MSR-TR-99-14.

94   Chen, X., H. Ma, J. Wan, B. Li, and T. Xia. 2020. "Multimodal Fusion for 3D Object Detection in Autonomous Driving: A Survey, Taxonomy, and Challenges." *IEEE Transactions on Intelligent Transportation Systems* 22(1): 3–30.

95   Chen, C., Y. Zhu, J. Zhang, and Y. Zhou. 2022. "Multimodal Medical Image Segmentation: A Survey and Future Directions."

96   Wachter, S., B.C. Stahl, and C. Mittelstadt. 2020. "Transparency in Machine Learning: Toward a Taxonomy. In *Proceedings of the 2020 ACM Conference on Fairness, Accountability, and Transparency (FAccT)*, 647–652.

97   Huang, S., Papernot, N., Goodfellow, I., McDaniel, P., & Sheldon, F. (2017). Adversarial Attacks on Neural Network Policies.

98   Diakopoulos, N. et al. 2016. FATML. "Principles for Accountable Algorithms and a Social Impact Statement for Algorithms. www.fatml.org/resources/principles-for-accountable-algorithms.

99   Rudin, C. 2019. "Stop Explaining Black Box Machine Learning Models for High Stakes Decisions and Use Interpretable Models Instead." *Nature Machine Intelligence* 1(5): 206–215.

100   National Research Council. 2019. "The National Academies of Sciences Engineering, and Medicine." *Foundational Techniques in Risk Assessment and Management.*

101   Padilla, S. June 14, 2024. Businesses Want Insurance for AI Risks, but Insurers Are Still Figuring Out How to Offer It. *Inc.*

102   Costanza-Chock, S., E. Harvey, I. Raji, M. Czernuszenko, and J. Buolamwini. 2022. "Who Audits the Auditors? Recommendations From a Field Scan of the Algorithmic Auditing Ecosystem." *Proceedings of the 2022 ACM Conference on Fairness, Accountability, and Transparency*, (1571–1583)

About the Author

Tom Petro brings decades of boardroom leadership and strategic insight to artificial intelligence, drawing from his experience as a CEO, corporate director, and venture investor. As managing partner of 1867 Capital Partners, he oversees investments in bioinformatics, fintech, and tech-enabled services. Tom has led two public and two private companies, including a NASDAQ IPO.

Tom chairs the Risk Management and Trust committees at Univest Financial Corporation (NASDAQ: UVSP) and serves on the boards of Fintegra, NovaData, Derstine's Inc., and the NACD Philadelphia chapter. He also helps global firms launch venture studios as a board member-in-residence for Mach49. Tom's AI expertise is demonstrated through his directorships with companies commercializing AI in life sciences, legal, insurance, and financial services. His articles on AI governance have appeared in Directors & Boards and NACD's Directorship magazine, and he is a frequent panelist. He holds a BS in Business Management from Point Park University and a CERT Certificate in Cybersecurity Oversight from Carnegie Mellon. He is a NACD Board Leadership Fellow and Directorship Certified.

Index

Adversarial example defense, 66
Agentic AI, 69–70
Aggregation bias, 191
AI governance frameworks, 114,
    149–150
  decision-making, 144–145
  feedback mechanisms, 148–149
  oversight strategy, 137
    board-level expertise, 138–140,
      142–144
    restructure/reassign responsibili-
      ties, 140–142
    situationally tailored oversight,
      137–138
  readiness assessment (see Readiness
    assessment)
  reporting, 148–149
  risk governance
    assurance, 135–136
    audits, 135–136
    business strategy, 125
    data management, 130
    development life cycle, 130
    incident response, 133–134
    liability insurance, 136–137
    model validation, 131
    operating plans, 125
    policy scope, 125
    privacy and regulatory compli-
      ance, 134–135
    readiness assessment, 119–124
    risk appetite, 125–126
    risk assessments, 126–129
    roles and responsibilities, 125
    third-party AI systems,
      129–130
    training data validation, 131
    tracking mechanisms, 145–148
Algorithmic bias, 24, 190–192
Algorithmic vigilance, 33
Artificial intelligence (AI), 1
  decision-making, 19–21

deep learning (see Deep learning
    (DL))
  ethics, 30–31
  framework, 17–18
  impact, 1–2
  knowledge representation and
    reasoning (KRR), 13
  language-based, 13–14
  machine learning (ML) (see
    Machine learning (ML))
  perceptual intelligence, 14
  risk categories, 32, 38–39
    bias and discrimination, 23–25
    drift, 35–37
    hallucinations, 26
    messy data, 39–40
    missing data, 37–39, 65
    privacy and security, 27–30
    safety and reliability, 33–34
    social impacts, 41–42
    transparency and explainability,
      34–35
    unintended consequences,
      40–41
  strategic boardroom leadership, 2–4
  taxonomy, 13–16
Attention networks, 201–202
Automated content generation, 99

Bayesian model averaging (BMA), 197
Benchmarking, 147
Bias
  algorithmic bias, 24, 190–192
  data bias, 24, 189–190
  deployment bias, 25, 193–194
  metrics bias, 24, 192–193
Board director checklist, 165–168
Board governance checklist, 169–172
Board-level AI Governance expertise,
    138–140, 142–144
Board oversight checklist, AI, 157–
    159

California Consumer Privacy Act
(CCPA), 123
Chatbots, 99
ChatGPT, 89
Classification-based supervised
learning, 62
Claude, 90
Clustering-based anomaly detection,
64
Compliance readiness, 122–124
Computer-aided design (CAD)
systems, 56
Computer vision (CV), 14, 77–81,
179–180
Content-streaming recommendation
systems, 64
Continuous learning, 147
Convolutional neural networks
(CNNs), 14, 72, 74, 75, 77,
79, 80, 87
Credit scoring, 60
Cross-functional oversight, 147
Cultural readiness, 122
Customer segmentation, 64

DALL-E 2, 90
Data
assets, 44
handling, 43–44
integrity, 33
quality, 51–52
training, 52–54
types, 49–51
validation, 53–54
Data bias, 24, 189–190
Data governance, 49
boards in, 54
data access and usage, 47–48
data lifecycle management (DLM),
48
data privacy, 47
data quality and consistency, 44–45
data security, 45–46
data stewardship, 48–49
metadata management, 45
Data lifecycle management (DLM),
48

Decision-making framework, 144–
145
Deep learning (DL), 14, 72
challenges, 74–75
decision-making paradigm, 76–77
governance questions, 178–179
risks, 75–76
use cases, 73–74
Deep Q networks (DQN), 72
Deployment bias, 25, 193–194
Deterministic artificial intelligence,
19–20, 36, 38–39
Distortions, 26
Document clustering, 64

E-commerce, 60
Email spam filtering, 60
Ensemble learning, 14, 108–109
governance questions, 186–187
homogeneous, 109–111
multimodal, 111–115
Enterprise risk management (ERM),
124
Evaluation bias, 192
External threats, 34
External validation, 147

Feedback mechanisms, 148–149
Financial fraud detection, 56, 109
Fraud detection, 56, 60, 109

Gemini, 90
Generative adversarial networks
(GANs), 14, 72
Generative AI (GenAI), 14, 102–103
challenges, 104–106
decision-making paradigm, 108
governance questions, 184–185
large language models (LLMs),
89–91
vs. natural language processing
(NLP), 91
opportunities, 104–106
reshaping, 103–104
risks, 106–108
General Data Protection Regulation
(GDPR), 134
GPT-4, 89

Gradient boosting machine (GBM),
    196

Historical bias, 189
Historical data, 50
Homogeneous ensemble learning
    applications, 110
    Bayesian model averaging (BMA),
        197
    governance questions, 186
    gradient boosting machine (GBM),
        196
    Random Forest, 195
    risks, 110–111
    stacked ensemble, 196–197
    XGBoost, 195–196
Human-centered AI, 117
Human-in-the-loop (HITL) principle,
    131–132

Impact-based risk assessment, 127
Incident response, 133–134
Intelligent tutoring system (ITS), 56
Insurance, 136–137
Investment analysis, 147–148

Jasper.ai, 91
Jukebox, 91

Knowledge representation and
    reasoning (KRR), 13

Labeled data, 50, 51, 61
LaMDA, 90
Language-based artificial intelligence,
    13–14, 87–89
    generative AI (GenAI), 89–91,
        102–108
    large language models (LLMs),
        97–102
    natural language processing (NLP),
        91–97
Large language models (LLMs), 13,
    87, 97–98
    advanced natural language
        processing, 98
    automating text-based tasks, 98

data-driven insights and analysis,
    98
decision-making paradigm,
    101–102
enhanced language understanding,
    98–99
generative AI (GenAI), 89–91
governance questions, 183–184
risk, 100–101
use cases, 99–100
Learning bias, 191
Legal document review, 99–100
Legal systems, 57

Machine learning (ML), 13, 59–60
    deep learning (DL), 72–77
    reinforcement learning (RL),
        67–72
    supervised learning, 60–63
    unsupervised learning, 63–67
Measurement bias, 190–191
Medical diagnosis, 56, 61, 109
Metadata management, 45
Metrics bias, 24, 192–193
Midjourney, 90
Milestone reviews, 146–147
Misidentification, 26
Model-based risk assessment, 127
Multimodal ensemble learning,
    111–112
    advantages, 112–113
    attention networks, 201–202
    governance questions, 186–187
    multimodal generative models, 199
    risk, 114–115
    transformers, 200–201
    variational autoencoders (VAEs),
        201
    vision-language models, 199–200
MuseNet, 91
MYCIN system, 56

National Artificial Intelligence
    Initiative Act of 2020
    (NAIIA), 27
Natural language processing (NLP),
    13, 87

challenges, 93–94
decision-making paradigm, 95–97
generative AI (GenAI) *vs.*, 91
governance questions, 182–183
risk oversight issues, 94–95
use cases, 92–93

OpenAI Codex, 91

Perceptual intelligence, 14
  computer vision, 14, 77–81
  sensor fusion, 14, 81–86
Perplexity, 90
Phantom detections, 26
Phased evaluation, 146–147
Prediction-based supervised learning,
  62
Probabilistic artificial intelligence,
  20–21, 36, 38–39

Qualitative-based risk assessment,
  127–128

Random Forest, 195
Readiness assessment, 119
  AI uses, 121
  compliance readiness, 122–124
  core system fitness, 120–121
  cultural readiness, 122
  data governance, 119–120
  defensive posture, 121–122
  impact-based risk assessment, 127
  market analysis, 121
  model-based risk assessment, 127
  qualitative-based risk assessment,
    127–128
  talent, 120
  threat-based risk assessment, 127
  vulnerability-based risk assessment,
    127
  workforce readiness, 122
Real-time data, 50
Recurrent neural networks (RNNs),
  14, 72, 88
Reinforcement learning (RL), 13,
  59, 67
  challenges, 70–71

decision-making paradigm, 71–72
governance questions, 177–178
use cases, 68–69
Reporting, 148–149
Representation bias, 190
Responsible AI (RAI) governance
  principles, 117–119
Risk management
  audits and standards, 154
  case law and regulation knowledge,
    151–152
  intellectual property (IP) risks,
    151–153
  security and privacy risks, 154
ROI tracking, 147–148
Rules-based financial analysis system,
  56
Rytr, 91

Selection bias, 189
Semistructured data, 50
Sensor fusion, 14, 81–82
  challenges, 83–84
  commercial applications, 82–83
  decision-making paradigm, 85–86
  governance questions, 180–181
  risks, 84–85
Sentiment analysis, 99
Small language models (SLMs), 88,
  89
Spam detection, 60, 109
Spreadsheets and traditional database
  management (DBMS), 45
Stable Diffusion, 90
Stacked ensemble, 196–197
Strategic boardroom leadership, 2–4
Structured data, 50
Supervised learning, 13, 59, 60–63,
  174–175
Supply chain optimization, 64
Symbolic learning, 13
  applications, 55–57
  conflict resolution, 57
  decision-making, 55, 58
  explainability, 58
  governance questions, 173–174
  interpretability, 58

knowledge base integrity, 57
System design fortitude, 34

Third-party AI adoption checklist,
    161–163
Threat-based risk assessment, 127
Three Lines of Defense model, 124,
    131–133
Tracking mechanisms, 145–148

Unlabeled data, 50, 51
Unstructured data, 50
Unsupervised learning, 13, 59, 63–
    67, 175–176

Variational autoencoders (VAEs),
    201
Virginia's Consumer Data Protection
    Act (CDPA), 123
Virtual assistants, 100
Vision-language models, 199–200
Vulnerability-based risk assessment,
    127

Word embeddings, 87
Workforce readiness, 122

XGBoost, 195–196

OTHER TITLES IN THE CORPORATE GOVERNANCE COLLECTION

John A. Pearce II, Villanova University and Kenneth Merchant, University of Southern California, Editor

- *Navigating the Human Side of Boardroom Interactions* by Thomas Sieber
- *Business Sustainability* by Zabihollah Rezaee
- *Corporate Sustainability* by Zabihollah Rezaee
- *A Primer on Corporate Governance* by Jose Luis Rivas
- *A Primer on Corporate Governance* by Andrea Melis and Alessandro Zattoni
- *A Primer on Corporate Governance* by Sibel Yamak and Bengi Ertuna
- *Managerial Forensics* by J. Mark Munoz and Diana Heeb Bivona
- *A Primer on Corporate Governance* by Jean Chen
- *A Primer on Corporate Governance* by Felix Lopez-Iturriaga and Fernando Tejerina-Gaite
- *A Primer on Corporate Governance, Second Edition* by Cornelis A. de Kluyver
- *Blind Spots, Biases, and Other Pathologies in the Boardroom* by Kenneth Merchant and Katharina Pick
- *A Director's Guide to Corporate Financial Reporting* by Kristen Fiolleau, Kris Hoang and Karim Jamal

Concise and Applied Business Books

The Collection listed above is one of 30 business subject collections that Business Expert Press has grown to make BEP a premiere publisher of print and digital books. Our concise and applied books are for...

- Professionals and Practitioners
- Faculty who adopt our books for courses
- Librarians who know that BEP's Digital Libraries are a unique way to offer students ebooks to download, not restricted with any digital rights management
- Executive Training Course Leaders
- Business Seminar Organizers

Business Expert Press books are for anyone who needs to dig deeper on business ideas, goals, and solutions to everyday problems. Whether one print book, one ebook, or buying a digital library of 110 ebooks, we remain the affordable and smart way to be business smart. For more information, please visit www.businessexpertpress.com, or contact sales@businessexpertpress.com.

www.ingramcontent.com/pod-product-compliance
Lightning Source LLC
Chambersburg PA
CBHW061147220326
41599CB00025B/4392